Black Ice:
The Invisible Threat of
Cyber-Terrorism

Dan Verton

McGraw-Hill/Osborne

New York Chicago San Francisco
Lisbon London Madrid Mexico City Milan
New Delhi San Juan Seoul Singapore Sydney Toronto

The McGraw·Hill Companies

McGraw-Hill/Osborne
2100 Powell Street, 10th Floor
Emeryville, California 94608
U.S.A.

To arrange bulk purchase discounts for sales promotions, premiums, or
fund-raisers, please contact **McGraw-Hill/Osborne** at the above address.

Black Ice: The Invisible Threat of Cyber-Terrorism

1234567890 DOC DOC 019876543

ISBN 0-07-222787-7

Publisher	Brandon A. Nordin
Vice President & Associate Publisher	Scott Rogers
Executive Editor	Jane K. Brownlow
Senior Project Editor	Carolyn Welch
Acquisitions Coordinator	Tana Allen
Copy Editor	Robert Campbell
Proofreader	Susie Elkind
Indexer	Claire Splan
Composition	Tara A. Davis
Illustrator	Lyssa Wald
Series Design	Jean Butterfield
Cover Design	Bryan Walton

This book was composed with Corel VENTURA™ Publisher.

For Neil ...
and Justy—sweet, happy life

About the Author

Dan Verton is a senior writer and veteran investigative reporter with *Computerworld* in Washington, D.C.

As one of the leading technology journalists in the country, Verton traveled around the world in 1999 and 2000 covering the NATO-led war in Kosovo and the use of cyberwar tactics by the U.S. military. He has interviewed and written profiles of hackers, Kosovo refugees, and military cyber-warriors from around the world, and has traveled with former U.S. Secretary of Defense, William Cohen. His career has taken him from the front lines of military cyber operations to the front lines of hacker wars in the U.S.

A former intelligence officer in the U.S. Marine Corps, Verton earned an M.A. in Journalism from American University in Washington, D.C., a B.A. in History from the State University of New York-Binghamton, and has attended the University of Pennsylvania.

Verton is the 2003 Winner of the Jesse H. Neal National Business Journalism Award for Best News Coverage for a groundbreaking series of reports on wireless network security threats at some of the nation's largest airlines and airports.

CONTENTS

FOREWORD

The essence of terrorism is terror. What made the attacks on September 11, 2001 in New York, Northern Virginia, and Pennsylvania so devastatingly effective as tools of terror was not only the monumental loss of life and property damage these attacks caused, but the way they have changed the face of American society. People have, at least temporarily, lost confidence in their security and well-being.

The attacks also prompted vast changes in the way U.S. law enforcement and intelligence communities work, the technologies they employ, the methods they use to cooperate with one another, and how they transfer information and knowledge. Legislation was passed that gave sweeping new powers to domestic law enforcement and intelligence agencies, while shifting the traditional balance of power away from the judicial branch in favor of a much more powerful executive branch. All of this was achieved by an enemy with a bit of intelligence and planning and devices no more sophisticated than a dozen box cutters.

As important as the buildings attacked on that day were—both in terms of the lives of the people who lived and worked in them and their value as symbols of economic and military power—the true underpinnings of their power lay beneath them: in hundreds of thousands of miles of coaxial and fiber optic cables and the computers they link together; in the electrical power grid that feeds and nourishes these computers; in the water supply that feeds both the hydroelectric plants and the people who operate the computers; in the bus, rail, truck, and highway systems that supply the parts for these infrastructures; in the telecommunications networks that allow these computers to communicate with each other and allow people to go about their daily lives; and in the financial systems of banks, insurance companies, brokerages, and other financial institutions that fund and insure these technologies and depend on them in turn for their own lifeblood.

These critical infrastructures, which can be attacked from thousands of miles away, are essential for the continued success of this experiment in democracy we call America. These infrastructures are inherently co-dependent. Without electricity, there is no telephone service; without either, there is no useable Internet. The scope of these interdependencies is only now being fully appreciated. Certainly, we could survive a temporary and partial disruption of some of these infrastructures.

Little more than a week after the September 11 attacks, a computer program traveled across the Internet flooding and congesting thousands of critical computer networks. Since then, malicious and destructive computer programs—with names like NIMDA, CODE RED, and SLAMMER—have caused hundreds of millions of dollars of loss to critical corporate infrastructures. And these attacks have been relatively benign; the programs themselves destroyed no data and had no malicious "payload." Is this the next forum for a terrorist attack?

The goal of the September 11 attacks was to inflict symbolic injury on the United States. In the future, the goals of terrorists are likely to be more insidious. What makes the United States strong is not only its people, its military, and its values, but also the hardware, software, and financial infrastructure that support its economic development and growth. Al Qaeda has made no secret of its intention to attack that infrastructure. The goals of the next terrorist attack will be to cripple our economy and economic base, thus undermining the confidence and trust the American people place in their fundamental institutions and way of life.

The next terrorist attack may well be launched—at least partially—in cyberspace. Much of our economy depends on the proper functioning of this digital medium. Typically, we think of cyberspace as "the Internet"—the global interconnections of computers that facilitate electronic commerce (e-banking, securities trading, and online sales) and electronic communications. If this were the only function of the new digital medium, this nation would remain at risk. However, much more than the World Wide Web is at risk of a terrorist attack. Virtually everything we do is in some way impacted by the new electronic world.

Without properly functioning computers and the networks that connect them, there would be no ability to generate electricity, whether from nuclear power plants, coal or natural gas powered facilities, or hydroelectric plants. Even if electricity can be generated, attacks to computer networks can disable the ability to transmit power if the computers that control the electrical distribution systems are not functioning properly. Cell phones, landline telephones, and other forms of communication (including those used by the military) are computer controlled. Medical information systems, inventory control, ordering, processing, manufacturing, and distribution systems are all controlled by computer technologies. Insurance, banking, investment, and financial services are all heavily dependent upon both the availability and reliability of information systems.

A terrorist attack need not destroy these systems to wreak havoc. Substantially impairing the operation of these systems could undermine consumer confidence, and have a debilitating effect on the economy. Corrupting data or preventing access to data could devastate the financial services sector.

To launch a conventional attack similar to September 11, an enemy, whether a foreign government or a terrorist organization, would likely need a physical presence within the United States, either directly or through "sleeper" cells present in the United States. And the presence of such sleeper cells requires infrastructure, finances, planning, and substantially increases the risk that members of the organization will be caught. Unlike conventional attacks, however, network-based attacks can be launched remotely from thousands of miles away, decreasing the likelihood that the attackers will be discovered. Future terrorists may be unwilling to sacrifice their lives for their causes, and will undoubtedly be tempted to launch attacks from the safety and security of countries that offer them refuge—and a high-speed Internet connection.

There are tens of millions of people currently on the Internet. If only a small fraction of these individuals have the necessary skills and training essential to launch destructive network-based attacks, this still means that there are thousands if not tens of thousands of individuals with such capabilities. Terrorist organizations recognize the importance of computer training, and are actively recruiting people with the necessary skills. Information about hacking, cracking, and attacking is freely available. There are some 30,000 hacker-related Web sites on the Internet, and even more active bulletin board and newsgroup sites. The number of attacks and their costs go up every year. To date, more than 50,000 computer viruses have been created, and up to 400 are active at any one time.

Just as the September 11 attackers received training in aviation security vulnerabilities and technical training in how to pilot aircraft, terrorist organizations with access to training, research, and money have the ability not only to train a corps of cyber attackers, but can purchase their services of "hackers for hire" in the open marketplace. The collapse of the former Soviet Union and the ready availability of technically trained individuals in Asia, Eastern Europe, and the Middle East, increase the risks and threats to our critical infrastructures.

But we continue to make it easy for would-be attackers. We publish vast amounts of data about our infrastructures in publicly accessible Internet archives. Information about vulnerabilities is widely disseminated, but companies and government agencies are slow to install the patches necessary to respond to these vulnerabilities. We continue to use insecure software, cobbled together on publicly accessible and insecure networks, without adequately monitoring new risks, threats, vulnerabilities, and incidents. We make our corporate and government networks accessible by attaching wireless devices that broadcast critical data to anyone within "earshot." Millions of home computer users with high-speed Internet connections fail to secure these connections, and become potential "jumping off" points for terrorists or other malicious hackers.

For ease of use or convenience, we make critical "command and control" systems accessible over the Internet, often with disastrous results. These systems—called SCADA systems—could control things like heating, air conditioning and ventilation systems, energy generation or transmission facilities, and highway or railway traffic control systems. SCADA systems could even control experiments on the Space Shuttle. Successful attacks on such systems could—and likely would—invoke terror on a grand scale. In caves in Afghanistan, U.S. troops found plans for al Qaeda to attack these very SCADA systems.

Current U.S. policy relies on the economic marketplace to provide the basis for securing our critical infrastructure. It has been estimated that 80 percent of this infrastructure lies not in the hands of the military or government, but in private institutions—from your local bank to the drug store down the block. Unfortunately, this strategy has not proven effective, at least not yet. The marketplace has already defined the level of security it deems "adequate," just as the marketplace before September 11 defined the level of airline security that it deemed cost effective.

Companies within the critical infrastructure must as a matter of business necessity increase the level of training, awareness, and protection of these critical infrastructures. They must continually monitor the health and security status of all of their networked resources and effectively share information with each other and with appropriate government agencies about new incidents, threats, and vulnerabilities.

Government must be willing to do the same and more. Governments must remove barriers to security, develop and share new security technologies and research, and encourage—through grants and tax reform—new investment in creating a secure environment. Just as no one would have expected the Port

Authority of New York and New Jersey to invest in putting a Harrier jump jet on top of the Twin Towers, no one should expect industry to go it alone.

As this book points out in chilling detail, to inflict genuine terror (as opposed to merely inconvenience), the next terrorist attack to come from cyberspace is likely to be coupled with a physical attack. Terrorists could attack the electronic infrastructure with destructive computer programs (viruses, worms, or Trojan horses), flood the Internet and telecommunications networks with vast amounts of electronic traffic to render them essentially unusable, or virtually attack them with high-energy devices (electromagnetic waves or high-energy radio waves) to remotely destroy data on computer networks. This electronic attack could mask, exacerbate, or confuse a physical attack—a bombing, chemical attack, biological attack, or nuclear related attack—and compound its terror-inducing effect. Essential government response services would be crippled by such a dual attack.

Lawmakers have responded to terrorism by restricting civil rights, giving government greater access to individuals' personally identifiable information, and assembling, accumulating, analyzing, and sharing bits of data that may or may not result in a safer and more secure society but certainly represents a tremendous invasion of the privacies and civil liberties our nation has taken for granted.

This may be the most insidious part of terrorism—not what the terrorists do to us, but what we do to ourselves to respond to the threat of terrorism. As the government moves more toward "Total Information Awareness," connecting disparate government databases with commercial databases and developing detailed "profiles" of the movements, habits, and preferences of citizens and non-citizens, the open society we are trying to preserve becomes more a thing of the past.

What follows is a chilling scenario of cyber and physical terrorism that is altogether too real. These are descriptions of what could happen—not necessarily what would happen—if we do not take action. We do not truly know the capabilities or intentions of our adversaries, or even who those adversaries are. Businesses' primary concerns about the bottom line and government agencies' concerns about growing deficits mean new pressures on security spending.

In *Black Ice: The Invisible Threat of Cyber-Terrorism,* Dan Verton examines in detail the threat of terrorism and the capabilities of terrorist cells and networks, as well as the responses or lack of responses from government and the private sector to the terrorist threat. In a thoroughly researched and documented treatise, the book presents a chilling reminder of what could happen if such an attack were to take place. It reminds us that in the post-September 11 world, it is not only our buildings and people who are at risk, but also the critical physical and digital infrastructures that support them. Hopefully, legislators, policymakers, and regulators as well as industry executives will stand up and take notice.

Mark Rasch

July 2003

Mark Rasch *is the Senior Vice President and Chief Security Counsel of Solutionary, Inc., a managed and monitored security service provider (MSSP) headquartered in Omaha, Nebraska. Rasch is the founder and former head of the Department of Justice's computer crimes unit.*

ACKNOWLEDGMENTS

I want to thank the entire McGraw-Hill/Osborne team who worked on this book including Jane Brownlow, executive editor; Carolyn Welch, senior project editor; Robert Campbell, copy editor; Tana Allen, acquisitions coordinator; and the entire Creative Services department (art and graphics). I could not have asked for a better team of professionals to work with. A special thanks goes out to Robert Campbell for lending his expertise in Arabic.

I also want to acknowledge those current and former members of the White House and National Security Council staff who gave me their time and shared their expertise. In particular, I want to thank Richard Clarke, the nation's first counterterrorism coordinator, cybersecurity czar for two presidents, and a powerful intellectual force who will be sorely missed in the tumultuous days ahead. Likewise, Howard Schmidt and Roger Cressey of the President's Critical Infrastructure Protection Board, and Ron Dick, the former director of the FBI's National Infrastructure Protection Center (NIPC), were instrumental in helping me to understand the Bush administration's response to the September 11, 2001 terrorist attacks as well as the overall challenges facing the nation in terms of defending privately owned critical infrastructures. And few, if any, of those discussions would have happened without the assistance of Tiffany Olson and Julia Conroy.

Special thanks also go to Brenton Greene, the director of the National Communications System (NCS), without which the recovery effort from the attacks of September 11, 2001 would have been nearly impossible, and to former Virginia Governor James S. Gilmore III, who graciously shared with me his thoughts on cyber-terrorism and the nature of the cyber threat facing America.

I also want to extend my appreciation to Vince Cannistrano, the former chief of operations at the CIA's Counterterrorism Center, and Larry Johnson, a former CIA officer and deputy director of the U.S. State Department's Office of Counterterrorism, for helping me better understand the motivations and methods of operations of terrorist organizations. Others who shared their expertise with me and whose knowledge is directly reflected in the pages that follow include Ruth David, former CIA deputy director of Science & Technology and now president of Analytical Services, Inc., Ed Badolato, the former deputy assistant secretary for energy emergencies at the Department of Energy, and Joe Weiss, a consultant and expert in real-time control systems.

Last, I want to extend my greatest appreciation to Dr. Paula Scalingi of Scalingi & Associates. Paula has served as the director of critical infrastructure protection at the Department of Energy and has been responsible for some of the most important tabletop exercises designed to test the nation's ability to respond to physical and cyber-based attacks. She was directly involved in the planning and execution of the Pacific Northwest Economic Region's Black Ice exercise, from which the title of this book is derived, as well as other follow-up exercises that have benefited our country immensely. I owe much of my understanding of these issues to Paula.

Today, the cyber economy is the economy. Corrupt those networks and you disrupt this nation.

Condoleezza Rice,
National Security Advisor to President George W. Bush,
speaking at a conference on security on March 22, 2001

We cannot do business in this country today and we cannot defend this country today without the Internet.

Richard Clarke,
former chairman of the President's Critical Infrastructure
Protection Board and senior advisor for cybersecurity

It is very important to concentrate on hitting the U.S. economy through all possible means...look for the key pillars of the U.S. economy. The key pillars of the enemy should be struck...

Osama bin Laden, December 27, 2001

INTRODUCTION

Within hours of the tragic events of September 11, 2001, America's television screens filled with dozens of talking heads prepared to give their analyses of how and why America had been caught by surprise. One of the earliest messages to come out of the mouths of the so-called experts and political commentators was that nobody ever imagined that terrorists would use commercial airplanes as precision strike weapons. America had been taken completely by surprise because the tactic was so unusual, according to their line of reasoning. The tactic of deliberately crashing commercial airplanes into large office buildings was so dastardly that nobody ever thought for a minute that a terrorist could or would attempt it.

Of course, we were wrong. But so was the initial analysis that painted September 11 as a unique occurrence in the evolution of terrorist tactics. The truth of the matter is that while most Americans were taken by surprise, the national security community had not been (or should not have been). Al-Qaeda had a long history of attempting to use airplanes as precision strike weapons. In fact, that history dated back nearly eight years. But America had been sleeping the deep sleep of the comfortable and the free.

In 1994, for example, the CIA and French authorities disrupted an al-Qaeda plot to crash a commercial Air France jetliner into the Eiffel Tower in Paris. That same year, the CIA was successful in preventing terrorists from crashing an airplane into the agency's Langley, Virginia, headquarters complex.

By 1999, the National Intelligence Council had gone as far as to prepare an intelligence estimate for then President Bill Clinton warning of the threat that al-Qaeda and other terrorist groups were interested in using commercial airliners to strike at American landmarks and the government's center of gravity in Washington, D.C. "Al-Qaeda's expected retaliation for the U.S. cruise missile attack against al-Qaeda's training facilities in Afghanistan on August 20, 1998, could take several forms of terrorist attack in the nation's capital," the report warned. "Al-Qaeda could detonate a Chechen-type building-buster bomb at a federal building. Suicide bomber(s) belonging to al-Qaeda's Martyrdom Battalion could crash-land an aircraft packed with high explosives (C-4 and semtex) into the Pentagon, the headquarters of the Central Intelligence Agency (CIA), or the White House."[1]

After participating in the first World Trade Center bombing on February 26, 1993, Ramzi Yousef, a 25-year-old al-Qaeda operative, returned to Manila, in the Philippines. There he plotted a complicated scheme he called "Project Bojinka," which involved planting virtually undetectable bombs aboard U.S. passenger airliners using Casio digital watches as timing switches and light bulb filaments to ignite cotton soaked in a nitroglycerine explosive. On December 9, 1994, Yousef carried out a practice run on Philippine Airlines Flight 434, bound for Tokyo. His bomb killed a Japanese tourist and wounded ten others who were seated near the explosive, which he taped under a seat.

In March 1993, prosecutors in the U.S. indicted Yousef for his role in the WTC bombing. And when Manila police, responding to fears that he was plotting to kill Pope John Paul II, raided Yousef's room in Manila on January 6, 1995, they discovered explosives, a map of the Pope's route, clerical robes, a computer disk describing the plot against the Pope, and plans for attacks against U.S. airlines. But Yousef had vanished.

On February 8, 1995, authorities in Peshawar, Pakistan got lucky and managed to arrest Yousef in Islamabad, where he was staying in the Su Casa guesthouse owned by a member of Osama bin Laden's family. When they arrested him, authorities discovered bomb-making materials and flight schedules for United and Delta Airlines. His plans included using Said Akhman as a suicide pilot to crash an aircraft packed with powerful explosives into the CIA headquarters in Langley, Virginia, as well as blowing up 11 U.S. commercial airliners simultaneously as they approached U.S. airports.

Then in 2000, an Italian newspaper printed an interview with an alleged al-Qaeda operative who stated on the record that he and others were undergoing pilot training to conduct kamikaze-style attacks.

The indications and the warnings that al-Qaeda was trying to find a way to use aircraft as weapons were clearly available to the U.S. intelligence community and to members of the Clinton administration and Congress. But nobody was paying attention. Nobody had recognized the subtle shifts that were taking place in the attack modes of terrorists.

---

[1]   See Rex A. Hudson, "The Sociology and Psychology of Terrorism: Who Becomes a Terrorist and Why?" A report prepared by the Federal Research Division, Library of Congress, September 1999.

-.-. -.-- -... . .-. - . .-. .-. --- .-.

Unfortunately, the same tragedy may be playing itself out today in the cyber-realm. The same stodgy thinking that led to the attacks of September 11, 2001, may soon lead to another devastating and crippling economic attack in cyberspace. The indications and warnings are appearing now that suggest groups such as al-Qaeda understand the usefulness of cyber-weapons to the larger strategic goals of international terrorism. The only question that remains to be answered is if America will throw off the shackles of inflexible thinking and accept the reality of cyber-terrorism.

Like the views of the vast majority of terrorism observers, and even many experts, my view of terrorism has been formed by the world's collective historical experience with terrorism and with little or no appreciation for the fact that terrorism, like warfare, is in a constant state of evolution. The problem with terrorism, however, is that it evolves at tectonic speeds over many decades, making the process of discerning subtle changes in tactics extremely difficult, even for the trained eye. But there is a danger to this. Like seismologists who fail to detect the movements of the earth's tectonic plates and the increasing pressure those movements cause, we can be caught by surprise by a massive, life-threatening earthquake when we fail to pick up on the subterranean changes in terrorism.

Terrorism, as we have come to know it, is a form of political violence that strikes fear in the hearts and minds of people because of its destructive power and its ability to wreak havoc and physical pain on unsuspecting innocent people. Few people will ever forget the horrific scenes from Lockerbie, Scotland, where in 1988 a bomb ripped apart Pan Am Flight 103 in midair, killing all 270 passengers. Likewise, the 1983 bombing of the U.S. Marine barracks in Beirut, Lebanon, that killed 241 Marines and sailors, and more than 100 others, serves as a timeless reminder of what the destructive forces of terrorism are all about. The same can be said of the 1995 bombing of the Alfred P. Murrah Federal Building in Oklahoma City, Oklahoma, which killed 168 people and wounded more than 500. And, of course, no book on terrorism would be worth the paper it's printed on if it did not mention the attacks against the World Trade Center in New York and the Pentagon on September 11, 2001, and the new operational standard that may have been established on that day for terrorist organizations throughout the world to emulate.

However, we judge the future of terrorism solely on the basis of these historical examples at our own peril. We cannot afford to discount future terrorist tactics or targets merely because we are unable or reluctant to discern subtle changes in the operational modes of global terrorism, especially in the age of information and the Internet. While violence will always be a key pillar of international terrorism, we cannot disregard the use of new and innovative tactical measures that are designed to augment the psychological and even physical impact of traditional violent terrorist attacks. And the tactical measures I am referring to include the use or targeting of information age technologies, such as computers and the Internet, to destroy or disrupt the critical infrastructures that our economy and national security depend upon.

It is in that spirit that I introduce to you *Black Ice: The Invisible Threat of Cyber-Terrorism*, a book about the unthinkable and the art of the possible.

Cyber-terrorism may be one of the most misunderstood and misused terms to ever come out of the information age. Generally speaking, cyber-terrorism is the execution of a surprise attack by a subnational foreign terrorist group or individuals with a domestic political agenda using computer technology and the Internet to cripple or disable a nation's electronic and physical infrastructures, thereby causing the loss of critical services, such as electric power, emergency 911 systems, telephone service, banking systems, the Internet, and a host of others. The goal of a cyber- terrorist attack is not only to impact the economy of a region or country, but to amplify the effects of a traditional physical terrorist attack by causing additional confusion and panic throughout the general population.

However, cyber-terrorism can also take the form of traditional terrorism, whereby critical Internet, communications, and electric power nodes are physically destroyed, causing widespread, cascading failures of electronic systems that can threaten both the health of the economy and the safety of the public. Few observers of cyber-terrorism have acknowledged the fact that a successful cyber-terrorist attack can be conducted without ever touching a computer keyboard or employing traditional computer hacking techniques. A cyber-terrorist attack, therefore, must be analyzed in terms of its intended goal and its impact, and not solely on the mode of attack. A recent article in *CIO Magazine*, for example, illuminates the widespread misunderstanding of what cyber-terrorism really is and how most people lack a sophisticated understanding of modern terrorist organizations—a situation that invariably leads to inaction. "The real threat is to critical data, not to property," the article states. "That's what [chief information officers] should be focusing on."[2] Such analysis represents a classic underestimation

---

[2]   See Scott Berinato, "The Truth about Cyberterrorism," *CIO Magazine*, March 15, 2002.

of the threat, most often perpetuated by nonexperts in military or paramilitary operations who approach every cyber-related threat as if its mode of attack must be confined in total to the Internet.

According to the FBI's National Infrastructure Protection Center (NIPC), a special unit established at FBI headquarters in Washington, D.C., to detect, warn of, and prevent major cyber-based attacks against U.S. critical systems, the goal of cyber-terrorism is "to create fear by causing confusion and uncertainty within a given population."[3] Terrorist organizations "generally use symbolic means to attack the sanctity of the society. If attacks on these symbolic targets are successful, the terrorists will have accomplished their goal of isolating individuals from the society in which those individuals formerly felt secure. Such actions result in confusion and uncertainty about a government's ability to protect its citizens. This is when citizens are most vulnerable to influence by others."

Yet, a fertilizer bomb set off outside of a major regional switching station or a series of chemical or biological attacks that make key Internet or electric power facilities uninhabitable can lead to problems that can create the same denial of service effects as an electronic-based attack using malicious viruses or worms. The violent destruction of a physical plant, particularly one that relies on computers and networks for its day-to-day operations, can and does have cyber-ramifications. In fact, the physical cyber-terrorist attack (particularly in the nuclear, biological, or chemical arenas) plays to the terrorist's advantage in that it creates the potential for both a mass- casualty and mass-panic event that will get the attention of the national or global news media while at the same time degrading or destroying key economic infrastructure systems—another key objective of the post–September 11 terrorist threat. In Chapter 1, I offer a fictional scenario based on real-world analyses of the physical connection to cyber-infrastructure. The fictional scenario is actually based on a real-world exercise, code-named Black Ice (Chapter 2), that used a combination of cyber- and physical terrorist attacks to cripple key economic infrastructures throughout a five-state region. The lessons that came out of that exercise included the potential for prolonged loss of electric power, massive financial damage, and the inability of local emergency responders to effectively manage the crisis.

In Chapter 3, we look at a classified government exercise known as "Eligible Receiver" that tested the ability of hackers to use computers to bring down critical services and infrastructures. It was during that exercise that the reality

---

3 See *National Infrastructure Protection Center Highlights,* June 15, 2001, p. 2.

of the cyber-threat first came to the forefront of our thinking about national cybersecurity and the implications of terrorism in this new age.

"The most likely perpetrators of cyber-attacks on critical infrastructures are terrorists and criminal groups rather than nation-states," warned the Second Annual Report of the Advisory Panel to Assess Domestic Response Capabilities for Terrorism Involving Weapons of Mass Destruction, popularly known as the Gilmore Commission, named after the panel's chairman, former Virginia Governor James Gilmore.

In an earlier study on the evolution and future of modern global terrorism, Clark L. Staten, the executive director and senior analyst at the Emergency Response & Research Institute, summed up the cyber-terror threat to the U.S. as follows: "Even a country as large and sophisticated as the United States could suffer greatly at the hands of an educated, equipped, and committed group of fewer than 50 people. At the present time, such an attack could realistically be expected to cause an effect vastly disproportionate to the resources expended to undertake it."[4]

Some say a surprise electronic attack that has strategic national security implications, often referred to as an "electronic Pearl Harbor," is impossible. Others argue vehemently that it is inevitable. As in most debates, however, the truth can be found somewhere in the middle, where the art of the possible lives and breathes. And as we discovered on September 11, 2001, the ever-changing threat of terrorism knows only the art of the possible. Terrorists live and die carrying out attacks that people fail to anticipate or discount as too difficult or too technically challenging. But the attacks of September 11, 2001, and the new operational benchmark established on that fateful day speak to a different reality. The management sophistication of Osama bin Laden's al-Qaeda global terror network and its focus on creating task-oriented global alliances capable of attacking on a variety of fronts using a multitude of weapons, also points to a different reality. That reality is simple: The attack the experts say cannot happen or that terrorists are not interested in pursuing is simply an attack that hasn't happened yet.

Cyber-terrorism is not an abstract concept, as you will learn in Chapter 3. It is not a theory that academics are wrestling with behind closed doors in ivory towers far away from the gritty streets of the real world. And it is not

[4]   See Clark L. Staten, "Asymmetric Warfare, the Evolution and Devolution of Terrorism; The Coming Challenge for Emergency and National Security Forces," Emergency Response & Research Institute, April 27, 1998.

something that journalists like myself use to craft fear-mongering headlines that will sell more newspapers (although that certainly has happened). It is real, a logical extension of traditional forms of terrorism, which are continuously being adapted by a thinking enemy to the realities of the modern world. In short, cyber-terrorism exists because it is in the cyber-realm that most industrialized nations are weakest. All of the things we take for granted in our everyday lives, such as electricity, telephone and Internet service, the 911 emergency system, air traffic control systems, banks and ATM machines, credit card systems, real-time financial market transactions, waterways and railroads, hospitals and critical life-saving medical equipment, a large percentage of the Pentagon's national defense capabilities, and a host of other so-called "critical infrastructures," rely on computers and computer networks for their management and continued operation. And increasingly these networks are becoming more connected and more dependent on each other, creating a situation where a failure in one network can cause cascading failures throughout many other networks.

"Today, the cyber-economy is the economy," said President Bush's national security advisor Condoleezza Rice, in her first major policy address on the topic of cybersecurity on March 22, 2001. "Corrupt those networks and you disrupt this nation," said Rice.

The threat of cyber-terrorism has not only struck a chord with officials in the U.S., but it has also become a front-burner issue for government leaders in Great Britain. The Terrorism Act of 2000, passed in the U.K., extends the traditional definition of terrorism to cyber-forms of terrorist activity. According to the text of the legislation, the new law is aimed at people who "seriously interfere with or seriously disrupt an electronic system."

The wired and wireless Internet (covered in Chapter 4) and the ever-growing number of linkages and interdependencies that exist in the modern world of computers and computer networks have become the soft underbelly of our national defense. And terror is like a shark in the ocean that must constantly move in order to breathe—a top-feeder that strikes without warning from the murky depths below. It never stops searching for wounded or vulnerable prey and it will strike wherever it finds it, using whatever tools are most appropriate for the job. Rest assured, global terrorism in the post-9/11 world is a thinking, learning enemy.

For the first time in our nation's history, the government alone cannot defend its citizens. With more than 85 percent of the nation's most critical computer networks and infrastructure in the hands of private companies, the front line of the war against cyber-terrorism runs through corporate America and Main Street USA. This is unprecedented in American history.

For more than 200 years, the United States has enjoyed the security provided by two massive oceans and peaceful land neighbors to the north and south. However, the Internet, invented by the U.S. military during the early days of the Cold War as a means to provide for redundant communications in the event of a nuclear first strike by the now-defunct Soviet Union, has effectively eliminated those natural security barriers. The Internet and global electronic business know no borders. Our current and future enemies also know no borders.

Furthermore, the globalization of information technology has created an international information warfare arms race that is not subject to treaties or control regimes. The weaponization of information technologies has been achieved, with at least a half-dozen nations (the U.S., Russia, China, France, India, and Israel) actively pursuing information warfare capabilities and stockpiling digital weaponry and intelligence data. While terrorist groups have proved their ability to easily obtain state-of-the-art information technologies, the information warfare arms race that is now underway (and that will likely continue for many years to come) and the significant economic pressures bearing down upon a multitude of the world's population have combined to produce a pool of willing information warriors for hire. Just as al-Qaeda was able to hire an Egyptian nuclear scientist to assist it with its nuclear weapons program, so too can it and other terrorist organizations hire world-class hackers to conduct both offensive and intelligence gathering operations on the Internet. In Chapter 5, I offer a view of al-Qaeda's evolution toward the use of cyber-weapons.

In addition to the easy access that terrorist groups now have to inexpensive software, hardware, Internet connectivity, and a growing pool of young supporters with formal training in software programming and computer science, cyber-terrorists are also reaping the benefits of the United States' growing electronic vulnerability. And, as you will learn in Chapter 6, America has a tendency to post its most sensitive information about its critical infrastructures on the Internet for all to see. Perhaps the most electronically advanced society in the world, the U.S. continues to move more and more critical services to the Internet for reasons of improved efficiency, cost savings, and convenience. Deregulation in the energy industry, for example, has forced many utility companies to move their operations to the commercial Internet. The problem, of course, is that energy is the first domino in a cascading failure of infrastructures. Nothing works without electricity. And when things don't work (business computers, Internet facilities, office lights, heating systems, banks, etc.), the economy begins to slow. And when the power throughout a major metropolitan region of the country remains off for prolonged periods of time, the economy begins to grind to a halt.

"In World War II, countries flew heavy bombers over the enemy's cities to blow up communications nodes and electrical power stations," said Richard Clarke, the former National Coordinator for Security, Infrastructure Protection, and Counterterrorism at the National Security Council during the Clinton Administration, who at the time of this writing was serving as the chairman of the President's Critical Infrastructure Protection Board. "In the next war that effort may not be necessary. Electrical power grids and telecommunication grids are computer-controlled and linked over fairly open-access communication systems. It is now possible to hack one's way into such systems, take control of the controlling computer systems, and disable electrical power grids and telephones as surely as if they had been destroyed."[5] Therefore, the rapid push for ubiquitous computing is a double-edged sword. The more dependent we become on computers and the Internet, and the more interconnected our critical services and infrastructures become, the more vulnerable we are to failures—either man-made or natural.

In addition to the telecommunications sector, electricity and commercial Internet technologies are critical to the effective management and continued operation of chemical and oil refineries; nuclear power plants; water treatment plants; dams; aviation control towers; railroads; and the command, control, and communications networks of our nation's military and intelligence agencies. Border surveillance and security operations also depend on computer networks, as do navigation devices for recreational boaters, commercial fisherman, and international cargo vessels. Hospitals rely on computers and networks to treat and monitor patients, alert doctors to incoming traumas, and store highly sensitive personal medical data. And most important of all, the lifeblood of our nation's economy, better known as the stock market, also depends on the uninterrupted flow of electricity to power its computers, networks, and trading systems, all of which must remain safe from computer viruses, worms, and hackers. And while many of these infrastructure sectors have contingency plans and disaster recovery plans either in place or in development that call for backup means of delivering power, it is a fact that diesel fuel-powered

---

[5]   Prepared remarks by Richard Clarke at the Policy Conference at Lansdowne Conference Center, The Washington Institute for Near East Policy, October 16, 1998.

backup generators do not last forever and are dependent on the ability to import additional fuel to the region of the disaster—something that is not always possible in a timely manner, as we learned during the attacks of September 11, 2001. Should a future terrorist attack involve a radiological or chemical agent, significant physical restrictions on travel may be put in place, thereby making it impossible to deliver fuel and other needed equipment to the businesses and government organizations in the affected area.

Despite the reality of our ever-increasing dependence on information technologies and computer networks, and our vulnerability to malicious or terrorist-sponsored attacks in cyberspace, there are those who contend that terrorists are not interested in the silent, nonbloody tactics of cyber-terrorism. This is a myopic view of international terrorism that, as I said earlier, seeks to foresee the future course of terrorism solely in terms of its history. Underestimating a thinking enemy, especially the new type of thinking enemy that is represented by al-Qaeda, is also dangerous. Al-Qaeda represents an unprecedented threat to the United States and its allies not only because of its ability to carry out massive terrorist attacks around the world, but because of its management sophistication and its long-term view of terrorism. Al-Qaeda has shown that as an international conglomerate it is capable of adapting to new weapons, including nuclear, chemical, and cyber-weapons.

In fact, al-Qaeda may now be actively shifting from using information technologies as a command, control, and communications medium to using technology as an offensive weapon system, especially after the attacks of September 11, 2001. The communications failures that resulted from the attacks in New York had a demonstrative effect on the growing crop of future young al-Qaeda members and supporters that cannot be ignored. To accept modern global terrorists as a thinking enemy is to accept the fact that terrorist organizations study the aftermaths and the impacts of their attacks and learn from them. Therefore, it is highly likely that al-Qaeda and other terrorist organizations around the world have studied the unintended consequences of the September 11, 2001 attacks, particularly the impact the attacks had on the U.S. electronic infrastructure located in and around New York and Washington, D.C. Chapter 7 provides a behind-the-scenes look at the cyber-ramifications of the attacks of September 11, 2001.

A well-balanced combination of high-tech and human intelligence is also vital to any homeland defense strategy that aims to prevent terrorist attacks in the future. Federal, state, and local governments, together with private-sector organizations, share an unprecedented task of improving electronic information sharing pertaining to imminent terrorist threats. In Chapter 8, we look at the technology-based intelligence failures that may have contributed to the successful attacks of September 11, 2001, and why real-time electronic information sharing is critical to the short-term goal of stopping the next major attack.

Cyber-terrorism must also be viewed in a multidimensional fashion. To simply look at cyber-terrorism from the perspective of the potential for offensive use of cyber-weapons is to look out at a world that doesn't quite exist yet and to conclude wrongly that there is nothing to worry about. Cyber-terrorism, therefore, must be analyzed in terms of the full range of possible attacks and even the supporting role that commercial information technologies might play in traditional physical attacks. More importantly, we can look at the war against terrorism as a cyber-war of our own, waged with the help of the United States' own arsenal of information technology. In fact, many experts have argued that the technologies capable of making Americans more secure from the ravages of terrorism at home have long existed. In Chapter 9, therefore, we look at the concept of using commercial information technology to build a "defense in depth," which includes everything from an overseas early warning capability to protecting our ports of entry and monitoring our cities, landmarks, public places, corporate office buildings, and even our transportation industry from the threat of nuclear, chemical, or biological terrorism.

"The issue of homeland defense must be taken seriously," warned Richard Clarke, three years before the attacks of September 11, 2001. "Why would people conduct terrorism in the United States? One reason is blackmail. A major terrorist attack occurs involving chemical weapons or computers, then someone reliably says they did it and adds that, if the United States continues its support for Israel or eradicating coca on the Upper Huallaga valley in Peru or whatever, it will happen again. Perhaps their motive is revenge. Maybe attacks in the United States would be part of a regional war, just as in the Solar Sunrise scenario [a code name for a government investigation into a major hacker attack against the Pentagon's global network in 1998], where the United States may be rushing troops to another part of the world and someone wants to make that difficult to do."[6]

Of course, all of these efforts to defend against terrorism introduce new threats to the very old traditions of personal privacy and civil liberties. In the

---

[6]   Ibid.

aftermath of the attacks on September 11, 2001, we were bombarded with the mantra that to change our way of life and to give up our liberty and freedom is to allow the terrorists to win. In Chapter 10, we look at the various government efforts underway to use information technologies to battle terrorism at home and abroad and we analyze the threats to privacy and liberty. For example, are the new powers gained by the Justice Department to conduct electronic monitoring really a threat to the personal privacy of average citizens? Can antiterrorism operations really be conducted without some form of racial profiling, even with the assistance of modern software and data mining technologies? Are we fast becoming a database nation of mass background checks? And are all Muslims, especially those in the high-tech industry, automatically suspected of taking part in illicit money laundering on behalf of al-Qaeda?

While these questions of personal privacy loom large in our national consciousness, they do so amid massive change in the federal government and the private sector. Both the government and the private sector companies that own and operate the bulk of the critical systems that the terrorists of the future will endeavor to target have been hard at work on a national plan to defend America against these so-called asymmetrical threats. And with terrorist operations averaging an 18-month cycle between major events and information technology roughly doubling in performance and capability at the rate of every 12–18 months, it is easy to see why the future is now.

"For years terrorism has been viewed as the exclusive domain of national security. That view requires a reality check," according to Gilmore Commission chairman James Gilmore. "Our preparedness for cyber-terrorism must be broader, to include all levels of private and public activity."

The Gilmore Commission and various other expert panels have warned and rebuked us for allowing previous warnings of our vulnerability to terrorist attacks within the U.S. to go unheeded. Therefore, it is imperative that we not make the same mistake when it comes to preparing for the future of terrorism. We must look closely for the warning signs that exist in the ether, and in our own vulnerabilities, and ensure that the high-tech future of terrorism does not become like black ice stretched across the information superhighway—alerting us to its presence only after we are spinning out of control.

Dan Verton
Washington, D.C.
2003

1

Cyber-Terrorism: Fact or Fiction?

Terrorists are strategic actors. They choose their targets deliberately based on the weakness they observe in our defenses and our preparedness. We must defend ourselves against a wide range of means and methods of attack. Terrorists continue to employ conventional means of attack, while at the same time gaining in expertise in less traditional means, such as cyber attacks.

—**National Strategy For Homeland Security**
—The White House, July 2002

Sometime in the Future
Somewhere in the Pacific Northwest, U.S.

The operation had finally entered the execution phase after two long years of collecting intelligence, conducting covert surveillance, and preparing a detailed, multipronged strategy. The men were happy to be done with the difficult, tedious aspects of planning the attacks. Now it was simply a matter of receiving the order to set the plan in motion. And they were eager to sacrifice for the cause.

This assault would be like no other. It would be unrivaled in its coordination and technical sophistication, and it would show the world, especially the United States, that al-Qaeda remains a cunning enemy that is capable of adapting rapidly to the new operational realities it faces around the world. The lessons of the September 11 attacks, available in startling detail in the news media and on Web sites throughout the U.S., had not been lost on the architects of these planned assaults. They took those lessons and adjusted their strategy for conducting mass casualty attacks accordingly; taking into consideration the importance of precisely timed supporting strikes on America's digital infrastructure. This time, the chaos, confusion, and fear would surge outward from the epicenter of the main attack like a digital shockwave from an earthquake. Blood would be spilt, but not only human blood. The goal of this assault was to sever economic arteries as well.

Supreme command of the operation fell to 44-year-old Abdul Salah. A well-dressed, soft-spoken, handsome man with a slight tint of gray hair, Salah had emigrated legally to the U.S. from Saudi Arabia in the 1980s and quickly linked up with wealthy business professionals and various charity organizers who supported al-Qaeda in Brooklyn, New York, New Jersey, and Chicago.[1] He was chosen for this assignment because of his organizational and managerial skills, as well as his technical expertise in engineering and his devotion to Osama bin Laden's radical, perverted interpretation of the Islamic religion.

But the foot soldiers under Salah's command were of a different breed, a new generation of terrorists. They were as adept at using modern technology to plan, coordinate, and launch their attacks as they were at strapping dynamite around their waists and walking into a crowded café. More importantly, these twenty-first-century al-Qaeda-bred youth were as motivated by the prospect of destroying America's digital economy, and hence its ability to engage the world and respond militarily, as they were to carry out martyrdom missions. Unlike the founders of the radical Islamist movement, this was a generation that understood the futility of waging a war of attrition against the U.S. and took a long-term view of al-Qaeda's political and fanatical religious goals. Some were born and schooled in the U.S., melting into their communities. Others were schooled in madrassas around the world that mixed radical Islamist teachings with computer science and electrical engineering. Despite the mindless hatred and intolerance that was part of their indoctrination into al-Qaeda, this new crop of terrorists knew that spilling blood was no longer enough to bring about change in the modern world. For this new brand of terrorism to work, the bloodshed had to be accompanied by attacks that caused mass disruption, damage, or destruction of the cyber-infrastructure

---

[1]   Details of al-Qaeda's ties and infrastructure in the U.S. can be found in Ronan Gunaratna's Inside Al Qaeda (Columbia University Press, 2002), pp. 101–116.

that feeds the economy and the army of the enemy infidels. Although young in age and somewhat lacking in experience, Salah's men understood that an army moves on its belly. And America's belly was its digital economy.

The new terrorism's call to arms, which Salah hung proudly on the wall above his desk in the one-bedroom apartment he rented in Chicago, could be found in Osama's own words spoken a few months after the attacks of September 11, 2001, that killed thousands in New York, Washington, and Pennsylvania: "It is very important to concentrate on hitting the U.S. economy through all possible means...look for the key pillars of the U.S. economy. The key pillars of the enemy should be struck...."[2] Terrorism had not only become more destructive, it had become savvier in its target selection.

Salah exercised strategic control of four cells, each with five operatives. Three of these cells were based in the U.S., and one cell had recently arrived from Southeast Asia aboard a foreign merchant vessel with the help of a bribed port official. With a few exceptions, most cell members never met each other and did not know the identities of any other cell member. This was how the larger, decentralized cell structure maintained operational security. Should one member be uncovered and arrested by the FBI, he would have no knowledge of who the other cell members were or what their specific missions were. Instead, the individual tentacles of the loose-knit group were coordinated through Salah, who would meet with each senior cell leader in person to exchange data only when absolutely necessary. He preferred to exchange operational information through the use of encrypted, anonymous e-mail messages, obscure password-protected Internet bulletin boards, online chat rooms that he rotated through weekly, and steganography—the process of hiding data in digital files, such as images. Since the passage of the USA Patriot Act, which gave the FBI massive new powers to monitor cell phones and other forms of digital communications, telephone conversations were deemed too risky and therefore were used only in emergencies.

Salah read the newspapers and the technology trade journals in the U.S. religiously, and he knew that most people, especially the so-called experts in Internet security, still doubted al-Qaeda's interest in and ability to leverage information

---

[2]   Osama bin Laden, quoted in an Arab newspaper on December 27, 2001, and
       referred to during multiple Congressional hearings in the U.S. as evidence
       of al-Qaeda's future plans.

technology for offensive purposes. But Salah knew the truth about the world of modern terrorism. He knew that most Americans, even the experts, thought of terrorist organizations that rely on suicide bombers as nonthinking enemies. That was the problem with America; there were too many experts given free airtime by a pervasive media culture. The American media and their experts never seemed capable of revealing the true level of al-Qaeda's sophistication. This was an inherent weakness in the American enemy that Salah knew he could take advantage of. America was great at responding to and analyzing catastrophes, but it was terrible at preventing them from happening.

The media and the horde of Internet security analysts in America seemed to be intoxicated with the picture of al-Qaeda as a typical, single-minded, bloodthirsty, rag-tag army of terrorists. In reality, however, al-Qaeda had evolved into a task-organized, multinational paramilitary organization that valued formal training and education. One underestimated al-Qaeda's willingness and ability to adapt at one's own peril.

Many years earlier, Salah had attended training in computer programming, encryption, and various intelligence-related electronic surveillance and hacking techniques in a guesthouse belonging to Osama bin Laden in Hyatabad, a neighborhood in Peshawar, Pakistan. When he arrived, the al-Qaeda instructors asked him if he was an engineer. Having not yet finished his schooling, he answered no. Surprised and somewhat annoyed by his answer, the instructors told him to go back to school at "the institute" in Bebi, another region of Peshawar, and earn his degree in electrical engineering. Only then would he be allowed to attend computer training, they said.[3]

All of the terrorists under Salah's command had specialties, and they were split evenly throughout the four cells. There were four cell leaders; four explosives experts; four reconnaissance, surveillance, and intelligence specialists; four computer programmers with secondary training in small arms and explosives; and four specialists in developing crude chemical, biological, or nuclear weapons—the so-called dirty bombs. Except for the senior cell leaders, all were in their mid-twenties. But what really made these cells unique was that each of the U.S.-based cells

---

[3]   The event described here actually happened and is described in the testimony of L'Houssaine Kherchtou in United States of America v. Osama bin Laden, United States District Court, Southern District of New York, February 7, 2001.

had a member who had been born, raised, and schooled in the U.S.—a red-blooded American citizen. This was another subtle change that had gone unnoticed by the terrorism experts, who operated under the assumption that the longer a radical terrorist was in the U.S. living a normal life as a sleeper agent, the less radical he or she became. But Salah and the others had taken a lesson from the Soviet KGB playbook, which encouraged sleeper agents to live normal lives and even enlist in the U.S. armed forces. It was a tactic that seemed logical—use America to produce homegrown al-Qaeda operatives.

The cell members who were not U.S. citizens had entered the country previously either as students or under the auspices of H-1B work visas, a favorite hiring tool of the high-tech industry. Along with their American counterparts, they worked at various high-tech companies that preferred hiring low-wage foreign workers. That was a lot cheaper than paying American citizens a living wage. But in the process of saving a little money, those companies had opened up their corporate enterprises to malicious insiders. But these insiders were different. They weren't interested in stealing or destroying the data of any one company. That would be too easy. To the contrary, what these insiders wanted was a legitimate way to study and learn about the corporate entity known as network America.

In addition to having studied computer science at colleges in the U.S., several of Salah's men had attended training in weapons handling at an al-Qaeda camp named al-Farouk in Afghanistan.[4] Their trips to the camp were made through Pakistan and went unnoticed by authorities in the U.S. In addition, none of the foreign-born terrorists were native Afghans. To the contrary, they were organized along "family" lines. Salah had under his command an Egyptian family, a Yemeni family, a Moroccan family, and a combination Pakistani-German family. In fact, Salah had worked at a computer company based in Hamburg with the senior member from the German family.[5]

---

[4] See Philip Shenon, "U.S. Says Suspects Awaited an Order for Terror Strike," New York Times, September 15, 2002, p. 1. Five members of a suspected al-Qaeda cell were arrested in Buffalo, New York; all were in their mid-twenties and born in the U.S. This underscores how we must revise our understanding of radical terrorist movements. The conventional wisdom has been that the longer radical terrorists are living in the U.S., the less radical and dedicated to the cause they become. This must now be rethought.

[5] See Gunaratna's *Inside Al Qaeda*, pp. 95–166, for a detailed description of al-Qaeda's global network.

The plan was perfect. Salah's men were the ultimate sleepers. The authorities in the U.S. would never suspect that radical Islamists could once again enter the U.S. undetected or be recruited within the U.S. itself, thought Salah. His massive, decentralized cell had, in essence, become the definitive "American" family within al-Qaeda.

But Salah also held a few wild cards in his hand. A dozen world-class computer hackers from Russia, known in Moscow and St. Petersburg as "khakkers," had been hired to launch a series of devastating cyber-attacks against the computer networks that manage and control various critical infrastructures in the region where the planned assaults were to take place. Russia, with its failing economy, had become not only a source of out-of-work nuclear scientists but also a one-stop shop of computer hacking talent. These hired guns came from a power base of organized crime syndicates and corrupt business and government officials. They were members of the true "black hat" underground hacker community, with ties to hackers and virus writers in places like Malaysia and India. Many had once worked for the FAPSI, the Russian equivalent of the U.S. National Security Agency. Their capabilities were well known throughout intelligence circles, especially in the U.S., where the banking industry had suffered at their hands repeatedly.

Perhaps the biggest force multiplier in Salah's plan was a handful of disgruntled insiders who worked at some of the control centers that housed critical computer systems for managing the electric and natural gas grids. These men were all secret members of right-wing radical groups that had taken hold throughout many states in the northwest of the U.S. This was the first time that al-Qaeda had reached out to non-Muslims— another change in tactics that Salah knew the experts would never expect. And it was easy. Salah took yet another lesson from the old Soviet KGB espionage playbook, which instructed agents that Americans can be bought. And when cold, hard cash failed to convince them to take part, Salah turned to blackmail.

All of the pieces were in place. The weapons were moving toward their targets and the electronic back doors to the various critical facilities had been identified and logged. Now it was simply a waiting game. When the time was right, Salah would order the wheels to be set in motion.

-.-. -.-- -... . .-. - . .-. .-. --- .-.

If they *were to form an independent nation tomorrow, the Pacific Northwest U.S. states of Alaska, Idaho, Montana, Oregon, and Washington, and the Western Canadian provinces of British Columbia, Alberta, and the Yukon Territory would immediately become the eleventh largest industrial economy in the world, with a gross domestic product valued at more than $350 billion and a population of more than 18 million people.*

Like most regions of the U.S. and Canada, the Pacific Northwest is an information-based economy kept alive not only by tourism, trade, and forestry products, but also by computers, software, and the Internet. The advance of technology has erased the international border between the two nations, creating critical linkages that most people have no idea exist. All of the so-called critical services that people take for granted in their daily lives—such as telephone service, electric power, the Internet, air travel, water systems, and banking facilities—depend to varying degrees on computers and computer networks to operate properly. It is a reality of the modern world that not even the hearty inhabitants of the vast frontier region of the Pacific Northwest could escape.

But there are consequences that come with this new reality. Technology is a double-edged sword, slicing through complexity and inefficiency with one blade and cutting holes in personal and organizational security systems with the other. Digital connections that never existed before now form the high-speed avenues of approach for America's enemies. And even the most obscure organizations, some of which never once considered the threat of being targeted directly by an international terrorist organization, are now subject to the same level of destruction and disruption as the nation's major cities and symbolic landmarks. This is the essence of the new national security challenge, a challenge fueled by what some call the unintended consequences of information technology. That is a familiar concept for Salah, who is about to give the U.S. one of its first major lessons in what those unintended consequences can be.

-.-. -.-- -... . .-. - . .-. .-. --- .-.

The crisp *winter air concealed the telltale stench of death, destruction, and confusion that was now on the move.*

The explosions were timed for maximum, sudden impact on a regional scale. And they were massive; making use of hijacked fuel trucks that had been monitored closely during the past year for predictable route and delivery patterns. The drivers had become the first casualties of the attacks, and their trucks had been transformed into 18-wheeled, explosive-laden bullets. Surprisingly, a biometric access device protected one of the trucks by scanning the driver's fingerprint before allowing the engine to start. However, the technology had not yet evolved to the point that it could discern the difference between a finger that was attached to a living person and one that was attached (or not attached) to a corpse.

The first explosion occurred just north of Washington state highway 547 and the Sumas River at the U.S.-Canadian border. The blast catapulted a fireball high into the air, creating a thick, black plume of noxious fumes. In the center of the fiery rubble lay the remains of one of the most important natural gas interconnection points in the region. A series of metering stations, pumps, and compressors channel that natural gas south, parallel to the Burlington Northern Santa Fe rail line, through the states of Washington, Oregon, and into California, providing critical energy for electric power stations, which were already operating under great stress due to the region's energy crisis.

To Salah's pleasure, a cryptic message appeared on one of the password-protected bulletin boards that he used to communicate with various cell leaders, especially the corporate insiders at the various utilities. "We used sand to clean up the oil. It worked very well," the message stated. To a stranger, the message meant nothing. But to Salah, it spoke volumes. It told Salah that at least some of his American recruits had taken action against the electricity generators at the facilities where they worked. Sand was placed in the bearings, oil was drained from the system, and a wrench had possibly been dropped into a maintenance port. Time would tell how successful the attacks had been.

The next three attacks, targeting 500,000-volt long-haul transmission substations at key power plants throughout the region, occurred in rapid succession. It took the attackers less than ten seconds to cut their way through the chain link fence surrounding the facilities, and a mere 60 seconds to place the shape charges in strategic locations. Acting with the precision of a trusted insider, the Russian hacker contingent initiated a simultaneous cyber-onslaught against remaining utility control centers that penetrated critical Supervisory Control and Data Acquisition (SCADA) systems—the digital brains of the electric grid and natural gas pipelines. The Russians attacked from multiple points around the globe, injecting viruses and worms into the networks. They did so by exploiting remote dial-in and Internet-based administrative connections that lead directly into the unprotected SCADA systems. Once they had broken in, the hackers modified control programs and operational commands, and injected false commands into the networks. Valves in the natural gas system that should have been open were now closed. Unstable pressure waves in the pipelines, known as a hammering effect, were created and threatened further explosive damage to the system. Throughout the regional telecommunications network, malicious software automatically altered the configuration of critical nodes and initiated denial of service attacks that blocked vital management messages from reaching other areas of the network. The digital meltdown had begun.

On a national level, malicious software code that had never been seen before in the wild began attacking 10 of the 13 core domain name servers that direct traffic on the Internet. All of the DNS systems under attack were located in the U.S. The sophistication of these attacks, drawing as they did on Russian intelligence work that had been done for years as part of the Russian information warfare program, made all previous cyber-attacks on the DNS infrastructure pale in comparison. These failures began to build upon each other, like an avalanche.

Technicians could only guess about the origins of the disruptions. Nobody knew for sure if the failures were the result of a series of software glitches or a deliberate attack somewhere in the massive network. After all, simple glitches had caused serious problems in the past. The older, more experienced technicians remembered the 1990 crash of the AT&T long-distance network and how an error in three lines of code caused a massive failure that authorities initially thought was the work of hackers. Likewise, a distributed denial of service attack against several of the U.S.-based DNS servers had taken place in October 2002, and hardly anybody noticed. The Internet infrastructure had built-in redundancies that made such devastating attacks improbable. Of course, they were not impossible, simply improbable, especially without the right intelligence and hacking talent. Regardless, clear-cut answers to what was happening were hard to come by. It was the fog of war. And it was that type of uncertainty that the terrorists had hoped to create.

The lack of power generation and the inability to import additional energy forced authorities across multiple counties and states to institute rolling blackouts. Businesses and government agencies that had well-planned and tested disaster recovery and continuity of operations plans, including secondary diesel-powered electric generators, fared well during the initial power outages. Thousands of others were not so lucky and were forced to put their operations on hold. But the attacks were just getting started, and their full impact had yet to be felt.

-.-. -.-- -... . .-. - . .-. .-. --- .-.

In the *heart of Seattle, explosives are detonated in a residential apartment building, ripping through the guts of the structure and killing, maiming, and trapping dozens of innocent people. Before the debris settles from the first series of blasts, another, less dramatic explosion takes place on a fifth-floor balcony of an adjacent building. This time, however, the explosive device is an electromagnetic pulse (EMP) bomb—the dreaded e-bomb. One of Salah's men has placed a large cache of conventional explosives in a copper tube that is wrapped in copper wire. A battery charges the coil and creates an electromagnet. As the bomb explodes, the electrically charged coil short-circuits and compresses the magnetic waves, sending out an electromagnetic pulse similar to what is produced by a nuclear explosion, only without the massive physical destruction to people and property. The pulse produces an ionization effect that impairs radio transmissions throughout a large swath of the city. The weapon also fries all of the delicate electronic circuits and computer equipment sitting in offices and stores throughout its kill zone. The lack of EMP defenses in commercial computers subjects every business and government computer network within a two-mile radius of the attack to catastrophic failure. Business transactions come to a halt. Those failures are immediately followed by malfunctions in vehicle ignition systems, major Internet data centers, heart pacemakers, and industrial control applications, including traffic and railroad signaling systems. Communications equipment that is critical to search and rescue efforts doesn't work. Salah's men built the weapon for about $1,500, relying on rudimentary engineering skills.*

As quickly as the invisible pulse of energy penetrates the dense Seattle air and destroys the electronic circuits that keep the city communicating, the al-Qaeda operatives that had been stowed away aboard a commercial shipping vessel arrive at their target several hundred miles to the south. Like their counterparts, they have dynamite strapped to their bodies beneath their clothes and are sitting in the cab of a large fuel truck weighted down by thousands of gallons of gasoline.

They stop at the corner of West San Fernando and Market Street in San Jose, one block north of Cesar de Chavez Park and the same distance south of their target. San Jose, better known as the capital of the digital universe and the heart of the Silicon Valley, is nothing like what Salah's men had imagined. The streets are relatively empty. There are still plenty of expensive cars parked along the side of the road, plenty of traffic, and a few overweight Internet executives sipping decaf lattes as they walk down the street, but this is not the digital Land of Oz that the terrorists had expected to find.

Two of the five operatives get out of the truck as if acting on cue. One is holding a brown shoe box, the other a concealed handgun. They proceed to walk north on Market Street. The driver, 27-year-old Muhammad al-Sudani, alias Muhammad al-Assan, alias Abu Fadl, removes a photograph from an envelope and places it against the steering wheel. He checks the photograph against what he sees through the windshield. The two views are the same. The gold, mirrored building at the corner of Market and Post Street appears exactly as it does in the photo. "That is it," he says to the others, who begin to pray as the truck lurches forward slowly.

The building in their sights is home to one of the two largest and most critical Internet nodes in the world. National security experts know the place simply as MAE-West, the namesake of one of the most famous and curvaceous bombshells of 1930s Hollywood. But to MCI WorldCom, the owner and operator of the west coast Metropolitan Area Ethernet (the real meaning of MAE-West), the tenth-floor facility houses a critical Internet switching center that major Internet service providers connect to as a means of sharing data across networks. Millions of Internet sessions, billions of bits of data per second—by some estimates as much as 40 percent of total U.S. Internet traffic—flow through the electrically charged office space. Massive batteries rest on steel-reinforced floors that vibrate to the low drone of air conditioners. A maze of chain-link cages surrounds ceiling-high racks of routers and shelves of modems, and equipment that belongs to independent ISPs.

Al-Sudani nudges the truck forward slowly, giving the operatives carrying the shoe box time to make their way far enough into the lobby of the building that the release of the white-powdered, anthrax-laced substance will be most effective. The deeper the contamination spreads through the building, the tougher it will be to remove. And the tougher it is to remove from the building—at least whatever is left of the building when the final assault is carried out—the longer the psychological damage will linger throughout the community.

As the brothers approach the building, al-Sudani signals to one of the other operatives seated to his right. The other reaches into his left shirt pocket and removes a cell phone. The number he is calling is stored in memory and he connects in seconds. "Now. 911," he says. The cryptic message has nothing to do with the September 11 terrorist attacks and everything to do with America's reliance on a new generation of cell phone technology—a third generation, to be exact. In seconds, the Russians will launch a devastating worm that will infect thousands of unprotected cell phones and cause them all to dial 911 simultaneously. The network will quickly become overloaded from the massive denial of service attack. Real emergencies, like the one that is about to happen, will go ignored until the network can be restored.

Once the operatives disappear into the bowels of the building and with a clear view of the target, al-Sudani presses the accelerator to the floor. The truck belches a thick column of black smoke from its exhaust pipe and begins to rumble uncontrollably toward what will soon be ground zero. When al-Sudani and his al-Qaeda brethren detonate the explosives strapped around their bodies, the blast sets off a chain reaction that ignites the 10,200 gallons of gasoline in the tanker. Bodies vaporize and tear apart. The face of the building is ripped into shreds, exposing its skeleton. Glass shatters, sending razor-edged shards slicing through the air. Metal and steel melt and bend in the 1,700-degree inferno. However, mistaken for the smoke and debris of the blasts is a sinister white substance that hangs ominously in the air like a genie released from its bottle. The true nature of the substance will remain unknown for days until dozens of survivors begin arriving at hospitals complaining of flu-like symptoms and strange, dark lesions on their skin.

But the hospitals in the region have another, more immediate problem on their hands. Patients are becoming critically ill, and some are dying from incompatible blood transfusions. When the first patient received the wrong blood, doctors simply chalked it up to a nursing mistake. For that lucky soul, the error was caught in time. But when dozens of other critically injured patients began to succumb to incompatible blood, hospital authorities realized that they were facing a vastly more sinister and complicated problem. Prior to launching their denial of service attacks, Salah's Russian hackers had succeeded in compromising medical records that were stored on computers at various hospitals throughout the region. They changed the blood types in dozens of patient records and deleted critical test results and doctors' orders in others. This was perhaps the easiest task of all for the hackers. Hospitals everywhere have for years been moving their operations onto computers, and these computers are often connected to the Internet to allow pharmacists and doctors to interact with each other and conduct business remotely.

Security precautions, however, are costly and often stand in the way of what most medical professionals would call efficient care.

Meanwhile, the impact of the attack against MAE-West combined with the denial of service assault on the Internet's DNS infrastructure is felt immediately throughout the region's Internet infrastructure. Many major ISPs lose all connectivity. Others fall back on peering agreements—a practice by which two ISPs connect to each other's networks for mutual benefit. However, even with peering arrangements in place, hundreds of Internet links slow to a crawl. As traffic is rerouted around the devastated interconnection points, congestion begins to take its toll on other regions of the national infrastructure. Once again, business transactions slow or fail completely.

News reports of the attacks begin to filter out of the region to the rest of the country. Salah's final stroke of genius was actually one of the first stages of the attacks that until now went unnoticed—the defacement of Web sites belonging to several major news organizations. The attacks replaced the legitimate content of the Web sites with a photo of Osama bin Laden and an admission of responsibility for the attacks. The defacements summarize in surprising detail the intended economic and psychological impact of the attacks. As Internet services slowly return, online news organizations and their consumers are met with the following message:

> Divide their nation, tear them to shreds, destroy their economy, burn their companies, ruin their welfare, sink their ships and kill them on land, sea and air....[6] That is our mission and we've proven that we are capable of standing up to the U.S. Your dependence on technology makes you weak. More brothers await orders to attack again. They will attack your powerful companies, like Microsoft, from the inside and you will not know when or how. Through these attacks your power will fail, your communications will fail, your businesses will starve, your economy will crumble, your people will panic, your military and firemen will be immobilized and, God willing, you will one day be incapable of sustaining the sinful deployment of your infidel army throughout the land of the two holy places.

---

[6] Quote attributed to Muhammad Atef, the former military commander of al-Qaeda, and Ayman Muhammad Rabi' al-Zawahiri, founder of the Egyptian terrorist group, Islamic Jihad, who became a close, influential confidant of bin Laden. Quoted in Gunaratna's Inside Al Qaeda, p. 47.

-.-. -.-- -... . .-. - . .-. .-. --- .-.

In Washington, *D.C., it's already too late. There were no indications or warnings of what had just transpired. Once again, America was responding to a successful attack, rather than acting to prevent one.*

At the White House, the President's National Security Advisor sends word to her staff that she wants answers that she can take to the president and she wants them now. Working through the Secretary of Homeland Security, her demand for information gets passed down through the National Security Council and on to the government's Cyber Incident Coordination Group (CICG)—a select group of cyber-intelligence experts from the CIA, the National Security Council, the Critical Infrastructure Assurance Office, and the FBI. The mission of the CICG is to coordinate the government's response to any cyber-incident that poses a threat to national security.

Almost immediately, intelligence experts throughout Washington are exchanging data and analysis on the attacks using secure video conferencing networks that link the various national security agencies together for just such contingencies. At CIA Headquarters in Langley, Virginia, the 24-hour, high-tech Terrorism Watch Center has been turning around requests for information in an average of 35 minutes. In this case, however, they're looking at closer to 90 minutes—still well within the center's two-hour response requirement.

With little information about the origin of the cyber-attacks or the possible terrorist links of those responsible for the physical attacks, officials turn immediately to the FBI's National Infrastructure Protection Center for an answer to the one question they know the president will ask—what are the larger regional and national implications of these attacks and how long will it take to get back to relative normalcy? The director of the NIPC, a career FBI and counterintelligence agent, orders an emergency impact analysis based on information that is flowing in from the private-sector information sharing and analysis centers. The assessment that will reach the president paints a dismal picture of the resilience of the infrastructure.

The power outages last for weeks, in some areas, for months. System failures begin to cascade out of control and are felt as far south as California. The voltage collapse in the power grid combined with the bombing of the MAE-West facility leads to communications failures on a massive scale. The combined effects of the EMP explosion, telecommunications failures, denial of service attack against local 911 systems, and a surge in wireless cell phone use impair the ability of emergency *first-responders to coordinate rescue and response operations. Coming as they do in the dead of winter, the attacks and the massive failures of the computerized, interconnected, and interdependent infrastructures forces authorities to mobilize the National Guard to attend to the elderly and the shut-ins living in remote areas that are now without electricity and telephone service, and possibly without heat.*

Medical facilities quickly enter crisis mode as they are forced to rely on back-up power generators for critical care systems. Complicating matters further is the lack of an integrated, nationwide warning and analysis system that medical officials can use to spot suspicious outbreaks of unusual diseases. Such systems exist and are often deployed to local hospitals during major events, such as the Super Bowl or World Series, but most hospitals do not have the luxury of tapping directly into the expertise of the Centers for Disease Control. Likewise, the lack of telecommunications makes coordinating medical emergencies and sharing data on the possible biological or chemical cases nearly impossible.

Businesses, banks, government offices, industrial plants, and manufacturing firms are also starved of connectivity. Some will be forced to close their doors for good. The defacements of the national news media Web sites also send shock waves through Wall Street. Microsoft stock tumbles as fears grow that it may be next on the terrorists' target list, or worse, that al-Qaeda sympathizers may have infiltrated the company. Then, news reports indicate that at least a half dozen other companies are attributing declines in stock prices to suspected hacking intrusions that made subtle changes to press releases.

Failures and disruptions ripple through potable water control systems, the computers that manage sewage treatment plants, and chemical and oil refineries. And the hardest hit businesses, the utilities that had been directly targeted, go about the difficult task of rebuilding the destroyed systems, eradicating the malicious software viruses from the remaining command and control computers, and rerouting electricity and natural gas loads where possible. The replacement of equipment alone can take weeks or longer because America doesn't manufacture many of the industrial systems that make up the electric infrastructure.

-.-. -.-- -... . .-. - . .-. .-. --- .-.

This is *the face of the new terrorism. It is a thinking man's game that applies the violent tactics of the old world to the realities and vulnerabilities of the new,* *high-tech world. Gone are the days when the only victims are those who are unfortunate enough to be standing within striking distance of the blast. Terrorism is now about smart, well-planned indirect targeting of the electronic sinews of a nation. The architects of the new terrorism have finally learned what perhaps is the most important lesson of all: America's national security depends upon its economic security. And the vanguard of both is a weak, unprotected corporate-run digital nervous system.*

2

Black Ice: Cyber-Terrorism's Hidden Dangers

Our society presents an almost infinite array of potential targets, allowing for an enormously wide range of potential attack methods. Terrorists may seek to cause widespread disruption and damage, including casualties, by attacking our electronic and computer networks, which are linked to other critical infrastructures such as our energy, financial, and securities networks.

—*National Strategy For Homeland Security*
—*The White House, July 2002*

The scenario outlined in Chapter 1 is, admittedly, a work of fiction. Although not impossible, the odds are not in favor of a terrorist group such as al-Qaeda being able to conduct such a widespread, massive, coordinated attack within the continental U.S. As impossible as that scenario may seem, however, all of its component parts, such as the vulnerability of systems to physical attacks and cyber-attacks and the cascading effects of widespread power outages, were taken from real-world simulations and exercises conducted within the last three years by the U.S. government as well as by private-sector entities. Likewise, the biographical information provided on the fictional terrorists was taken from factual court testimonies of actual

17

al-Qaeda operatives who have been tried for previous terrorist attacks, as well as from the works of respected terrorism experts. The point of the scenario, therefore, is simple: America's critical infrastructures, which power our way of life and our national security, depend on computer systems and networks that are increasingly connected to each other via the Internet and are becoming increasingly vulnerable to a wide array of attacks, both cyber and physical. And America's enemies are actively studying new ways to inflict damage to the nation's economy and weaken its resolve.

The first major infrastructure interdependency exercise took place in November 2000 in preparation for the 2002 Winter Olympics in Utah. Known by its code name, Black Ice, the simulation was sponsored by the U.S. Department of Energy and the Utah Olympic Public Safety Command. The goal was to prepare federal, state, local, and private-sector officials for the unexpected consequences of a major terrorist attack or a series of attacks throughout the region, where tens of thousands of athletes and spectators from around the world would gather. When it was over, Black Ice demonstrated in frightening detail how the effects of a major terrorist attack or natural disaster could be made significantly worse by a simultaneous cyber-attack against the computers that manage the region's critical infrastructures.

The Black Ice scenario takes place on February 14, during the second week of the Olympics. A major ice storm topples power lines across seven counties in Utah and disrupts microwave communications in the Salt Lake City area. It also damages the high-voltage bulk transmission lines in several states, including transmission lines north and south of Salt Lake City. The damage to the transmission system isn't extensive, but the ability to import electricity to the seven-county area is hindered significantly. The lack of power generation forces authorities to conduct rolling blackouts.

As the rolling blackouts begin to take their toll, the Supervisory Control and Data Acquisition systems, which control the power grid and other key industrial-sector facilities, experience widespread failures. The source of the disruption is unknown; it could be a hacker, a terrorist, an insider, or the result of storm damage. Regardless, the failures begin to ripple throughout the rest of the regional infrastructure.

Telecommunications networks are the first casualties of the massive disruptions in the power grid. To their dismay, the more than 225 exercise participants discover that prolonged power outages, particularly outages that last for several hours or longer, quickly degrade the performance and survivability of the multitude of other infrastructures that depend on power—which is just about everything.

And it's not only telecommunications that succumbs to the systemic failures that ripple throughout the vital organs of the digital infrastructure. Water systems rely on electric power, as do the natural gas industry and the natural gas–powered electric utilities in the region. Those systems also begin to experience greater than normal stress, and as a result, many fail. Emergency responders struggle through the chaos that results from Internet outages, cell phone overload, and telephone failures—similar to what happened during the September 11, 2001, attacks in New York (see Chapter 7).

The ice storm that the exercise planners injected into the scenario could easily have been replaced with multiple bombings, hijackings, or other physical catastrophes. The important lesson is that Black Ice showed the growing number of critical interdependencies that exist throughout the various infrastructure systems and how devastating combined cyber-attacks and physical attacks can be. It proved for the first time that the terrorist's mode of attack is irrelevant when it comes to cyber-terrorism. Terrorist groups that want to amplify the chaos and confusion of physical attacks or directly target the economy can succeed by launching traditional-style terrorist assaults against the nation's cyber-infrastructure.

Many Internet security analysts and observers have refused to acknowledge the physical aspects of cyber-terrorism, mostly because of a lack of formal education and experience in holistic approaches to security. Fortunately, many of the most senior members of the Bush administration understand the problem in all of its aspects. For example, Richard Clarke, former chairman of the President's Critical Infrastructure Protection Board and the de facto cybersecurity czar, spent his entire career in the national security arena. Prior to being picked for the cybersecurity post, Clarke was the nation's first counter-terrorism chief in the executive branch during the Clinton administration. His deputy, Howard Schmidt, the former chief security officer at Microsoft Corporation, is also a military veteran who was once in charge of the physical security of Microsoft chairman Bill Gates and other key executives. Neither Clarke nor Schmidt has chosen to approach cybersecurity with blinders on.

"We have to take a holistic approach to security," said Schmidt. "There's a cyber-dimension to the physical world and there's a physical dimension to the cyber-world," he said. "If indeed there was a physical event, whether it was deliberate or an act of nature, and at the same time there was a disruption in the cyber-world, the situation could be a lot more problematic than if one or the other event happened in isolation," said Schmidt. "So, we have to be cognizant of both of those aspects in order to do a better job of protecting ourselves."[1]

Paula Scalingi is a former director of the Department of Energy's Critical Infrastructure Protection Office and played a central role in planning the Black Ice exercise as well as a follow-on exercise code-named Blue Cascades that took place in June 2002. Scalingi, who now heads her own security consulting firm located outside of Washington, D.C., witnessed first-hand the chaos, confusion, and coordination failures that plagued the hundreds of exercise participants, all of whom were actual officials from the government and private organizations that are responsible for responding to such attacks and system failures. Her assessment is straightforward and chilling: There's no question that such attacks and disruptions are achievable.[2]

"The infrastructure system providers did not understand the interdependencies among their systems," Scalingi said. "If you talk to state and local governments and local utilities, they'll tell you they have great response plans. The problem is, they write them in isolation."

One of the recommendations to come out of the Black Ice exercise called on the private-sector owners of critical-infrastructure systems, such as the utility companies, to build a database to identify the various levels of

---

[1]   Author's interview, September 25, 2002.

[2]   See Dan Verton, "Black Ice Scenario Sheds Light on Future Threats to Critical Systems," *Computerworld*, October 18, 2001. (http://www.computerworld.com/securitytopics/security/story/0,10801,64877,00.html)

interdependency among their systems. Utah emergency planners also proposed developing a secure database to create an inventory of infrastructure information that could be used in times of emergency. The database would have included geographic information system technology that would have enabled officials to view a graphic representation on a map of the status of various infrastructure systems and how they connect. However, concerns about the security of proprietary industry data put the project on hold.

-.-. -.-- -... . .-. - . .-. .-. --- .-.

As was mentioned, Black Ice was followed by a sister exercise code-named Blue Cascades. Sponsored in June 2002 by a host of organizations, including the Pacific Northwest Partnership for Regional Infrastructure Security, the U.S. Navy, the Federal Emergency Management Agency, and Canada's Office of Critical Infrastructure Protection and Emergency Preparedness, Blue Cascades uncovered many of the same problems and vulnerabilities that were highlighted during Black Ice.

Participants in Blue Cascades included federal and state officials as well as companies such as Bonneville Power & Light Company, The Boeing Company, Pacific Gas & Electric Company, Verizon Communications, Qwest Communications International, Inc., and a multitude of other companies from both the U.S. and Canada. The exercise focused on linkages between infrastructures that could make the Pacific Northwest, including regions of Canada, vulnerable to cascading failures in the event of an attack or disruption that could complicate quick response and disaster recovery operations. The critical infrastructures studied in the exercise included energy (electric power, oil, and natural gas), telecommunications, transportation, water supply systems, banking and finance networks, emergency services, and government services. And what made the exercise and its results even more interesting was the fact that the companies and government agencies that took part drew on their own worst fears and concerns to write the scenario.

The final report on the lessons learned from Blue Cascades outlined how terrorist attacks or other physical disasters could disrupt the region's electric power for weeks, and in some cases for months, leading to region-wide power outages that could spread quickly to other Western states. It also envisioned follow-on disruptions to the region's telecommunications and at least two natural gas distribution systems, as well as threats to a major municipal water system and the region's seaports.

"In the case of Verizon, it wasn't an attack that caused damage, but a cyber system failure that was caused by the prolonged electric power outage, resulting in an emergency situation at one of their key facilities that took out the Internet," said Scalingi. "It was a very realistic scenario."

But the vulnerabilities that exist in the electric power industry predate Blue Cascades and Black Ice. For example, few critical components of electric power substations in the U.S. are actually manufactured in the U.S. Therefore, getting replacement parts when they are needed is often a lengthy process that extends the duration of the power outage. "For decades there's been no economic incentive to stockpile these components," which are very expensive and difficult to transport, according to Scalingi. One of the recommendations to come out of the Blue Cascades exercise is to create a stockpile of critical components that can easily be replaced in the event of damage. But with little or no immediate return on investment, the strategic stockpiling of critical systems may fall to the government. For the U.S. companies that own and operate approximately 85 percent of the U.S. critical infrastructure systems, being able to guarantee survival before a disaster occurs does not translate into a return on investment.

-.-. -.-- -... . .-. - . .-. .-. --- .-.

As in the fictional scenario presented in the preceding chapter, the disruptions of critical services that took place during the Blue Cascades exercise affected other important operations and facilities, including transportation, emergency services, hospitals, law enforcement operations, and even water services. Given the interconnected nature of the western grid system (including electric, natural gas, and water), prolonged failures and disruptions would likely extend as far south as southern California. It is the vast number of interconnections made possible by computer technology that have created these hidden vulnerabilities. However, the analytical tools do not yet exist that can give officials an accurate picture of exactly how far the system failures and damage would extend if major utility companies were taken off line through either a surgical cyber-attack or physical destruction of cyber-control systems.

According to the final report on the lessons learned from the exercise, government and private-sector participants "demonstrated at best a surface-level understanding of interdependencies and little knowledge of the critical assets of other infrastructures, vulnerabilities and operational dynamics of these regional interconnections, particularly during longer-term disruptions."[3] Moreover, most companies and government officials failed to recognize their own "overwhelming dependency upon IT-related resources to continue business operations and execute recovery plans," according to the report.

One such overwhelming dependency that continues to take hold throughout the entire country is a movement by state and local governments to transfer emergency communications systems to the Internet. Many state and local law enforcement and emergency responder organizations speak proudly of their state-of-the-art Internet-based communications and coordination architecture. However, the wholesale push to move critical communications functions to the Internet demonstrates a complete lack of understanding of the interdependencies that exist between the telecommunications sector and other industrial sectors of the economy. Few local planners have stopped to think about the implications of indirect cyber-attacks or physical attacks against other infrastructure systems, such as the natural gas grid, and the impact such disruptions may have on local Internet connectivity.

Scalingi says that most companies and even some government officials have a hard time accepting the notion of cyber-terrorism and even fewer

---

3   Report of the Pacific Northwest Economic Region, Partnership for Regional Infrastructure Security Interdependencies Tabletop Exercise "Blue Cascades," July 18, 2002.

are capable of acknowledging their own vulnerability to such a security threat. Most have deluded themselves into believing that this thing called cyber-terrorism "is somehow distinct or separate from terrorism or disruptions" or that such cyber-forms of terrorism occur only in the cyber-world (i.e., on the Internet). What Scalingi found during both the Black Ice and Blue Cascades exercises is that most private companies "… can't resonate with cyber-terrorism and they're not interested in what they think is cyber-terrorism."

In fact, most participants in the exercises were reluctant to include physical attacks as part of the scenarios that were used to test their responses to such crises. What they were most interested in, says Scalingi, was learning how their systems and services could be disrupted electronically. This shows a fundamental misunderstanding of security in the information age, particularly with respect to the post–September 11 environment.

Such intellectual inflexibility is rampant throughout the private sector, particularly in the upper echelons of corporate leadership. In fact, prior to the September 11 terrorist attacks, many companies told crisis management experts and security consultants that the possibility of a plane crashing into their building or other facility was too bizarre to even consider.[4] Likewise, officials at some nuclear facilities refused to use security exercise scenarios that involved a deliberate plane crash.[5]

The intellectual inflexibility that to date has hamstrung corporate America has also taken hold in the one area that presents the best chance of preventing such devastating, cascading failures from occurring: public-private sector information sharing on everything from current and future threats to ongoing cyber-attacks.

This is perhaps the most important issue facing U.S. national security in the information age. As of this writing, the private companies that own and operate the bulk of the nation's most critical infrastructure systems continue to balk at sharing with the government the lion's share of information about cyber-vulnerabilities and security incidents. Most fear that

---

[4]   See Dan Verton, "Corporate America Must Confront Terrorism, Security Experts Say," *Computerworld,* September 12, 2001. (http://www.computerworld.com/news/2001/story/0,11280,63751,00.html)

[5]   Ibid.

the government, through Freedom of Information Act requests, will inadvertently disclose proprietary company data to competitors. Congress has been debating this issue for years, trying in vain to balance the deluge of lobbying by special interest groups with the legitimate need of government security professionals to have access to the data. And while information sharing has improved dramatically with the establishment in various economic sectors of private sector–run Information Sharing and Analysis Centers (ISACs),[6] the reality is that many of the companies that should be taking part in ISACs, such as the manufacturers of critical system components, are not. In addition, competing interests in the form of a multitude of industry associations that claim to offer critical information sharing services to member companies have added to the confusion that comes with redundant efforts and have hindered cross-sector cooperation.

The tectonic speed at which the information sharing issue is being acted upon is symptomatic of the failure of both the federal government and private industry to come to grips with the new realities of national security in the Internet age. In multiple interviews with senior members of the Bush administration's National Security Council, particularly those officials working in the cybersecurity arena, the concept of allowing market forces to dictate security requirements remains the centerpiece of the administration's policy on national cybersecurity. Clarke, Schmidt, and others from the NSC have said repeatedly that government regulation of Internet and software security requirements is out of the question—music to the ears of computer hardware and software manufacturers, as well as the companies that use the equipment. I've been present at speeches given by Clarke to industry groups where his assertions that the government would not seek to improve cybersecurity and critical infrastructure protection through regulation were met with resounding applause. But the government's position that industry needs to engage in self-regulation when it comes to cybersecurity is tantamount to abandoning its national security responsibilities.

---

6 ISACs have been established in the IT, telecommunications, energy, banking, and other industry sectors through a joint government–private sector effort. Companies share information on threats and security incidents as a means of enhancing the common defense against cyber-based threats to infrastructure.

However, the free market is driven by the bottom line, not security. And that was the message delivered to the president and Congress on December 15, 2002 by the Advisory Panel to Assess Domestic Response Capabilities for Terrorism Involving Weapons of Mass Destruction led by former Virginia Governor James S. Gilmore III. During a press conference announcing the completion of the commission's fourth annual report, Gilmore said, "So far, pure public/private partnerships and market forces are not acting ... to protect the cybercommunity." Relying on the private sector's willingness to do the right thing when it comes to security is simply not an answer, he said.

-.-. -.-- -... . .-. - . .-. .-. --- .-.

The pervasive intellectual rigidity that surrounds the issue of cyber-terrorism has created two competing camps of thought. One camp, consisting mostly of individuals with years of formal training and experience in national security from a holistic point of view (i.e., the relationship between physical security and cybersecurity, and the adaptive nature of international terrorism), accepts the notion that America is facing a thinking enemy that is far more capable than most people are willing to accept. The other camp, consisting mainly of self-proclaimed experts, industry "analysts," neophyte media commentators, and Internet security professionals whose expertise is limited significantly to the virtual realm of the computer, remains the last, fading bastion of hope for those who want desperately to hang on to the conception of traditional terrorism as the only legitimate form of terrorism. This latter group falls into the same category as those who, prior to September 11, 2001, considered airborne threats to physical infrastructure too bizarre to spend time and resources preparing for.[7]

This brings us back to where we started, focusing on the questions of whether cyber-terrorism is real and, if it is real, if we truly understand what it is and what it entails. If we go back to one of the earliest definitions,

---

[7] Yet, on at least three different occasions—two in 1994 and one in 2000—intelligence officials uncovered al-Qaeda plots to use aircraft to attack physical structures, including the Eiffel Tower in Paris and CIA Headquarters in Virginia.

offered in 1997 by Mark Pollitt, a special agent for the FBI, cyber-terrorism is defined as follows:

> *Cyber-terrorism is the premeditated, politically motivated attack against information, computer systems, computer programs, and data which results in violence against noncombatant targets by subnational groups or clandestine agents.*[8]

Pollitt's definition is particularly useful because it does not make the mistake of pigeonholing the term "cyber-terrorism" as strictly a cyber-based phenomenon. If you read between the lines of Pollitt's definition, the "attack" against computer systems or data can take either a physical form or a cyber-based one. This is the more sophisticated, long-term view of cyber-terrorism and of terrorism in general. And for those who still find it difficult to break out of the narrow understanding of the term, there have already been many low-level examples of what we can expect to see taking place in the future as international terrorism continues to evolve. While the examples that follow may not be terrorism as defined by Pollitt or by myself, they should be taken as low-level indications and warnings for the future.

For example, in November 2001, a 49-year-old Australian man was sentenced to two years in prison for using the Internet and stolen control software to release up to one million liters of raw sewage into public parks and creeks throughout Queensland, Australia's Sunshine Coast. The man, who had been a consultant on the water project, conducted the attack after he was refused a job with the company that installed a computerized sewerage system for Maroochy Shire Council. The creek water turned black, and an untold number of precious marine animals died. More telling is the fact that the facility failed to notice the attacker's 44 previous break-in attempts.

The U.S. Congress was alerted in February 1998 to attempts by Islamic extremist organizations to develop a hacker network to support their activities as well as possibly engage in offensive information warfare attacks

---

[8]   Mark M. Pollitt, "Cyberterrorism: Fact or Fancy?" *Proceedings of the 20th National Information Systems Security Conference*, October 1997, pp. 285–289.

against key U.S. government computers.[9] Several months later, news reports indicated that a member of a militant Indian separatist group attempted to purchase military software from a hacker group that claimed to have stolen the software from a U.S. Defense Department network. The group in question, Harkat-ul-Ansar, was one of the dozens of organizations on the U.S. State Department's terrorism list.

Some writers and analysts have characterized the 1998 e-mail flood attack launched against Sri Lankan embassies by ethnic Tamil guerrillas as the first known attack by terrorists against a country's computer systems. The guerillas swamped Sri Lankan embassies with thousands of electronic mail messages that read, "We are the Internet Black Tigers and we're doing this to disrupt your communications." The so-called "e-mail bombing" campaign consisted of about 800 e-mail messages a day for two weeks. While the impact of the deluge of e-mail messages may have been negligible, especially from a terrorism perspective, the intent of the attackers is consistent with an accurate understanding of cyber-terrorism.

In 1997, a teenage hacker disabled a key telephone company computer, cutting connectivity to an airport in Worcester, Massachusetts. Although the teen had little or no knowledge of what he had done, the airport control tower lost critical services for six hours, forcing incoming airplanes to rely on radio communications and other airports to provide landing instructions. That same year, a technician at a Virginia Internet service provider inadvertently injected errors into the ISP's routing tables, causing critical Internet routers to crash.

In London, eight members of the Irish Republican Army (IRA) were arrested in 1996 for conspiring to blow up six key electric substations, gas valves, and pipelines. Had they succeeded, the attackers would have disrupted power to major portions of London for months. The gang researched the national electric grid in libraries and used open sources of information to select the key nodes that would have had the most impact on the grid. A police raid uncovered 36 explosive devices.

---

[9] Clark Staten, testimony before the Subcommittee on Technology, Terrorism, and Government Information, U.S. Senate Judiciary Committee, February 24, 1998.

Since the start of the U.S. War on Terrorism, a significant amount of evidence has been unearthed throughout Afghanistan and various other al-Qaeda hideouts around the world that indicates terrorism may be evolving toward a more high-tech future at a faster rate than previously believed. In January 2002, for example, U.S. forces in Kabul discovered a computer at an al-Qaeda office that contained models of a dam, made with structural architecture and engineering software. The software would have enabled al-Qaeda to study the best way to attack the dam and to simulate the dam's catastrophic failure. In addition, al-Qaeda operatives apprehended around the world acknowledged receiving training in how to attack key infrastructures.

By June, working on intelligence from the Central Intelligence Agency, the Bush administration was warning Americans that al-Qaeda had far more interest in cyber-terrorism than previously believed. "We were underestimating the amount of attention [al-Qaeda was] paying to the Internet," Roger Cressey, chief of staff of President Bush's Critical Infrastructure Protection Board, told *The Washington Post* in an interview.[10]

More than a year after the terrorist attacks of September 11, 2001, the warnings about the vulnerability of America's critical infrastructures to both physical attacks and cyber-attacks continue to flow. One of the most recent and significant studies comes from the Council on Foreign Relations, which sponsored an independent task force headed by former Senators Gary Hart and Warren Rudman to study the progress of America's homeland security efforts. The conclusion of the task force, which was turned into the title of the final report, was simple and straightforward: "America Still Unprepared—America Still in Danger." More importantly, as is evident from the following paragraph, the detailed findings of the Hart-Rudman task force confirmed the findings of the Black Ice and Blue Cascades exercises.

> *Sixty percent of the Northeast's refined oil products are piped from refineries in Texas and Louisiana. A coordinated attack on several key pumping stations—most of which are in remote areas, are not staffed,*

---

10 Barton Gellman, "Cyber-Attacks by Al-Qaeda Feared," *The Washington Post*, June 27, 2002, p. A01.

and possess no intrusion detection devices—could cause mass disruption to these flows. Nearly fifty percent of California's electrical supply comes from natural gas power plants and thirty percent of California's natural gas comes from Canada. Compressor stations to maintain pressure cost up to $40 million each and are located every sixty miles on a pipeline. If these compressor stations were targeted, the pipeline would be shut down for an extended period of time. A coordinated attack on a selected set of key points in the electrical power system could result in multi-state blackouts. While power might be restored in parts of the region within a matter of days or weeks, acute shortages could mandate rolling blackouts for as long as several years. Spare parts for critical components of the power grid are in short supply; in many cases they must be shipped from overseas sources.[11]

For the most part, these dire warnings have gone unheeded by the private-sector companies that own and operate these infrastructure systems. Senior executives view such scenarios as something akin to a Hollywood movie script. However, throughout the entire post-September 11 security review process, a process that continues to this day, administration experts and other senior members of the U.S. intelligence community were quietly coming to the conclusion that they were witnessing the birth of a new era of terrorism. Cyberspace, with its vast invisible linkages and critical role in keeping America's vital infrastructures and economy functioning, was fast becoming a target and a weapon of terror.

---

[11] "America Still Unprepared—America Still in Danger," Report of an Independent Task Force Sponsored by the Council on Foreign Relations, p. 26.

3

Terror on a Wire:
The Internet as Weapon

Peace really does not exist in the Information Age.

> —Air Force Lt. Gen. Kenneth Minihan
> Director, National Security Agency
> Testimony—Senate Armed Services Committee
> June 4, 1998

It is conceivable that terrorists could mount a cyber attack against power or water facilities or industrial plants—for example, a commercial chemical plant that produces a highly toxic substance—to produce casualties in the hundreds of thousands.

> —Second Annual Report of the Advisory Panel to Assess Domestic Response
> Capabilities for Terrorism Involving Weapons of Mass Destruction
> December 15, 2000

In summer 1997, the U.S. Joint Chiefs of Staff organized what is known as a "no-notice" exercise that would test the Pentagon's ability to detect and defend against a coordinated cyber-attack against various military installations and critical computer networks. It would involve dozens of world-class computer hackers and last for more than a week. The Joint Chiefs gave the highly classified exercise the code name "Eligible Receiver." The operational details of how the "Red Team" of pretend-hackers would carry out their attacks were left to senior officials from the super-secret National Security Agency.

Prior to launching their attacks on June 9, officials briefed the team of 35 NSA computer hackers on the ground rules. They were told in no uncertain terms that they were allowed to use only software tools and other hacking utilities that could be downloaded freely from the Internet through any one of the hundreds and possibly thousands of hacker Web sites. In other words, the Pentagon's own arsenal of secret offensive information warfare tools, which the NSA certainly had, could not be used. And while they were allowed to penetrate various Pentagon networks, the Red Team was prohibited from breaking any U.S. laws.

The primary target of the exercise was the U.S. Pacific Command in Hawaii, which is responsible for all military contingencies and operations conducted in the Pacific theater, including the tension-racked Korean Peninsula. Other targets included the National Military Command Center (NMCC) in the Pentagon, the U.S. Space Command in Colorado, the heart of the Pentagon's logistics operation at the U.S. Transportation Command in Ohio, and the Special Operations Command in Tampa, Florida.

Posing as hackers hired by the North Korean intelligence service, the NSA Red Team dispersed around the country and began digging their way into military networks. They floated through cyberspace with ease, mapping networks and logging passwords gained through brute force cracking and the more subtle tactic of social engineering—sometimes it was just easier to call somebody on the telephone, pretend to be a technician or high-ranking official, and ask for their password to the network. The team gained unfettered access to dozens of critical Pentagon computer systems. With that level of access, they were free to create legitimate user accounts for other hackers, delete accounts belonging to authorized officials, reformat the server hard drives and scramble the data, or simply shut the systems down. They were able to break through the paltry network defenses with ease, after which they could conduct denial of service attacks, read or make minor changes to sensitive e-mail messages, and disrupt telephone services. And they did so without being traced or identified.

The results of the exercise stunned all who were involved, including the senior NSA officials responsible for running it. The bottom line was that the NSA Red Team, using hacking tools that were available to anybody on the Internet, could have crippled the U.S. military's command and control system for the entire Pacific theater of operations. From a military perspective, that alone was a nightmare. But it soon became clear that the exercise had revealed much broader vulnerabilities that could have catastrophic implications for the rest of the U.S. national infrastructure.

During the course of analyzing what the Red Team had accomplished, NSA officials discovered that much of the private-sector infrastructure in the U.S., such as the nationwide telecommunications and electric power grid, could easily be sent into a tailspin using the same tools and techniques. More importantly, one former high-ranking NSA official indicated in a recent interview that the exercise revealed it would be possible to cause "strategic damage to the U.S. money supply."[1]

Contrary to previous press reports, no private-sector networks were directly targeted or tested during Eligible Receiver, according to a senior NSA official involved in running the exercise. However, the vulnerabilities were so clear that NSA could confidently "infer" that such damage and disruption was possible. It was something that "took everybody by surprise," according to the NSA official.

Word of the exercise did not leak out to the press until April 1998. However, it had an immediate impact on federal efforts to organize and tackle the issue of computer and Internet security. Briefings were held shortly after the exercise with the vice president and the Department of Justice. In addition, the Pentagon created for the first time the position of Chief Information Officer, who would also serve as the assistant deputy Secretary of Defense for Command, Control, Communications, and Intelligence (C3I). Art Money, the first person to hold that post, became the Pentagon's point person for improving computer security and ensuring that the Internet did not become the Achilles heel of the most powerful military in the world.

"Eligible Receiver. . .succeeded beyond its planner's wildest dreams in elevating the awareness of threats to our computer systems," said Defense

---

[1]   Author interview. See "Experts Predict Major Cyber Attack Coming," *Computerworld*, July 8, 2002.

Department spokesman Kenneth Bacon, during a press briefing at the Pentagon. "We did learn that computer hackers could have a dramatic impact on the nation's infrastructure, including the electrical power grid," said Bacon. "That, of course, is why there's a whole commission set up to deal with that, the Commission on Critical Infrastructure."

-.-. -.-- -... . .-. - . .-. .-. --- .-.

The President's Commission on Critical Infrastructure Protection had been formed a year prior to Eligible Receiver. Its purpose was simple: study the national security implications of the mind-numbing pace of information technology development and, specifically, the breakneck speed at which critical infrastructures throughout U.S. society were being migrated to the Internet. Those infrastructures had been identified by presidential Executive Order 13010 as "critical" due to the potential debilitating impact their destruction or disruption could have on a regional or national scale. Eight infrastructure sectors were identified in this order: telecommunications; electrical power; gas and oil storage and transportation; banking and finance; transportation; water supply; emergency services (including emergency medical services, police, fire, and rescue); and government services.

The Commission delivered a report to the president in October 1997 that, although far less dramatic than the results of Eligible Receiver, described in detail the potentially devastating impact that lack of attention to computer security could have on the nation's overall security and economic stability.[2] As is evident in the following paragraph, the report, *Critical Foundations,* offered a clear picture of the combined nature of physical and cybersecurity:

> *A satchel of dynamite or a truckload of fertilizer and diesel fuel have been frequent terrorist tools. The explosion and the damage are so certain to draw attention that these kinds of attacks continue to be among the probable threats to our infrastructures. Today, the right command sent over a network to a power generating station's control*

---

[2]   *Critical Foundations: Protecting America's Infrastructures, the Report of the President's Commission on Critical Infrastructure Protection,* October 1997.

computer could be just as effective as a backpack full of explosives, and the perpetrator would be harder to identify and apprehend. A variety of groups around the world would like to influence U.S. policy and are willing to use disruptive tactics if they think that will help. Both physical and cyber attacks on our infrastructures could be part of a broad, orchestrated attempt to disrupt a major U.S. military operation or a significant economic activity.

The Commission's report was one of the earliest official documents to recognize what until that time had been an unspoken level of vulnerability and a seemingly endless number of physical and cyber-threats to the nation's digital backbone. But what it also did was describe for the first time the domino-like effect that a cyber-failure in one sector of the nation's infrastructure could have on all other sectors. The Internet, stated the Commission, was to blame for this unprecedented level of vulnerability.

The PCCIP report was followed on May 22, 1998, by a presidential directive that made it the official policy of the U.S. government to take all the necessary steps to ensure the security of the cyber-systems that run the nation's most critical infrastructure components. Signed by President Bill Clinton, Presidential Decision Directive 63, or PDD 63, identified the various infrastructure systems that are critical to the minimum essential operations of the government and the economy. The directive also called for the formation of a public-private partnership between the government and the private companies that own and operate the bulk of the critical infrastructures. However, the Clinton policy (which remains basically unchanged under George W. Bush) sought to enter into a partnership with the private sector to identify and fix gaps in the nation's cybersecurity as a means to avoid government regulation. In essence, the private sector's participation was completely voluntary, and the level of effort put forth was dictated by the financial condition of individual companies as well as their own particular views of the threat. The result was a national effort that was and continues to be lead by industries that differ drastically in their level of preparedness and willingness to make the needed investments in security measures.

For the first time in U.S. history, America's national security was in the hands of thousands of privately owned companies that were free to dictate their own security procedures. The government, fearful of alienating important campaign contributors, remained steadfast in its commitment to allowing "market forces" to drive investment in cybersecurity. While some can legitimately argue that government regulation of private industry would have a negative impact on the economy as a whole, the failure of the government (Clinton and G.W. Bush) to require even a minimum investment in cybersecurity as a condition of doing business equates to an abdication of its national security responsibilities.

Rather than increase government regulation, the government opted instead to appoint a federal representative for each major sector of the economy (e.g., telecommunications, transportation, energy) to help coordinate and spearhead efforts made in those sectors to eliminate cyber-vulnerabilities to the nation's infrastructures. By January 2000, the Clinton administration released the first "National Plan" to defend cyberspace. In reality, however, the plan was a typical government "road map" that defined a perfect world of the future but mandated nothing that would help make it a reality.

-.-.   -.--   -...   .   .-.   -   .   .-.   .-.   ---   .-.

Early one December morning in 2000, I sat down to breakfast at a nondescript hotel restaurant located around the block from the White House. With me sat a senior member of the National Security Council in the Clinton administration. We talked in low voices over coffee about the state of cybersecurity in the private sector, particularly at the companies that owned and operated systems that were critical to our way of life and economic vitality.

"Cyber-terrorism is real," he said. "It's not an abstract concept or something taken from a Hollywood movie script."

I responded that I too believed the threat to be real, but that a majority of Americans didn't think the administration had made its case, especially since groups like al-Qaeda had yet to show any interest in the relatively non-bloody tactics of Internet-based attacks. The official agreed but alluded to significant evidence that certain groups and individuals had tried to conduct very sophisticated attacks over the course of the millennium New Year celebration. I pressed the official for details, but he refused.

However, he did offer insights into other, more immediate threats to the nation's critical Internet-based infrastructure. A few weeks prior to our meeting, he said, a newly formed group of intelligence and national security experts from the Washington, D.C., area, called the Cyber Incident Coordination Group (CICG), had held a secure video teleconference to discuss fears that possibly tens of thousands of computers around the U.S. had been surreptitiously turned into what are known as "zombies"—computers that have been compromised with hidden code that an attacker can use at a later date to command the infected computer to attack other computers over the Internet.

The problem stemmed from the worldwide effort to fix computers for the Year 2000 bug, he said. While there was no need to worry about most computers and critical servers, there was plenty of reason to worry about the thousands of government and private-sector computers that were fixed with software patches that had been developed in India. A large number of IT services firms that had been hired by government agencies and private companies to work on the Y2K bug had actually outsourced a lot of the work to subsidiaries and other firms overseas. The potential was enormous for malicious code to have been implanted into thousands of systems, residing silently on the hard drive and waiting to be activated and commanded at a later date by a foreign agent to conduct distributed denial of service attacks against other U.S. networks. To date, there has been no known national effort to make companies aware of the need to scrub systems for malicious code that may have been injected into their networks and servers during the Y2K remediation period. So far, the fear has also proved unfounded as far as overt attacks are concerned. However, the potential for covert intelligence collection and other surveillance activities cannot be ruled out.

A few days prior to our meeting, I broke a story about a progress report that representatives from the various critical infrastructure sectors of the economy were preparing to deliver to the White House. The report, which I had managed to obtain through various sources, painted a disjointed picture of a dozen different private industries, each of which was moving at a different speed and with a varying degree of commitment to the government's call for greater cooperation on cybersecurity. Officials said the banking and energy industries remained ahead of many other sectors in security preparedness. However, at least one industry official acknowledged to me that corporate concerns regarding shareholder value and increased competition may have been getting in the way of security progress at some banks, airlines, and telecommunications companies.

As I broached the subject of the status report with the NSC official, he acknowledged the unbalanced nature of the progress that was being made in the private sector. He characterized the banking industry as "clannish" and sometimes uncooperative, and warned of the long-term effects of deregulation in the power industry. "For years, there's been a systematic lack of investment in grid capacity in the electric power industry," he said. "The grid, for example in California, is already operating at a highly stressed state," he said, referring to recent mandatory rolling blackouts caused by the increased demand for energy to power computers and data centers, and the inability of the existing grid to keep up with that demand. Combined with the industry's incessant appetite for Web-based applications that link everything from buying and selling systems to real-time control systems, the effects of mergers and acquisitions and the lack of grid capacity were producing what the official called a "potentially perilous security situation." It was a situation where even minor cyber-intrusions and disruptions could have catastrophic consequences for an energy system that experts say is in its worst condition in more than three decades.

I walked away from that meeting with the understanding that the energy industry in general was the first domino in a vast array of dominos that had the potential to take down the larger infrastructure. Should the energy sector experience a major failure or disruption, everything else that depends on energy would suffer. And there are few things in this modern world of ours that do not run on some form of energy—oil, natural gas, or electricity. And interdependencies have increased even within these three energy categories, such as the growing reliance of electricity generating stations on natural gas—the "clean air" alternative—to power the turbines.

-.-. -.-- -... . .-. - . .-. .-. --- .-.

The focus on the increased threat of terrorist attacks against the energy infrastructure dates back to the 1980s. Public hearings on the subject were later documented in an official government report titled "Physical Vulnerability of Electric Systems to Natural Disasters and Sabotage." Since then, energy companies have compiled internal lists of their critical assets and spare components, and they have recently formed an industry-led Information Sharing and Analysis Center (ISAC) for sharing cyber-threat data with each other and with the government. Likewise, the Defense Department and the FBI started a program called the Key Asset Initiative to help identify and keep tabs on the most critical facilities. Yet, as you learned from the Black Ice and Blue Cascades exercises outlined in Chapter 2, the pace at which the Internet is creating unexpected, hidden vulnerabilities has outpaced our ability to understand what those vulnerabilities are and what future vulnerabilities might look like. Despite our best efforts, we find ourselves standing at the brink of disaster.

For example, during any given year the average large utility company experiences about one million cyber-intrusions that require investigation to ensure that critical system components have not been compromised.[3] In addition, data collected by Alexandria, Virginia–based Riptech, Inc., on cyber-attacks during the six months following the September 11 terrorist attacks showed that companies in the energy industry suffer intrusions at twice the rate of other industries. And many of those attacks appear to be sponsored by governments or organizations in the Middle East.[4] Out of the 5.5 billion firewall logs and intrusion-detection system alerts reviewed, approximately 129,000 were identified as validated cyber-attacks. More importantly, the data revealed that power and energy companies averaged 12.5 severe or critical attacks requiring immediate intervention per company. That rate was more than twice the average rate of attacks for all 300 companies surveyed. Release of the Riptech study came on the heels of an internal law-enforcement warning issued January 16 by the FBI's

---

[3]   See "Utility Companies Face Barrage of Cyberattacks," *Computerworld,*
      January 21, 2002.
[4]   See "Vulnerability Assessment Triggers Alarms," *Computerworld,* January 21, 2002.

National Infrastructure Protection Center about potential Internet-based attacks targeting utilities and municipal and state government information systems.

Internet-based vulnerabilities are almost as pervasive as physical vulnerabilities. The energy industry and many other industrial sectors of the economy have opened their enterprises to a vast array of cyber-disruptions by creating inadvertent Internet links (both physical and wireless) between their corporate networks and the digital crown jewels of most industrial processes—Supervisory Control and Data Acquisition (SCADA) systems. These are the systems, including real-time programmable logic controllers, that manage the actual flow of electricity and natural gas and perform other critical functions in various industrial control settings, such as chemical processing plants, water purification and delivery systems, wastewater management facilities, and a host of manufacturing firms. Control, disruption, or alteration of critical commands, instructions, and monitoring functions performed by these systems can be an issue of regional and possibly national security.

The influence of deregulation and the increased focus on the bottom line has forced utilities and other companies to move more and more operations to the Internet as a means of improving efficiency and reducing costs. In addition, there has been a simultaneous increase in the number of remote dial-in connections established between mobile and home systems belonging to technicians and the actual SCADA systems. And even if those connections are dismantled, multiple hidden connections may still exist between the SCADA network and the utility's administrative networks that are used for buying and selling capacity and trading with business partners.

In a white paper prepared by Riptech in January 2001, the company detailed how the power industry's demand for remote access has encouraged many utility firms to establish connections to SCADA systems. In addition, some utilities have added connections between corporate networks and SCADA networks in order to allow executives to obtain instant access to data about the status of their operational systems. "The security strategy for utility corporate network infrastructures rarely accounts for the fact that access to these systems might allow unauthorized access and control of SCADA systems," the white paper concluded.

The security challenges posed by the integration and interoperability of SCADA systems with corporate IT systems is, in some cases, institutionalized as part of the IT contracting and acquisition process at some utility companies. In other words, companies often force SCADA systems to be interoperable with corporate architectures (e.g., must be Windows 2000 and use the following password and logon structure...) before the systems can be purchased. All of these connections provide avenues of attack for hackers and terrorists online and also expand the universe of the so-called "trusted insider."

The energy industry has acknowledged the existence of these linkages and the imperative of protecting SCADA systems from unauthorized access. In December 2001, for example, the American Gas Association and the Gas Technology Institute met in Washington, D.C., to discuss the need for improved encryption to protect SCADA communications between key nodes in the natural gas grid. One of the slides used during the two days of presentations highlights the threats posed to SCADA communications from the use of commercial computer equipment, open communication protocols that are widely published and available to anybody, linkages and reliance on the public switched telephone network, and the ability to steal the hardware.[5] And while a major cyber-attack against the natural gas grid has never occurred (at least as of this writing), the representatives from the Gas Technology Institute warned of a different potential reality in the future. A cyber-attack is "technically feasible," they said. "Few SCADA communications are secure. . .most utility communication is [conducted in] plain text."

The reason for the lack of cyber-defenses for SCADA systems stems from the precise timing requirements that SCADA systems operate under. The electric power grid and other industrial control systems, for example, operate under very strict timing requirements that govern when critical control messages and data traffic must arrive at certain nodes in the network. The problem, however, is that the timing requirements are such that commercial IT security systems, such as firewalls, are in many instances

---

5   "A Manufacturer-Utility Dialogue on SCADA Encryption to Prevent
    Cyber-Attack," presented at a workshop sponsored by the American Gas
    Association and the Gas Technology Institute, December 4–5, 2001, slide 10.

incapable of supporting and operating effectively in such precise timing environments, where reliability is measured in milliseconds.

This is a reality that has not been lost on the Bush administration. As part of its National Strategy to Protect Cyberspace, released on February 14, 2003, the president's National Security Council announced a plan to invest in a long- term research and development effort to build commercial network security devices that are capable of protecting SCADA systems.

Of particular concern to the natural gas control community is the potential for hackers to conduct what is called a "man-in-the-middle" attack, whereby a system that is physically located between two other important nodes is compromised and used as a launching pad to issue false commands to subordinate systems or block legitimate traffic and, thereby, block legitimate control of a portion of the grid.

However, one of the biggest security problems facing the operators of SCADA systems remains a historical predisposition to approach security through obscurity. It used to be that information on industrial control systems was hard to come by. It was very specialized knowledge that pertained to systems that nobody cared about anyway. Today, however, that information is widely available on the Internet and, therefore, to terrorists.

Ed Badolato is a renowned expert on energy infrastructure security and a former Deputy Assistant Secretary of the U.S. Department of Energy who managed the largest industrial security program in the U.S., protecting the 58 DOE nuclear weapons facilities from espionage, terrorism, and theft. Two weeks after the September 11 terrorist attacks, Badolato wrote a brief study on the ability of the electric power industry to withstand a determined assault by terrorists or other criminals. According to Badolato:

> *Electric power systems are susceptible to attack with little risk to the attacker, a fact well recognized by saboteurs and military tacticians. Detailed maps of power systems are readily available in the public domain and on the Internet. Selecting points for attack and estimating the consequences is relatively simple. All components must be kept in operational harmony. Computers, telemetry, radio, and dedicated telephone lines continually monitor major system elements and transmit vital information to the control center. Most utilities are well prepared to handle a single contingency outage. They are not capable of reliable performance, however, when their major components are severely damaged on a widespread basis by deliberately planned acts of*

man. Virtually none are equipped or staffed to mitigate the consequences of multiple attacks against major components. The threat of coordinated malevolent acts either by domestic "home grown" terrorists, or by international terrorists, is a reality. By destroying relatively few critical nodes on the electric power systems, which supply our key defense and infrastructure assets, the stability of the population, the economy, and the security of the nation can be placed in jeopardy.[6]

Despite the warnings of experts, the necessary change in mindset and attitudes toward security has not taken place in all sectors that rely on SCADA systems for critical communications. That is the conclusion of a researcher from the water supply sector, which also relies heavily on SCADA systems in much the same way that the electric and natural gas grids do. "Good housekeeping practices are not always followed in SCADA operations," according to a paper published in the aftermath of September 11 by the Water Corporation of Western Australia.[7] "Simple things like enforced rotation of passwords, individual user logons, removal of accounts when individuals leave the job are frequently ignored. September 11 ensured we can never be as complacent again."

The truth of the matter, however, is that media accounts of SCADA vulnerabilities and other security threats to computer-controlled critical infrastructures in the U.S. are often filled with officials who are trying to talk people out of their fears rather than acknowledging that there are real problems that must be tackled.

The price of complacency in these areas may not be clear to many corporations and the average citizen, but it is exceedingly clear to most security experts. I spoke with Joe Weiss, a consultant with KEMA Consulting in Fairfax, Virginia, who formerly worked as the technical manager of the Enterprise Infrastructure Security Program at the Electric Power Research Institute, a nonprofit organization in Palo Alto, California. Weiss stated the issue succinctly.

---

[6]   Badolato, Ed, "Physical Security for Electric Power Systems—A Draft," (Contingency Management Systems Inc., September 27, 2001).

[7]   Ian Wiese, Principal Officer, SCADA Planning, "The Integration of SCADA and Corporate IT," (Water Corporation of Western Australia, 2002).

According to Weiss, if we as a nation do not take action immediately to improve the cybersecurity of SCADA systems, "The Web sites will be safe but the lights will be out, and water and oil won't flow. There have been vulnerability assessments done and these important control systems have been shown to be vulnerable. This is not in any way, shape, or form hypothetical."

For two days in July 2002, Weiss and about 140 other experts in real-time control systems and SCADA systems gathered in Vancouver to discuss war game scenarios in which SCADA and other critical control systems could be vulnerable to cyber-disruptions. "We proved the vulnerability of these systems," said Weiss. "There have already been more than 20 confirmed cases where control systems have been impacted by cyber-disruptions, and at least seven cases where inadvertent denial of service attacks have occurred," said Weiss, referring to cases where glitches and other internal system malfunctions caused internal system failures. At least one of those cases occurred at a nuclear power facility, he said.

And while none of those cases were traditional Internet attacks, such as the Code Red or Nimda worms, the internal failures and disruptions demonstrate the fragile nature of these systems and the potential for direct, concerted cyber-attacks to cause failures and disruptions on a massive scale.

The question we are left with—and a question that most companies want the media to simply not ask—is this: Are SCADA systems connected to the Internet? "Of course they are," said Weiss. "They have been for the past three or four years."

In fact, a recent network architecture plan released by a major company in the water and wastewater industry included the following requirements: Peer-to-peer networking over TCP/IP (Transmission Control Protocol/Internet Protocol—in other words, the Internet); software changes that can be downloaded from any node on the network; dial-in capabilities to all software functions; and a link to the existing pump station.

"This was a document that was supposed to be showing a state-of-the-art PC-based SCADA-controlled water and wastewater system," said Weiss. "Give me a break."

And the trend is not likely to end any time soon, said Weiss. "It's almost impossible today to get new control system or diagnostic hardware or software that isn't Web-enabled," he said. "Why? Because competition rules."

-.-. -.-- -... . .-. - . .-. .-. --- .-.

As was demonstrated during the Black Ice and Blue Cascades exercises, prolonged power failures have many casualties, the first of which is often the telecommunications infrastructure, including the Internet. But the telecommunications industry faces its own security challenges that, like those of the energy industry, are the product of market forces.

The Internet and telecommunications industry has assisted adversaries by making it easier for the infrastructure to be targeted and disrupted. "The vulnerability of the [Internet and communications] infrastructure to physical attack has increased as service providers have concentrated their operations in fewer facilities," states the report of the President's Commission on Critical Infrastructure Protection in 1997. "The availability of truck bombs, chemical agents, and biological agents has markedly increased the disruptive potential of physical attacks."

This remains a serious problem today, as many large data centers have been erected throughout the country that provide single points of failure, particularly from a physical attack perspective. Should those facilities be destroyed or severely damaged, hundreds and potentially thousands of companies that chose to outsource IT infrastructure or business processes could be left without mission-critical data and connectivity.

At the same time that there has been an enormous upswing in consolidation taking place throughout the telecommunications industry, the process of deregulation, which created the Baby Bell System, and the unbundling of local networks mandated by the Telecommunications Act of 1996 have spawned millions of new connection points into the infrastructure that adversaries, malicious hackers, and terrorists can use to exploit well-known vulnerabilities. In addition, nobody has studied the potential national security ramifications of the skyrocketing increase in the number of always-on broadband connections, such as cable modems, that are being installed in millions of homes throughout the nation. This rapid pace of change is taking place amid an unprecedented level of technology insertion and rising levels of complexity, both of which make the infrastructure more prone to man-made cascading failures.

History has already shown us the potential ramifications of this change. For example, the susceptibility of telecommunications switching equipment to software-based disruption became clear during the 1990 collapse of AT&T's long-distance service. A few lines of incorrect code caused a cascading failure of 114 electronic switching systems. And while that failure was the result of an internal system glitch, the Commission on Critical Infrastructure Protection concluded that the same type of failure "could alternatively have been triggered maliciously by relatively small individual actions." It went on to state that newer generations of switching equipment, which are entering service now or have already entered into service, are likewise "potentially vulnerable to remote access, alteration, or control by skilled attackers."

However, the term "skilled attackers" does not do justice to the level of threat now facing the United States and its allies. A dedicated, competent, and patient adversary, such as one of many of today's international terrorist organizations, can pose monumental challenges for homeland security, particularly cybersecurity. Most infrastructure industries, such as the telecommunications industry, have many years of experience dealing with temporary failures and reliability problems associated with the telecommunications grid. But the industry as a whole has very limited experience and knowledge of the impact that precisely targeted, deliberate, and repeated attacks of either a physical or cyber-nature can have on the infrastructure. It has only been in the last few years that organizations such as the Sandia National Laboratory have begun to produce studies using computerized models that will help us understand and predict the effects of such widespread events and cascading failures.

The process of recovering from major telecommunications failures can also be significantly complicated, particularly if the attack targets multiple infrastructure sectors. For example, many major Internet data centers, service providers, and electric utilities rely on back-up power generating systems to get them through a temporary outage. However, a coordinated series of attacks that targets natural gas pipelines in addition to telecommunications facilities could cause unexpected ripples in the supply of natural gas to the ever-increasing number of utilities that now use it to generate electricity. More important is the fact that most utilities and companies rely on natural gas or diesel fuel generators for back-up electricity generation. Those systems can run for a limited duration, and any prolonged interruption in the supply of natural gas or other fuels could mean a significant delay in energy deliveries for back-up power generators. A physical disruption to stop the shipment of supplies (e.g., a chemical attack that closes down major roads leading into and out of a city) could well lead to this situation.

-.-. -.-- -... . .-. - . .-. .-. --- .-.

Intentional, terrorist-induced failures or disruptions of regional power facilities and telecommunications networks will also have a dramatic economic impact, especially if the failures are prolonged by the inability to quickly import replacement parts and equipment from a vendor community that is increasingly foreign-owned. However, the economic impact of such failures would also likely stem from the overall dependence of the U.S. banking and finance sector on telecommunications networks and power to maintain normal operations. Likewise, the cost to individual companies of prolonged power and telecommunications failures can easily reach beyond the ability of the average firm to recover and stay in business.

Trillions of dollars change hands every day in the U.S. thanks to electronic transaction and payment systems running on computer networks that rely on uninterrupted sources of electric power. However, deregulation in both the energy and telecommunications industries has helped create multiple points of potential failure in the support networks that serve the financial community—support networks that were once operated end-to-end by single providers. Therefore, regional failures or disruptions of the energy and telecommunications systems that power the cyber-infrastructure of the financial community would have an immediate impact on banks, financial service companies, payment systems, investment companies, and securities and commodities exchanges.

The major threats to the overall reliability of the financial system remain largely physical in nature. It also is important to understand that individual hacking incidents targeting individual banks or financial institutions do not pose a strategic-level threat to the overall financial health and economic stability of the nation. However, a series of direct coordinated attacks, both physical and cyber-attacks, against the system's more vulnerable points could rise to the level of strategic terrorism. Furthermore, planning and conducting such attacks has been made easier by the increase in mergers and acquisitions in the financial sector that often result in centralization of operations centers. And while key organizations, such as the New York Stock Exchange, have undertaken efforts to increase diversity in support infrastructure as a means to spread out the risk to the system and make recovery easier, the attacks of September 11, 2001, proved that massive physical attacks that disable critical power and telecommunications infrastructure can stop the nation's financial dealings dead in their tracks.

The banking and financial sector also remains vulnerable to disruptions in the one system it relies upon most for its day-to-day operations—public confidence. Information warfare tools and techniques have significantly enhanced the ability of state-sponsored terrorism to be conducted in relative anonymity and, most importantly, with plausible deniability. Dozens of nations around the world, many of them harboring resentments toward the U.S. as well as outright hatred for the American way of life, have for years been actively developing information warfare arsenals designed to cripple the U.S. military's command and control capability as well as the U.S. economy. Such tools, which may include highly sophisticated computer viruses and worms, can easily be shared with terrorist groups that share a common dislike for America or given to individuals who are willing to operate as terrorist surrogates online. Should this cyber–arms race reach the point where competing powers are using their cyber-arsenals in a new, high-tech version of the Cold War, terrorist organizations could one day have easy access to capabilities never before dreamed of. And if that happens, the financial industry may be forced to deal with an unrelenting series of cyber-assaults designed to erode confidence in the U.S. banking industry's ability to protect citizens' assets and privacy from being stolen online. Such a scenario, which is completely within the realm of possibility given the state of the industry's focus on cybersecurity, would easily lead to an unprecedented drop in public confidence and possibly a collapse in large volumes of e-commerce activity. Just as physical terrorism in the form of sniper attacks led to a downturn in business at local gas stations and craft stores in the Washington, D.C., area in October 2002, so too can a series of massive cyber-heists and identity thefts in the financial industry lead to a downturn in online purchasing and banking activity by consumers. Combine the two forms of attack and you may soon have a localized cash economy focused strictly on the essentials, with little or no disposable cash going to luxury items or big-ticket items at local stores.

Disruptions to the cyber-powered energy and telecommunications networks also come with an economic price tag for businesses, even if the disruptions are not massive or accompanied by fear-inducing physical attacks. For example, a recent study sponsored by the Electric Power Research Institute and the Consortium for Electric Infrastructure to Support a Digital Society found that power outages, for example, cost millions of industrial firms and other companies that rely on data storage and retrieval for day-to-day operations roughly $13.5 billion a year in lost productivity and idle manpower.[8] Moreover, the cost of power outages and disruptions is directly proportionate to the duration of the failure. For example, the average cost of a one-second outage among industrial and so-called "digital economy" firms is about $1,477 and $7,795 for a one-hour outage. Given those figures, power outages on the order of what was described in the Black Ice and Blue Cascades exercises—outages that last for one month or longer—would result in financial damages in excess of $5 million per company, per month. Multiplied across the hundreds of thousands of businesses in any one region of the country that rely on digital economy "connectivity," such losses could easily surpass the trillion-dollar mark.

However, disruptions and economic damage to the banking and financial sector do not begin and end with electric power. This sector of the U.S. economy is also linked heavily to the telecommunications sector that carries its day-to-day, hour-to-hour, and minute-to-minute transactions. As you will see in Chapter 7, the physical or cyber-disruptions of critical regional data communications facilities can pose and have posed a serious threat to the stability of U.S. financial markets, particularly where those markets live—Wall Street. And, as you will learn in Chapter 5, to directly or indirectly cripple the U.S. financial infrastructure is a central tenet of the new terrorism.

---

[8] "The Cost of Power Disturbances to Industrial & Digital Economy Companies," (Electric Power Research Institute, June 2001).

-.-. -.-- -... . .-. - . .-. .-. --- .-.

We all take the so-called vital human services for granted. When we turn on the faucet in the kitchen, we expect not only water to flow but also that the water we use to drink and cook with will be free of dangerous chemicals and harmful contaminants. Likewise, when we call an ambulance or the fire department, we expect the call to get through and that the emergency responders will be able to coordinate their activities in a way that enables them to respond to our emergency and any other emergency that may happen at the same time. We also expect medical emergencies to be coordinated properly with local hospitals; outbreaks of suspicious diseases to be coordinated with the federally run Centers for Disease Control; and alerts on dangerous weather conditions or potential natural disasters to be communicated in a timely manner from the National Weather Service to local emergency personnel and weather officials. Also, although this is not necessarily a matter of life and death, millions of elderly and retired workers expect their social security checks to arrive on time.

But what most people probably don't realize is that all of these operations also rely heavily upon computers, the Internet, and automated databases that, in turn, rely on uninterrupted supplies of power and telecommunications support to operate properly. The same digital linkages that exist in the energy and telecommunications industry, including the use of Internet-enabled SCADA systems, are also in use throughout various forms of vital human services.

As mentioned earlier, one of the most critical areas from a public safety perspective is the water industry. Although most people don't think of computers and the Internet when it comes to water utilities, it is common knowledge among security experts that without electric power, uninterrupted telecommunications support, and Internet connectivity, local water systems will not function properly. And if potable water systems are not functioning, everything from drinking water to land irrigation and fire fighting operations could be impacted.

The water industry is similar to the natural gas industry in that it too relies on SCADA systems to manage almost every aspect of creating and delivering potable water to households, including decontamination and treatment and system pressure regulation and monitoring. And contrary to what some officials in the industry would like you to believe, these SCADA systems are increasingly being connected to the Internet or to corporate networks that have links to the Internet. Those links make our water systems vulnerable to a wide range of cyber-disruptions. For example, it is not beyond reason that an insider or somebody from outside the enterprise could manipulate or inject disruptions into the system that would impact the flow of water or pressure in the pipelines. And in many urban settings where the water infrastructure is older and in poor condition, such fluctuations in water pressure can easily result in fractured water mains. From a cyber-attack perspective, introducing a hammering effect into the pipelines (similar to the attack I described on the natural gas system in Chapter 1) by simply opening and shutting valves in rapid succession could lead to a series of rapid failures and fractures in the system. Likewise, disabling the electric power sources that run the pumps controlling flow and pressure could cause long-term outages. Although many water utilities have taken steps to install valves that can protect against such activity, many others remain vulnerable and continue to inadvertently open their operations to Internet-based disruptions.

A more sinister threat would be one that targets wastewater treatment plants or adjusts critical controls that manage the process of chlorinating drinking water. Such a threat doesn't even have to be real or possible for it to have a significant impact on public confidence and on the public psyche.

Any of these disruptions to the water system could impact any number of emergency response organizations. Even if the water system remains safe, however, these organizations also face a series of vulnerabilities stemming from their own incessant push to move more and more of their operations onto Web-based command and control systems and other systems that rely heavily on the public telephone network.

A prime example is the 911 emergency system, first deployed in Haleyville, Alabama, in 1968. Since that time, there have been several cases where computer viruses have been distributed to unsuspecting users that have overloaded local 911 services by ordering systems to place thousands of repeated calls simultaneously. More importantly, simple

failures or disruptions in the telephone system, whether as a result of prolonged power failures or cyber-disruptions, can also lead to the loss of 911
services.

Of course, 911 systems are susceptible to a wide array of other, less intentional disruptions. Everything from glitch-ridden software upgrades
conducted by the telephone company, to lightning strikes that damage
communications center equipment, water damage to 911 trunks leading
into a communications center, or inadvertent damage to underground
fiber-optic cable serving a major central office can disrupt 911 services.
And while such disruptions can be worked around by emergency organizations, the real damage from a terrorism perspective comes from the loss
of confidence and the psychological impact that such disruptions can have
on the general population.

The vulnerability of the nation's 911 system was demonstrated in 1996,
when a 19-year-old Swedish man, working from his home in Goteburg,
disabled portions of the emergency 911 system in southern Florida. He
was able to generate multiple, simultaneous telephone calls to the 911 systems throughout a dozen counties in Florida, including Pasco, Hernando,
and Citrus. But the important lesson that this case provides us is how interconnected our critical infrastructures actually are. This hacking incident
did not involve the 911 systems directly. Rather, the perpetrator used a
computer to hack into the public telephone network to generate the calls.
By making simultaneous calls, he was able to tie up all of the county 911
trunks, thereby blocking legitimate callers from getting the help they
needed.

According to a paper by the FBI's National Infrastructure Protection
Center dated April 18, 2001, a Massachusetts juvenile on March 10, 1997,
used his personal computer to access an optical digital loop carrier and interfere with telephone service to the community of Rutland, Massachusetts. The juvenile accessed the loop carrier and sent a series of computer
commands that altered and impaired the integrity of the data, thereby disabling the system. Public health and safety were threatened by the loss of
telephone service. According to the FBI's NIPC report:

> *911 and other emergency services communications traverse computers
> and switches that continue to be vulnerable to computer hackers and*

phone phreakers. Providing enhanced security measures to protect this equipment from unauthorized tampering, combined with the development and implementation of back-up procedures, should be a priority for 911 planners and those who rely on these services.[9]

In March 2000, the FBI's National Infrastructure Protection Center and the FBI Houston field office opened an investigation into a computer virus that allegedly targeted the 911 system for widespread disruption. Once activated, the so-called 9-1-1 virus would attempt to dial out on a modem in an attempt to tie up emergency lines. The virus, officially dubbed the "bat.chode" virus, would also attempt to erase the infected computer's hard drive on the nineteenth of the month. The potential existed for each infected computer to scan more than 2,500 computers simultaneously, creating in effect a massive denial of service attack against the 911 emergency system. Fortunately, the virus did not spread as fast as officials feared it could have. In May, a programmer for a bank in Houston was arrested for writing the virus and sentenced to five years probation.

Since the September 11 terrorist attacks, fears of such vulnerabilities have reached an almost frenzied state. However, it is often the subtle effects that such attacks and disruptions can and almost certainly will have that escapes the analysis of the skeptics—those who believe naively that terrorist-sponsored cyber-attacks are a thing of fantasy or that critical infrastructure systems are not vulnerable.

However, in April 2001, five months before the September 11 attacks, Ronald Dick, director of the FBI's National Infrastructure Protection Center, summed up the threat of relatively minor cyber-attacks and disruptions for a House subcommittee. According to the written testimony submitted by Dick:

Over the past several years we have seen a wide range of cyber threats ranging from defacement of websites by juveniles to sophisticated intrusions sponsored by foreign powers, and everything in between. Some of these are obviously more significant than others. The theft of national security information from a Government agency or the interruption of electrical power to a major metropolitan area would

---

[9] *National Infrastructure Protection Center Highlights,* Issue 4-01 (FBI, April 18, 2001), p. 3.

have greater consequences for national security, public safety, and the economy than the defacement of a Web site. But even the less serious categories have real consequences and, ultimately, can undermine confidence in e-commerce and violate privacy or property rights. A web site hack that shuts down an e-commerce site can have disastrous consequences for a business. An intrusion that results in the theft of credit card numbers from an online vendor can result in significant financial loss and, more broadly, reduce consumers' willingness to engage in e-commerce.

At a symposium on homeland security held in June 2002, Dick took the analogy one step further, acknowledging that his biggest fear "is a physical attack in conjunction with a successful cyber-attack on the responders' 911 system or on the power grid."

The indications and the warnings are out there. We ignore them at our own peril.

4

Terror in the Air: The Wireless Threat

Why is it that companies have sold [wireless] products that they know are not secure? And why is it that companies have bought them? We all ought to shut them off until the technology gets better.[1]

—Richard Clarke, Former Chairman,
President's Critical Infrastructure Protection Board

This is a serious problem that puts lives and the U.S. infrastructure at risk.[2]

—James Foster
Senior researcher at Guardent, Inc.
Commenting about the use of insecure wireless
networks at U.S. airlines

In winter 2001, not long after al-Qaeda succeeded in carrying out an unprecedented series of hijackings of commercial airlines, a mid-level manager at Fort Worth, Texas–based American Airlines tried to warn his superiors about other, less obvious security vulnerabilities that needed to be fixed immediately.

---

[1] Speech made September 30, 2002, at the annual Black Hat Security Conference in Las Vegas, Nevada.
[2] See "Wireless LANs: Trouble in the Air," *Computerworld*, January 14, 2002.

American Airlines was among the first airlines in the country to install wireless roving agent and curbside check-in systems. It was viewed as an indication of the airline's dedication to customer service. American had deployed wireless network infrastructures to support hand-held roving agent computers at 250 airports around the U.S. and curbside check-in computers that also used wireless devices at another eight airports. The systems allowed agents to check in passengers for flights anywhere in the terminal, including out on the street, helping frequent fliers and others to avoid the long lines at check-in counters. But the lack of even the simplest form of encryption on the systems and the fact that the mobile computers were integrated with the baggage check system, reservation systems, aircraft maintenance databases, and a host of other sensitive airline networks meant that the daily operations of the airline and even passenger safety were at risk. Terrorists could easily employ what is known as a sniffer program loaded onto a laptop computer to grab sensitive information, including user names and passwords, right out of the air. They could then use that information to gain access to the airlines' corporate control systems. From there, it was well within reason that a piece of baggage could be loaded onto an aircraft without its owner—a significant security violation. Even worse, the potential existed that the reservation system could be penetrated, allowing terrorists to manipulate names and identities so that hijackers went unnoticed by security watch lists.

At first, the airline manager was optimistic that the events of September 11 would force senior executives to study all security matters, regardless of their origin, with the same level of interest and concern. He knew that no issue was too minor to overlook when it came to security. But the type of security vulnerabilities that he had tried to warn senior airline executives about on several occasions were not a priority interest of his bosses at American. His warnings and requests to purchase new, more secure equipment fell upon deaf ears. The airline's adoption of wireless network technologies to support bag-matching operations was not a threat to safety, nor were the roving agent and curbside check-in systems, the executives told him. As in the rest of corporate America, the only threat that was real as far as these executives were concerned was one that had already been transformed into a catastrophe.

The manager continued his campaign to get the executives in his chain of command to listen to his concerns and to approve a request for new, more secure equipment. All of his warnings went ignored. It was then, after months of trying to fix what he believed to be a serious safety and security problem, that the manager contacted editors and reporters at *Computerworld*. In an interview, he detailed the glaring holes in American Airlines' wireless computer networks that could allow hackers working on behalf of a terrorist organization to help pave the way for another hijacking or bombing.

> *"You can't bring guns on board… theoretically… [but] now I don't need the gun. You've brought the gun to me [by giving me access to the identity of the undercover federal sky marshal on my flight]. From a cargo perspective, even if you match the bag to the person, you still don't know who that person is from a security perspective. Once I have an [Internet Protocol] address inside the network, I've got access to your switches, routers, Novell 3.1 server, your Web servers, Intranet, suppliers, you name it. You can sit at an airport and map the network for as long as you have electricity. If you really wanted to, you could… sit in the garage in a van and do it. Roving agent is Web-based, everything [unencrypted] in clear text, including username and password to the reservation system. You can log in as the agent [or] have the agent log in and then you got the username/password (by having someone else nearby sniff it). I've gotten signals from 1,500 feet [away] with an antenna out on the ramp.[3]*

With the sour taste of September 11, 2001, still lingering in the mouths of most Americans, the security implications of this news seemed endless. If the American Airline source was telling the truth, a skilled, patient hacker could gain access to the reservation system or bag-matching system of a major U.S. air carrier. With more patience, skill, and cunning, that same hacker could manipulate maintenance records, possibly causing critical safety issues to go unnoticed.

When editors at *Computerworld* asked me to join the effort to verify the source's claims, I was not at all surprised by his analysis of the vulnerabilities. I had been working for several weeks on another news tip that hackers

---

[3]   Confidential note sent to editors and writers at *Computerworld* from internal American Airlines source.

formerly employed by the Israeli intelligence service, Mossad, had successfully hacked their way through the public Web site of a major U.S. airline and were able to penetrate the back-end reservation and maintenance systems.[4] Through a hole in the Web site application code, the hackers were able to reach the airline's back-end corporate systems and were able to download the source code of the entire application. "We could have obviously obtained passenger manifests, maintenance systems and whatever was there,"[5] said Peggy Weigle, the chief executive officer of Sanctum, Inc., the firm that conducted the authorized security audit.

The success of Weigle's security experts was not lost on the White House or the Federal Aviation Administration (FAA). Shortly after learning of the incident, I called the FAA's chief information officer, Dan Meehan, and asked him how serious the FAA considered the breach to be from a public safety perspective. Meehan said he had been briefed on the audit and that the FAA and the White House were working on a more aggressive outreach program to raise the level of awareness throughout all other airlines that might be actively deploying wireless systems.

One airline that was not taking any chances was El Al Israel Airlines, based at Ben-Gurion International Airport in Lod, Israel. Sanctum had worked closely with El Al and other Israeli government agencies since November 2000, when pro-Palestinian hacker groups had launched what some characterized as a "cyber-jihad"—an Internet-based holy war—against Israeli and American Internet infrastructures, particularly e-commerce Web sites.[6] What eventually amounted to a series of poorly planned attacks was timed to coincide with the projected $19 billion online holiday-sales season in the U.S. For El Al, however, the commercial Internet, especially wireless technologies, had not yet proven secure enough to trust with the lives of Israeli citizens. "Since Sept. 11, any illegal access to data or transactions through our company Web site is viewed by us as a terrorist

---

4   See "Airline Web Sites Seen As Riddled with Security Holes," *Computerworld*, February 4, 2002.

5   Ibid.

6   See "U.S. May Face Net-Based Holy War," *Computerworld*, November 13, 2000.

act," said David Yaacobi, El Al's information systems security manager.[7] Because of the threat, El Al relies on proprietary network and communications protocols that are more difficult—but not impossible—to attack.

Despite all of the warning signs, the network security posture at U.S. airlines remained quite different. American Airlines' initial reluctance to invest in additional security precautions for a computer system was not a surprise; the September 11 attacks had made what was already shaping up to be a tough economic year for the airlines the worst in the aviation industry's history. For years, technology investment in the transportation sector of the economy had been geared toward enhancing business processes and improving the bottom line. Corporate America adopted new technologies with blinders on. Security was and remains an afterthought.

As the days wore on, the case against the airlines was building. By all indications, our source at American, now known inside *Computerworld* as "Deep Throat," was telling the truth. But we had to be absolutely sure. And the best way to do that was to ask a few ethical hackers to go to various airports around the country and find the answers to our questions. What they discovered sent shivers down the spines of all who worked on this story, and would lead the FBI's National Infrastructure Protection Center (NIPC) to issue a white paper on the importance of securing wireless networks.

-.-. -.-- -... . .-. - . .-. .-. --- .-.

The unending sky draped a crisp January air over the massive 53-square-mile sprawl of Denver International Airport. It appeared as a shining oasis in the middle of green and brown rolling plains, surrounded by mountain peaks of gray, blue, and white. The more than one million square feet of terminal area is among Denver's most recognizable landmarks, with a Teflon-coated roof that is shaped into 34 peaks of differing heights, symbolizing the Rocky Mountains. Inside the Great Hall,

---

[7]   See "Airline Web Sites Seen As Riddled with Security Holes," *Computerworld*, February 4, 2002.

a public atrium stretches longer than four football fields beneath a 126-foot-high translucent roof that soaks in the light from the stars at night.

Inside the nation's most advanced airport, harried travelers ran from gate to gate, trying to navigate their way through a quarter mile of ticket counters. The high-pitched sound of a crying baby punctuated the steady drone of luggage being dragged across the marble floor of the terminal area. The seating areas in front of each gate were an endless sea of drab suits, blinding ties, newspapers, cell phones, pagers, handheld digital organizers, and laptop computers. Business in America was no longer shackled by the availability of hard-wired pay telephones or dial-up Internet connections. To the contrary, this was the wireless age, a time when cell phones could exchange text messages and photos, and laptop computers could connect to the Internet using cell phone technology or wireless networking cards that could seek out a local Internet access point without the user having to plug a wire into a telephone wall outlet. Despite the new 24-hour work cycle that the technology had introduced into the lives of most Americans, people loved having the ability to roam about the country while staying connected to the "Net." And the best part was they didn't even have to think about it anymore. The wireless Internet was everywhere, and the devices that connected to it were promiscuous.

It was eleven o'clock in the morning when Thubten Cumerford parked his car at a nearby hotel and took the hotel's free shuttle to the airport. There were military guards stationed in and around the DIA parking lots, and he didn't want to risk a security search that would undoubtedly uncover his equipment and lead to a series of probing questions and heightened suspicions. This was a critical time for airport and airline security. The government's initial January 18 deadline to screen every checked bag for explosives was fast approaching. Tensions were high at airports all around the country, and it would certainly be a bad thing for a person without a ticket or a flight reservation to be caught carrying suspicious electronic equipment in a car parked outside the terminal. It was safer to go on foot.

The shuttle stopped at the entrance to the main DIA terminal, where half a dozen travelers got off and disappeared into the undulating sea of humanity. Thubten was last to get off the bus, stopping for a moment to survey the terminal from the curb. He was neatly dressed in formal business attire that made him appear as if he were en route to an important meeting. In his right hand, he carried a nylon laptop computer case, lending more credibility to his disguise as an on-the-go, always connected corporate executive.

He lifted his left arm and tilted his wrist to glance at his watch. But he already knew exactly what time it was. That was simply part of playing the role. The quick check of the time followed by a momentary look at a cell phone only added to the ordinariness of his false persona. Nobody thought to look at Thubten twice, which allowed him to walk with ease through the massive airport, where he stopped at a second-floor restaurant overlooking a large fountain in the center of the terminal.

Seated in the restaurant, Thubten placed the laptop on an adjacent chair and ordered a half chicken with a Caesar salad and iced tea to drink. The waitress delivered his iced tea and disappeared, as waitresses often do, promising to return when his main course was ready. Thubten reached down and opened the laptop case, exposing the computer and a well-concealed two-foot-long antenna that was connected via a short wire to a thin card that was inserted into one of the computer's PC Card slots. Once the computer booted up, Thubten opened an application called NetStumbler, which reached out through the antenna and began to automatically scan the airwaves for wireless Internet access points to connect to. By design, the application also picked up all unencrypted communications that were taking place between other wireless users in the vicinity and the airport wireless Internet access points. One hardly had to do anything overt to tap into the invisible streams of data that were flooding the airwaves. The devices simply looked for other devices to talk to automatically. Promiscuity was the nature of the wireless Internet environment. And Thubten was about to get lucky.

-.-. -.-- -... . .-. - . .-. .-. --- .-.

Thirteen hundred miles to the west, in the heart of the Silicon Valley, sits San Jose, California, a city better known as the Mecca of America's high-tech industry. It is also home to the only major airport in Santa Clara County. But the airport in San Jose is unlike many others. It is an airport in transition, caught between Scylla and Charybdis. In trying to avoid the scourge of terrorism, the airport has embraced information technology—technology that opens it up to a vast array of other, unseen vulnerabilities.

Jonas Luster knows all about those unseen vulnerabilities. He's been studying ways to take advantage of them for years. And today, he'll get his chance.

Dressed in black motorcycle boots, black jeans, and a black T-shirt, Jonas jumped out of his 2001 Jeep Wrangler on the second deck of the short-term parking lot, grabbed his Titanium Apple Powerbook laptop computer, and headed for the general departure area of the terminal. The tiBook had the advantage of a built-in wireless network card, which was far less obvious than carrying around a computer with a wire and an antenna sticking out of it. And maintaining a run of the mill profile was critical because security was tight.

Jonas moved slowly passed the baggage claim area and outside to the curb. He stood there for about ten minutes, pretending to fiddle with the computer, and then retreated to a waiting area inside the terminal to check the intercepted data. After checking the data, Jonas quickly programmed a few new filters for the sniffer software and headed back outside. Now he had a better idea of the type of data he was picking up and the type of data he was looking for. The curbside check-in stations for American Airlines and Southwest Airlines were not far from where he was standing, and he was confident that they were broadcasting signals to his laptop loud and clear.

-.-. -.-- -... . .-. - . .-. .-. --- .-.

Thubten finished his chicken and wiped his hands dry of the cold beads of water that had collected on the side of his glass of iced tea. He glanced down at the computer screen and watched as various wireless Internet users around the airport unwittingly emanated signals from their laptops. The streaming data painted for Thubten an intimate portrait of their digital lives. He watched a series of Web browsing sessions take place and also saw the system automatically identify several airport wireless network nodes. But this was not what he was looking for. Thubten wanted to know if the airport and the various airlines were sitting ducks for a wireless intrusion. And for that, he would have to get up and move about the terminal.

Thubten walked everywhere he was allowed to go without having to show a plane ticket to security personnel. He conducted the first sweep, with laptop in hand, throughout the main terminal area. He stopped in front of the American Airlines ticket counter and then in the lobby of the DIA administrative offices. There he observed an individual, most likely a contractor working on DIA computer systems, open his corporate e-mail.[8] The software even logged a suspected hacker attack on the network while he was observing the traffic flow. More surprising, however, was the fact that nobody questioned his presence or his activity.

From there, Thubten proceeded to walk out to the curbside check-in area run by American Airlines. The closer he got to the curbside check-in agent, the stronger the signal strength became. When he arrived outside, the signal strength had reached 100 percent. That meant he was standing virtually on top of the wireless access point. He noticed a skycap standing next to a computer terminal and realized that the signal he was picking up was coming directly from the curbside check-in station. Then he noticed two other similar computer terminals as he approached the skycap.

"What's this?" Thubten asked the young American Airlines employee.

"This is called a one-stop station," the employee responded enthusiastically.

"Oh. That's interesting. But I don't see any wires or anything. How does it work?"

"Well, it's battery-powered."

"Yeah, but how can you check in my bags without connecting this computer to the other computers?"

"Actually, this computer is connected. It's connected by radio to the ticketing and reservation computers inside," the skycap said.

---

[8] The person's name and company affiliation were also observed. For privacy reasons, however, that data is not provided here.

Thubten continued to feign interest, walking around to the front of the system to look at the screen. The skycap was only too happy to show him how it worked.

"Very cool," Thubten said, removing his Palm Pilot from his pocket and writing down the IP address that was taped prominently to the side of the workstation as well as on the one next to it. The IP address, or Internet Protocol address, was a series of numbers that acted as the Internet equivalent of a street address, denoting a computer's identity and location on a network. Thubten logged the numbers into his hand-held computer: 172.22.161.58 and 172.22.161.60.

Thubten's scan of the wireless systems in use at DIA, particularly at American Airlines, uncovered significant security gaps. The DIA administrative office area of the terminal was the only area of the airport where Thubten found wireless systems using encryption to protect communications from the prying eyes of hackers. Even in that case, however, the encryption in use was the standard 40-bit Wired Equivalent Privacy (WEP) encryption, which has been proven to provide woefully inadequate protection against hackers. But no WEP-protected connections were discovered in any other area of the airport. To the contrary, those wireless networks were sending data in the clear, with no protection whatsoever.

"In my judgment, any wireless networks currently being run by the airlines at DIA are severely insecure and are vulnerable to compromise," Thubten wrote in an e-mail message I received shortly after he completed his tests. The airlines' uses of these wireless networks "are putting themselves and our nation's security at risk," he said. Even when encryption is enabled, wireless networks "are a serious liability."

-.-. -.-- -... . .-. - . .-. .-. --- .-.

Meanwhile, Jonas Luster's undercover security audit at the San Jose International Airport began to produce results. In fact, there were so few safeguards in place to protect the wireless network connections in San Jose that had Jonas been willing to break the law, he could have done severe damage to the operations of several airlines.

Jonas was able to easily pick up signals and sensitive network information emanating from the wireless LANs belonging to American Airlines and Dallas-based Southwest Airlines Company. And like Thubten in Denver, Jonas was able to monitor American's curbside check-in operations. More importantly, his survey discovered that Southwest's networks were issuing information from back-end systems, including at least three Unix servers running the Solaris operating system.

It took Jonas only minutes to sniff out any data that he wanted from the airline networks. The real threat, however, stemmed from the fact that the routing infrastructure at both airlines was open to exploitation. The Routing Information Protocol (RIP) is a high-level language that transmits network routing updates at regular intervals. The problem is that it can be modified easily to assist a hacker. Jonas later concluded that by injecting a wrong RIP response, he could fool the network into declaring his laptop computer a legitimate, authoritative, and powerful node on the airlines' networks. As a result, all network traffic would be routed through his system, from which he would be able to manipulate or inject data at will.

During our investigation, we approached all of the airlines and several independent airline industry security analysts with the results of the audits. Most airlines, including Southwest, declined to comment, citing security concerns. However, the chief information officer at American Airlines had a lot to say about the findings of the security audit. Unfortunately, his explanation was cause for even more concern.

According to American, even if intruders penetrated the network, they could do little damage. That's because American's core systems are hosted by Fort Worth, Texas–based Sabre, Inc., on an IBM transaction processing facility (TPF) system that's generally viewed as extremely difficult to hack because of the rigid and arcane structure of TPF. That's right. American's official response was that hackers were not smart enough to figure out how their system worked. According to American, the only individuals who had the skills and knowledge to do any harm were those technicians and programmers who understood the system's unique and complex programming language and structure.

Given the national security implications of this story, I called my contacts at the FBI's National Infrastructure Protection Center in Washington.

The NIPC had been formed specifically to act as a cyber-threat analysis and warning arm of the government, particularly as those threats applied to the nation's critical infrastructures, of which the national transportation system was one. One senior official who was on loan to the NIPC from the CIA listened intently to the results of the wireless security audits that had been conducted as well as to the explanations provided by American Airlines. The official found sufficient need to immediately order a white paper and have a warning issued to critical infrastructure owners and operators pertaining to the use of wireless network devices. However, the veteran CIA analyst was perplexed by the airline's explanation that the back-end reservation system was too complex and arcane for outsiders to figure out. "I've made a lot of money over the years off of adversaries who thought like that," he told me.[9]

The CIA officer was not alone in his concerns. A senior executive in the network applications division of a major communications services provider owned and operated by a consortium of airlines also outlined significant security concerns pertaining to the safety and integrity of flight operations.[10] The executive's main concern was that a hacker could use an unprotected wireless network to hack his way into core airline operational systems, including flight operations, bag matching, and passenger reservations. Once the attacker gained access to the flight operations systems, it would be possible to do anything from injecting viruses to corrupting vital data that controls aircraft maintenance and flight dispatching.

From a terrorism perspective, however, the potential problems got much worse. The executive also expressed concern that access to a bag-matching system could allow an attacker to manipulate the system to show that luggage belonged to a boarded passenger when in fact it did not. This concern was of such an immediate nature that the communications company in question announced plans to abandon the industry-standard wireless bag-matching system it operated in favor of a proprietary system based on the more robust security measures provided

---

[9]   Personal interview.

[10] See "Wireless LANs: Trouble in the Air," *Computerworld*, January 14, 2002.

by Integrated Digital Enhanced Network (IDEN) voice and data terminals developed by Schaumburg, Illinois–based Motorola, Inc.

James Foster is a senior consultant and researcher at Guardent, Inc., a security firm in Waltham, Massachusetts. He has conducted several wireless security audits that have uncovered significant vulnerabilities in and around major airport facilities, including John F. Kennedy International Airport in New York and Boston's Logan International Airport. It was from Boston's Logan Airport that American Airlines Flight 11, along with United Airlines Flight 175, took off bound for Los Angeles before being hijacked and crashed into the North and South Towers of the World Trade Center. "Possible baggage system vulnerabilities do not surprise me," Foster told me during an interview for the investigative report.[11] "This is a serious problem that puts lives and the U.S. infrastructure at risk."

Although he wouldn't provide details about specific airlines, Foster's wireless security audits have shown that a skilled hacker with the right software tools would need only seconds to conduct a detailed reconnaissance of an airline's wireless network. "Most of the time these [wireless systems] are tied to back-end systems," he said. And regardless of how arcane or proprietary such a network may be, "it's only a matter of time until somebody figures out how it works, how it communicates, and how people authenticate," he said. "It would take no more than an hour to figure out how the system worked."[12]

-.-. -.-- -... . .-. - . .-. .-. --- .-.

Exactly one year after the September 11, 2001, terrorist attacks, additional security audits of the wireless networks in use at airports around the country revealed still more problems. A security survey conducted by Alpharetta, Georgia–based AirDefense, Inc., of wireless networks in operation at the major airports in Atlanta, San Diego, San Francisco, and Chicago O'Hare found that the passenger check-in and

---

11   Ibid.

12   Ibid.

baggage transfer systems were operating without the most basic security protections, such as encryption.[13]

Only 32 of the 112 wireless network access points detected during the audits had basic encryption security activated. More importantly, the Service Set Identifiers (SSIDs), critical codes that function as passwords for communicating through a wireless access point, hadn't been turned off on more than half of the access points discovered. All access points in a network must use the same SSID to communicate. Unfortunately, in the case of these airports many of the network access points were broadcasting unencrypted SSIDs, making it a simple matter for hackers to become authorized nodes on the network.

At San Francisco International Airport, wireless security audits picked up an unencrypted file directory of a Windows NT server and numerous PCs belonging to Northwest Airlines, Inc. The wireless hackers, who made sure they did not break any laws when conducting the impromptu scan of the wireless systems, said the Northwest network was set up in such a way that a hacker could have used the available information to learn the network's topology and steal passwords.[14]

Northwest's managing director of infrastructure for technology products and services said the airline had been testing a self-service check-in system at the San Francisco airport that used a wireless network to connect back to a server located at the airline's headquarters in Minneapolis. However, word of the security audit results led to the system being shut down. The executive from Northwest acknowledged that the airline made a mistake by not using even the most basic form of encryption on the system. However, security concerns about the use of wireless networks to support airline operations were enough to force Northwest to say it would use hard-wired connections for all future self-service check-in operations.

At Chicago's O'Hare International Airport, security tests uncovered several wireless network access points broadcasting an identifier named "X-ray" and transmitting unencrypted file requests. The obvious naming convention used in this case could easily lead an attacker to conclude that

---

[13] See "Airport WLANs Lack Safeguards," *Computerworld*, September 16, 2002.

[14] Ibid.

these access points were related to the systems used to support the airport's luggage X-ray machines—many of which are manufactured to support wireless access cards. Other common names for access points discovered included "baggage" and "gate a3."[15]

Security tests conducted at the airports in Atlanta and San Diego found wireless access points that were broadcasting Dynamic Host Configuration Protocol (DHCP) packets without encryption protection. Network administrators, who have access to the most sensitive operations of a computer network, use DHCP to automatically assign IP addresses to users of wireless networks. Hackers or terrorists could easily use this level of information to grant legitimate access to unauthorized computers.

In a final stroke of irony, another security consultant working for a firm that provides wireless technologies to the airline industry reported an incident where security personnel at an airline that had recently deployed a wireless system throughout its own area of the terminal inadvertently gained control of another airline's wireless security cameras.[16]

As of this writing, American Airlines has taken significant steps to lock-down all of its wireless check-in stations and roving agent systems. In fact, an audit of American's wireless systems conducted in December 2002 at Denver International Airport found no instances of American wireless systems operating without encryption. American had not only removed the IP addresses from its OneStop self-service kiosks, but it had also added Cisco Systems Inc.'s Lightweight Extensible Authentication Protocol (LEAP) authentication technology on top of the standard 40-bit Wired Equivalent Privacy (WEP) encryption. LEAP is an authentication algorithm that leverages the 802.1x framework and provides dynamic, per-user WEP keys to protect data in transit. However, public waiting areas throughout the airport remained hotbeds of potential hacking activity, since most users of wireless network technologies remained unaware of the amount of private data that was emanating from their laptop computers.[17]

---

[15] Obtained from actual audit report.

[16] See "DOD IT Projects Come Under Fire," *Computerworld*, May 20, 2002.

[17] See Dan Verton, "American Airlines Secures Wireless LANs in Denver," *Computerworld*, January 6, 2003.

-.-. -.-- -... . .-. - . .-. .-. --- .-.

Wireless security vulnerabilities at airports and airlines are certainly a serious public safety problem. However, the overall wireless threat to our nation's critical infrastructure and national security extends far beyond the airline industry. Almost every sector of the economy—from public utilities to manufacturing plants, chemical-processing facilities, nuclear materials processing operations, and railroad operations—is adopting wireless computer technologies at a rapid pace. And the faster these industries deploy such systems without the proper security protections in place, the faster they are putting themselves and the general public at risk.

In the government and national security arena, wireless technologies support the network of low-earth orbiting satellites that provide a wide variety of communications services, including back-up services for the land-based Internet. Satellite services also support applications such as mobile and cellular communication, telemedicine, cargo tracking, point-of-sale transactions, and Internet access. Federal agencies also use commercial satellites to support communications, data transmission, and remote sensing. For example, the Pentagon relies on commercial satellites to support its communications and information transmission requirements for non-mission-critical data and to augment its military satellite capabilities. NASA uses commercial satellites as an alternative means of transmitting launch commands and scientific data to spacecraft. The U.S. Secret Service uses satellite communications, as does the Federal Aviation Administration for global positioning system navigation and air traffic control.

The security ramifications of the government's reliance on commercial satellites, however, could be significant. The physical threat to satellite systems is found not in outer space (with the notable exception of the threat posed by a nuclear explosion in outer space that would produce an electromagnetic pulse [EMP] that could damage satellites without the proper level of EMP defenses built into their microprocessors), but on earth in the form of vulnerable control stations and communications equipment. Such facilities are vulnerable to natural disasters as well as deliberate physical attacks by terrorists.

Satellite control facilities are also vulnerable to a wide variety of cyber-threats designed to interfere with communications links between the satellite and its controllers on the ground. The attack scenarios are seemingly endless but most likely would take the form of denial of service, malicious software in the form of destructive computer viruses, unauthorized monitoring and disclosure of sensitive information resulting from data interception, or injection of fake signals or commands.

There have already been examples of security breaches and hacking incidents that reportedly compromised satellite control systems. In February 2001, for example, U.S. defense contractor Exigent International, Inc., acknowledged that an unknown number of hackers broke into a U.S. Navy computer system and downloaded source code that controls dozens of military and commercial satellite systems. The hacker intrusion occurred on December 24, 2000, and may have compromised a small portion of an older version of the company's OS/COMET software that was stored on a computer at the Naval Research Laboratory in Washington. OS/COMET is commercial software that allows ground station operators to monitor satellite systems and communicate commands to those systems. The incident was later traced to computers located in Sweden and on the campus of a university in Kaiserslautern, Germany.

The security breach, however, left a wide array of satellite systems potentially vulnerable to malicious software code. Experts feared that by downloading the source code, the attackers may have been able to figure out how to best write computer viruses and worms that would have an impact on the satellite systems that relied on the OS/COMET software. And there were many such systems. In addition to the Air Force's 24 NAVSTAR global positioning system satellites, OS/COMET was used by the entire constellation of more than 70 satellites owned by Reston, Virginia–based Iridium LLC; several NASA programs; direct broadcast and Internet satellite systems; and a Stratford, Connecticut–based manufacturer of electronic controls used by major restaurant chains and commercial appliance manufacturers.

In May 2002, I had the opportunity to accompany a wireless security expert on a drive around the nation's capital looking for open and vulnerable wireless networks—a so-called "war drive." He sat in the passenger seat of my sport utility vehicle, cradling his notebook computer in his lap. A small, gray box with a two-foot, flexible antenna sat on the dashboard in front of him.

After a relatively tense few hours of driving slowly through the terminal areas of Baltimore-Washington International Airport and Dulles International Airport, we proceeded to Arlington, Virginia. I turned down Courthouse Road, located in a residential area of Arlington, and parked across the street from a nondescript series of brick buildings surrounded by an iron security fence that was monitored by military guards and remote controlled cameras. The plainness of the buildings belied their true significance. We were parked across the street from the Pentagon's global network operations center.

The security analyst immediately began to pick up signals of a wireless network somewhere in the area. Without prompting, various Service Set Identifier (SSID) numbers of access points and numerous IP addresses for wireless devices began flooding onto his computer screen. Because none of the access points were protected with even the most basic encryption technology, we wondered if we were picking up a wireless network installed in one of the many homes in the area. That's when the technician noticed a system broadcasting an SSID named "AP-BLDG 12."

"Building 12 is right there," I said, pointing to the main headquarters building of the Defense Information Systems Agency with its large, white sign denoting the building number hanging on the wall facing the street.

It was soon clear that we had stumbled across a wireless access point for one of the security cameras in the compound. Had we been malicious hackers willing to break the law, we could have remotely monitored the very same picture of the parking area, front security gate, and security perimeter that DISA security personnel watched. DISA quickly denied that any of the wireless security cameras were linked to the agency's operational networks that monitored the security of the entire Defense Department computer infrastructure.

But the most sensitive and disturbing uses of potentially insecure wireless technologies may be taking place right in your own backyard, at dangerous facilities near your neighborhood, or in the middle of delicate natural wildlife areas.

Take, for example, the uranium mining operation located 54 miles southeast of Buffalo, Wyoming. That's one area where uranium is extracted from the soil through a process by which water is injected into the ground. The water flows along the bedrock and picks up the uranium that is in the soil. It is then pumped back out of the system where the uranium can be filtered out. The process sounds like a traditional, low-tech industrial job. However, a different picture emerges when you consider how control of the radioactive pumps is being achieved.

Because of the contamination, remote terminals are necessary to control and manage the pumps that move the water and extract the uranium. Commercial PC-based remote workstations now support critical monitoring functions, such as pump failure, pump status, temperature, speed, and even the pump's on/off condition. But the security implications are enormous. When pumps lose power, water pressure starts building up in the plant. Software has been programmed to automatically reset certain pumps to get the pressure out as fast as possible. And it's all being done in the name of cost-effectiveness.

Financial institutions, such as banks, brokerage houses, and credit unions, have also jumped headfirst into the information technology and wireless age out of an incessant desire to cut costs and improve customer service. Digital Internet and wireless systems today handle everything from electronic funds transfers (EFTs) to electronic data interchange (EDI), electronic benefits transfers (EBTs), and electronic trade confirmations (ETCs). As much as $2 trillion per day changes hands via EFT. In addition, EBT systems manage $500 billion in entitlement programs, such as Social Security payments and food stamps.

But more than 50 percent of all major hacking incidents in 2001 targeted banks and other financial institutions.[18] And increasingly, the hackers that target banks around the world are part of organized crime syndicates that have learned to digitize the traditional crimes of extortion, fraud, and identity theft. To date, hundreds of millions of dollars have been extorted or siphoned from bank accounts and credit cards by organized

---

[18] International Data Corporation statistics cited in "Electronic Security: Risk Mitigation in Financial Transactions" (The World Bank, June 2002).

criminals known and unknown. And wireless technologies may be playing a significant role in those cases.

For example, consumers are increasingly accessing personal and even organizational financial data through wireless access devices, such as wireless modems installed in home PCs, public kiosks, personal digital assistants, or cellular telephones. In the wireless world, however, new points of access to the various financial institutions and their third-party hosting companies that manage the banking transactions mean new vulnerabilities. One example is the use of Groupe Spécial Mobile (GSM) phones to initiate a banking transaction through an Internet connection to the financial service provider. Encrypted wireless data must pass through a gateway that, in turn, passes the data to the Internet. However, wired and wireless networks use two different protocols for communicating that encrypted data. As a result, once the data arrives at the gateway it is unencrypted for several seconds and then reen- crypted for transmission on the Internet. It is in those few seconds that hackers can intercept the transmission and in those few seconds that hundreds of millions of dollars can be compromised.

The U.S. railroad system's increasing use of wireless technologies may present one of the most immediate dangers to both national security and local safety. Given the system's long, winding network of radio, telephone, and computer assets, voice and data communications networks provide vital links between train crews, trackside monitoring and repair staff, and rail control centers. Total control of the massive network is accomplished through a communication system that integrates trackside maintenance telephones, trackside transponders, security cameras and monitors, passenger information displays, public announcements, the public telephone network, radio bases, and control center consoles. However, wireless SCADA systems are increasingly providing the management glue that keeps all of these systems running together.

One of the most critical and potentially dangerous areas where wireless SCADA systems are being employed in the rail system is in switching. Switches are mechanical devices that allow a train to switch from one track to another. Depending on the size of the rail line, railroads can have dozens or hundreds of switches in a network of track. Although switching technology has not changed much over the years, the one major change that holds significant implications in terms of security and safety is the use of remote communication technology to conduct the actual shifting and switching of the rails. Unfortunately, if a switch does not operate properly or changes the alignment of the rails unexpectedly, it can lead to either a derailment or a collision.

In the colder regions of the country, underground heaters keep the rails from freezing in winter. These operations are also being controlled and monitored by wireless SCADA computers. The use of modern technology in this case means that in the case of a failure, railroads no longer have to dispatch technicians in the dead of winter to remote locations where heating switches are usually located. However, it also means that the security of these switching operations may now have a new series of security challenges to deal with. This is of particular concern given the dangerous nature of some train cargo. In addition to passengers, many trains often carry a wide variety of hazardous materials, such as chemicals and fuels that could easily force the evacuation of tens of thousands of people in nearby communities should one of these trains derail.

Speaking of hazardous materials, some municipal water systems and wastewater treatment systems in the U.S. have upgraded their 1950s technology using wireless SCADA control computers. The City of Brighton, Michigan, is one example. Brighton is a city of only 6,500. But that population skyrockets to more than 70,000 each day due to a thriving business district and a boom in hotel space. However, beneath the streets of Brighton is a water and wastewater system that is controlled in part by wireless technology.

The remote terminals monitor pump run time, pump failures, flood sensors, high water level alarms, and power, as well as site intrusion alarms and manually activated panic buttons. The utility also planned to equip work vehicles with a controller connected to a laptop computer. "With critical data now available at just the click of a mouse, the laborious, time-consuming, and often hazardous, need for utility workers to make daily rounds to check pump status at each of the lift stations is a thing of the past," claimed marketing material from one of the contractors responsible for installing the equipment. The mobile controller would then allow utility engineers to monitor the waste water system while they're driving around the city.

Emergency 911 centers around the country are also moving at break-neck speed to install wireless SCADA systems to support remote monitoring of microwave communications infrastructures. Many local communities use digital microwave systems to interconnect their radio sites and their 911 centers. They use SCADA systems to monitor all of the various microwave system functions, as well as providing various alarms and status indications. And depending on the size of the area in question, some remote microwave sites can be located an hour or more away from the 911 emergency call center. However, the real danger arises from the increasing use of software such as "PC Anywhere," which allows technicians or the communications center supervisor to dial into the system from home to conduct routine maintenance.

In states throughout the Midwest, one can find oil wells arranged in a twelve-mile-diameter circle. They are part of what's known in the vernacular of the oil industry as a "water flood" operation. During drilling operations, thousands of gallons of salt water are pumped up with the oil and must be separated from the black gold. As drilling operations proceed and the well begins to curtail production, the salt water is pumped back into the lowest producing well to raise the underground pressure and boost the flow of oil to the remaining wells.

However, with such a large number of pumps and holding tanks to manage, drilling companies are increasingly turning their attention to wireless SCADA systems to monitor critical functions of the operation, including emergency systems that are designed to ensure environmental safety. For example, wireless SCADA systems are used to monitor pressure and flow rates in both oil and water pipelines. When flow rates drop below normal levels, the system is designed to turn on additional pumps. In addition, if pipeline pressure or tank levels exceed normal operating limits, the system will turn various pumps off. They are also used to monitor tank levels and overflow pit levels—a critical safety indicator that could have environmental consequences if it fails. And, as in the case of the 911 emergency systems, oil well managers and technicians also have remote dial-in connection capabilities.

Perhaps the most troubling development, however, is the increasing deployment of wireless networks in the health care industry. The U.S. health care industry spent $193 million in 2001 on wireless networking infrastructure and is projected to spend as much as $295 million by 2005. And the use of hand-held computers by doctors, nurses, and medical technicians is expected to triple in the same time frame. Hospitals of all sizes and in all areas of the country are deploying these systems to support everything from medical records management, diagnostics, charting, and pharmacy integration, to admissions, billing, and emergency services.

But this massive push to make hospitals more efficient in caring for patients also brings with it enormous risk for both the health care industry and the general public. Why? The simple answer is that the 802.11b standard commercial wireless technologies have become the wireless access technology of choice for most hospitals, doctors' offices, clinics, and pharmacies—despite its proven insecurity. Some hospitals, however, say the benefits of wireless outweigh the security concerns. For example, the North Shore–Long Island Jewish Health System in Great Neck, New York, which operates 18 hospitals, installed a wireless system in spring 2002 in its Manhasset hospital. But when asked if the hospital was concerned at all about security, North Shore CIO Patrick Carney told *Computerworld* magazine that while the publicity about wireless security problems has certainly made the hospital more skeptical about the technology, there were no immediate plans to end the so-called "order entry system" project that would allow a doctor to prescribe drugs through a laptop that's wirelessly connected to a server. "We haven't stopped, but we're more skeptical," he said.[19]

Hospital CIOs should be very skeptical, if not downright worried, about standard WEP-protected wireless networks. In fact, a random wireless security audit conducted in October 2002 of three hospitals in a major city in West Virginia found that each hospital's corporate network was wide-open to attack and sabotage from hackers who could simply sit in a car parked in the hospital's parking lot.[20] Other serious vulnerabilities that

---

[19] "IT Rolls Out Wireless LANs Despite Insecurity," *Computerworld,* March 25, 2002.

[20] Author interview with senior security firm executive who requested anonymity.

have yet to be addressed in detail by the health care industry include threats from insiders with authorized access to one of the several entry points into the electronic health care system (e.g., a doctor's office, insurance claims, diagnostics, a pharmacy).

Complicating matters for health care providers are the meager financial settings in which many hospitals now find themselves operating. Most hospitals and clinics have been forced for financial reasons to put all non–patient care projects on the back burner—and that means information technology security projects. And despite the October 2003 deadline set by the Health Insurance Portability and Accountability Act (HIPAA), which requires health care providers to adhere to national standards for electronic transactions as well as regulations to protect patient privacy, there has been little focus to date on defending health care institutions from hackers. Although HIPAA sets forth privacy rules, there are no minimum standards for security defenses. And why is that a problem? Well, consider the real-world implications of the fictional scenario outlined in Chapter 1, during which terrorist supporters compromise medical records and change blood types stored at hospitals serving the area where they are about to conduct a major physical, mass-casualty attack. In addition to the obvious physical and health consequences, the psychological impact on the general population of such an event could be enormous.

All of these examples point to a much broader problem of awareness. Tens of thousands of companies in all sectors of the economy are rushing to deploy wireless communications and Internet technologies with little or no focus on the security ramifications of doing so. What's worse, many companies are being unwittingly victimized by employees who deploy so-called "rogue" wireless access points throughout their work areas without the knowledge or permission of the firm's technology or security managers. Consider the potential ramifications of a determined insider working at one of the uranium mines or wastewater processing facilities mentioned earlier in this chapter. The proliferation of wireless systems presents one of the uncharted frontiers for criminals and terrorists who are looking for new ways to disrupt critical e-commerce transactions or conduct surveillance, espionage, or sabotage.

Unfortunately, the inherent vulnerabilities of wireless technologies have been clearly demonstrated to no avail. Few corporate executives believe that the wireless systems in operation at their company are of interest to an attacker, especially a terrorist organization. But security through obscurity has never worked in the past and will never work in a future security environment filled with thinking enemies. With the advent of wireless technologies, the concept of the Internet has changed forever. And so has the concept of security. The real challenge is getting the corporate owners and operators of the nation's critical infrastructures to recognize those changes, accept their own vulnerability, and take steps to mitigate that vulnerability.

5

Al-Qaeda: In Search of Bin Laden's Hackers

Hundreds of young men had pledged to him that they were ready to die and that hundreds of Muslim scientists were with him and who would use their knowledge in chemistry, biology and ranging [sic] from computers to electronics against the infidels.[1]

—Hamid Mir, editor of the Ausaf newspaper
Quoting from a statement by Osama bin Laden
September 2001

While bin Laden may have his finger on the trigger, his grandchildren may have their fingers on the computer mouse.

—Frank Cilluffo, Special Assistant to the President
and Adviser for External Affairs
Office of Homeland Security
Author Interview, June 2001

The search for Osama bin Laden's hackers does not begin in a dusty cave in a remote region of Afghanistan. Nor does it necessarily begin with the inner circle of al-Qaeda leaders or its 10,000 frontline fighters who have

---

[1] Quoted in "Threat Analysis: Al-Qaida's Cyber Capabilities" (Canadian Office of Critical Infrastructure Protection and Emergency Planning, November 2, 2001).

passed through its training camps. To find bin Laden's computer hackers, one simply needs to look at the state sponsors of terrorism, such as Iran and Iraq, or the Pakistani military intelligence service (the Directorate for Inter-Services Intelligence, or ISI). Likewise, one can also find bin Laden's hackers in the hundreds of *madrassas*, or religious schools, where young Muslim boys are sometimes fed a daily dose of hatred for the West along with their studies in computer science. In addition, one could also find ample evidence of bin Laden's computer hackers throughout the growing community of unemployed Russian scientists with training and experience in intelligence; or within organized crime syndicates in Russia, Malaysia, Italy, China, Japan, Columbia, or Mexico. And if after searching through those places you are still having trouble locating a bona fide al-Qaeda hacker, you can look through any number of online hangouts where hackers frequent. There, on the bulletin boards and in hacker chat rooms you will find plenty of skilled and potentially dangerous individuals who are willing to act as hacking surrogates on behalf of Osama bin Laden.

Americans have a difficult time understanding extremist groups, such as al-Qaeda, and are even less inclined to accept bin Laden and his cohorts in other extremist groups as a thinking, technologically sophisticated enemy. However, that reluctance is a fatal mistake that America must avoid at all costs. According to Roger Cressey, the former chief of staff of the President's Critical Infrastructure Protection Board and terrorism expert with the National Security Council, any characterization of international terrorist groups as technologically unsophisticated bands of thugs "would be a fundamental error."[2] The U.S. has underestimated the time that al-Qaeda dedicates to studying "the fissures" in the U.S. security apparatus, and it is clear that they and other radical groups are "pushing students into computer science" for these purposes, said Cressey. Likewise, at a Senate hearing on al-Qaeda terrorist operations held in December 2001, J.T. Caruso, the acting assistant director of the FBI's Counterterrorism

---

[2]   Author interview, November 19, 2002.

Division, characterized al-Qaeda as having "access to the money, training, and equipment it needs to carry out successful terrorist attacks."[3]

"They plan their operations well in advance and have the patience to wait to conduct the attack at the right time," Caruso stated. "Prior to carrying out the operation, Al-Qaeda conducts surveillance of the target, sometimes on multiple occasions, often using nationals of the target they are surveilling to enter the location without suspicion. The results of the surveillance are forwarded to Al-Qaeda HQ as elaborate 'ops plans' or targeting packages prepared using photographs, CADCAM (computer assisted design/computer assisted mapping) software, and the operative's notes."[4]

But to what end can this sophistication be used on the Internet to attack the electronic sinews of a modern society? Most people have a hard time accepting the notion of terrorism on the Internet—a legitimate argument, since nobody has or will ever be gunned down in a digital hail of ones and zeros shooting out of a computer, traveling across the Internet, and ripping through the side of a bus on its way to a religious celebration. But therein lies the fundamental misinterpretation that most people have about cyber-terrorism. In cyber-terrorism, the economy of the enemy nation is the target, and death and destruction are considered a welcome blend of collateral damage if the attackers can arrange it. In cyber-terrorism, the goal is to cut the digital arteries of the economy and the companies that make up the economy, leaving them to bleed money and resources into the streets.

It is worth taking a brief look at Osama bin Laden and the driving force behind al-Qaeda to understand this better and to see why cyber-terrorism is perfectly suited to the organization's goals.

The turning point in bin Laden's life came in 1990 during the Persian Gulf War. It was then that he witnessed American military forces building

---

[3] Statement for the Record of J.T. Caruso, Acting Assistant Director, Counterterrorism Division, Federal Bureau of Investigation, on al-Qaeda International. Before the Subcommittee on International Operations and Terrorism, Committee on Foreign Relations, United States Senate, Washington, D.C., December 18, 2001.

[4] Ibid.

encampments throughout Saudi Arabia, the land of the two holiest places of Islam. The al-Sa'ud family, the rulers of Saudi Arabia, maintained its legitimacy through an agreement with fundamentalist Islamic sects to guarantee the inviolability of Mecca and Medina. However, by allowing Western troops to be stationed on Saudi soil, the Saudi monarchy had, in bin Laden's opinion, betrayed that sacred trust. It was then that bin Laden used his personal fortune of approximately $50 million[5] as well as contributions from wealthy Saudi businessmen and charity organizations to move his operation to Sudan. And while he would eventually be forced to leave Sudan and take up camp with the Taliban in Afghanistan, bin Laden's goal of forcing America to withdraw its troops from Muslim lands and to curtail its support for Israel remained the constant driving force behind his actions.

For decades, observers have viewed individual changes in tactics and modes of attack as simply the latest flavor of traditional terrorism, which focuses primarily on fear and coercion. But with the attacks of September 11, 2001, al-Qaeda showed the world that terrorism's strategy had evolved to a new level. September 11 was an economic attack that had the added benefit for al-Qaeda of killing thousands of innocent people. And the evidence of this shift in strategic focus can be found in both bin Laden's own words, spoken only months after the September 11 attacks: "It is important to hit the economy of the United States, which is the base of its military power," said bin Laden. "If the economy is hit they will become preoccupied."

This is not to say, however, that mass casualty attacks and fear no longer play a role in global terrorism. What most observers fail to recognize is that fear and uncertainty are central themes of cyber-terrorism. Attacks on the financial infrastructure can create uncertainty and loss of confidence. Digital attacks on water systems that cause dangerous levels of chlorine to be released into drinking water can create fear in people who once felt secure from such remote enemies. The potential scenarios are endless, but all are economic in nature. And al-Qaeda's economic warfare strategy, which

---

[5]   Many authors have maintained that bin Laden inherited $300 million from his family. However, the most recent scholarship on this issue places his inheritance in the $30 million to $50 million range. See Ronan Gunaratna's *Inside Al Qaeda* (Columbia University Press, 2002).

bin Laden has reiterated many times since the attacks of September 11, is clear to many of bin Laden's staunchest supporters, including Sheikh Omar Bakri Muhammad, who I interviewed in November 2002.

Bakri stands out as an interesting figure in a sea of radicals who often make inflammatory statements that contradict everything they purport to believe in and stand for. Prior to the September 11, 2001 terrorist attacks, an FBI memo written by agent Kenneth Williams and e-mailed to the FBI's Washington headquarters on July 10, 2001, noted a connection between Middle Eastern men enrolled in Phoenix-area flight schools and Bakri's London-based al-Muhajirun organization. Bakri, a Syrian-born Muslim cleric, refers to al-Muhajirun as "the mouth, eyes, and ears" of bin Laden and claims to speak on behalf of bin Laden's International Islamic Front for Jihad Against Jews and Crusaders.

In 1998, Bakri was one of several individuals to receive a letter faxed from Afghanistan from bin Laden that outlined four objectives for a jihad against the U.S., including the hijacking of airliners. Also included in the fax was a statement urging Muslims to "force the closure of their companies and banks."

According to Bakri, Islam authorizes the use of all technologies for offensive purposes when Islam is under attack. The technologies mentioned by Bakri included military technologies, weapons of mass destruction, and even cyber-weapons designed to cripple the electronic systems that an enemy nation relies on for its day-to-day business.

"In a matter of time, you will see attacks on the stock market," said Bakri, referring specifically to the markets in New York, London, and Tokyo.[6] And while Jama'at al-Muhajirun is primarily focused on supporting the political goals of al-Qaeda and other radical Islamic groups, Bakri said the military wings of these various groups are also using and studying the Internet for their own operations. "That is what al-Qaeda is skillful with," he said. "I would not be surprised if tomorrow I hear of a big economic collapse because of somebody attacking the main technical systems in big companies," he said. "There are millions of Muslims around the world involved in hacking the Pentagon and Israeli government sites. I

---

[6]   Author interview.

believe that Osama bin Laden has earned his leadership and most [Muslim students] who are graduating in computer science and computer programming and IT technology are supporting Osama bin Laden. The struggle will continue," he said. "I would advise those who doubt al-Qaeda's interest in cyber-weapons to take Osama bin Laden very seriously. The third letter from Osama bin Laden a few months ago was clearly addressing using the technology in order to destroy the economy of the capitalist states. This is a matter that is very clear, and Osama bin Laden must be taken very seriously."

Bakri's statements on the potential use of cyberspace as a terror weapon are unique in that they signal the first time that a high-profile radical Islamic cleric with known ties to bin Laden, Hamas, Hezbollah, and other terrorist groups has openly acknowledged in surprising detail what the future of terrorism may hold. But in order to truly understand what the future holds, you have to know some of al-Qaeda's history in seeking and using high-tech equipment to help achieve its goals. And that history begins a decade ago in places like Pakistan and Kenya.

-.-. -.-- -... . .-. - . .-. .-. --- .-.

For thousands of years, Peshawar, the capital city of the Northwest Frontier Province of Pakistan and the guardian city of the Khyber Pass, has been known by many names. The earliest inhabitants called it the "City of Flowers," and then the "City of Grain." Under the rule of the Kushan Kings of Gandhara, Peshawar became known as "Lotus Land." History knows Peshawar as the meeting place of three of the world's great religions—Hinduism, Buddhism, and Islam—and home to some of the world's most ancient and diverse civilizations.

Today, however, among the Buddhist monuments, Hindu temples, Islamic palaces, tombs, and *qehwa khanas* with their shining teapots, Peshawar's central city beats to an underground digital pulse that connects it to the rest of Pakistan and to the rest of the world. Although the majority of Pakistan's rural population remains without access to the country's three million telephone lines, the nation's communications infrastructure has been growing and improving for years. Microwave radio relay stations, coaxial cable, fiber-optic cable, and cellular and satellite networks now dot the landscape and support more than 30 Internet service providers and 1.2 million Internet users. And among that growing pool of Pakistani digirati live and breathe supporters and full members of Osama bin Laden's global network of terror known as al-Qaeda. It is in Peshawar, with its relatively easy accessibility to what used to be al-Qaeda's center of gravity in Afghanistan, that bin Laden's lieutenants exploit the easy availability of telecommunications and the anonymity of the Internet to plan and coordinate their attacks.

Al-Qaeda's use of modern technology to support almost every facet of its terrorist operations dates back to the early 1990s. Recruitment and training for high-tech assignments were done very carefully, similar to how a military organization would assess both the intelligence and physical condition of volunteers for special operations units. But al-Qaeda's computer science program has progressed slowly, first focusing on technology as a command, control, and communications tool, then as a way to conceal plans. More recently, the organization's computer science efforts have focused on using advanced information technologies as a tool to study target vulnerabilities, such as the engineering weaknesses in bridges, dams, power plants, and buildings. But through this evolution, it is possible to discern a future capability road map that is likely to include more overt uses of the Internet as a weapon system.

L'Houssaine Kherchtou, a 36-year-old Moroccan, was one of al-Qaeda's early trainees in high-tech methods of surveillance. He had joined al-Qaeda in 1991 and worked for the group in Kenya. Kherchtou was sent to one of bin Laden's guesthouses in Hyatabad, near Peshawar, to receive training in photo surveillance techniques from Abu Mohamed al-Amriki (aka The American). Al-Amriki was a member of the Egyptian Jihad group, which had forged a close alliance with al-Qaeda and, in many ways, had come to form the backbone of bin Laden's organization. Kherchtou and seven others were separated into two groups of four and were first subjected to intelligence and physical fitness tests prior to being allowed to continue with training. Once training commenced, the course started with the basics of surveillance and then how to operate different types of camera equipment, particularly small cameras that could be concealed or used without having to look through a viewfinder.

Surveillance reports on potential terror targets were entered into an electronic database developed by Abu Anas al-Liby. The reports were produced in the same fashion as if they had been produced by a professional intelligence organization; classification markings were posted prominently at the top of each report, along with the date and a detailed description of the target. Al-Qaeda also put its students through rigorous final testing procedures before certifying them. For certification in photo surveillance training, for example, Kherchtou and the other students were dispatched on mock surveillance operations, starting with relatively easy targets such as bridges and major sports stadiums. The second stage of testing included police stations and foreign consulate buildings.

After his successful completion of photo surveillance training, Kherchtou proceeded to a nondescript building on Fey Street in Hyatabad. It was there that Abu al-Alkali and Salem the Iraqi ran al-Qaeda's electronics workshop—the heart and soul of al-Qaeda's research and development program in electronic document forging, and message encoding and decoding. Behind closed doors, the researchers worked on advanced encryption techniques, methods of breaking encryption, and processes to produce authentic-looking visas and government passport stamps.

Upon his arrival, Kherchtou was asked about his formal education in electronics and engineering. "They found out that I don't know anything about electronics, and they told me just to study from the beginning and to recognize...the different components," he said.[7] Kherchtou continued to attend the workshop, receiving on-the-job training of sorts. But when a more senior instructor arrived and asked Kherchtou for his engineering credentials, he was instructed to attend "the institute" in Bebi, another region of Peshawar, Pakistan. Although he would not graduate, Kherchtou studied at home and attended classes at the institute for six months, attending the al-Qaeda workshop in between. The example of Kherchtou is an important one. It demonstrates al-Qaeda's commitment to formal education and training in highly technical subjects.

By 1995, Kherchtou had returned to Sudan and al-Amriki (aka The American) returned to the United States, where he studied computers and

---

[7]   Court transcript, U.S. v. Osama bin Laden, February 21, 2002.

worked at an undisclosed computer company.[8] Al-Amriki maintained close contact with Anas al-Liby in London via e-mail and informed his associates that he was doing very well in the U.S. "He is good in computers," said Kherchtou. "Very good."[9]

-.-. -.-- -... . .-. - . .-. .-. --- .-.

In January 1995, Ziyad Khalil enrolled at Columbia College in Missouri. He chose computer science as his major. In his spare time, Khalil fought for the rights of his fellow Muslim students on campus. Although he refused to shave off his beard and blend in more with traditional American life, there was nothing particularly unusual about the young student who had made the dean's list. After all, this was America, the land of opportunity and of tolerance. People were not required to check their culture at the door. Khalil was fighting, therefore, for the one thing that truly made America strong—its diversity.

But what was not immediately obvious was Khalil's links to radical elements on campus. Through a group called the Committee for the Defense of Legitimate Rights, Khalil made known his connection to a London-based organization that fervently opposed the U.S. military presence in Saudi Arabia. It was there, in the land of the two holiest places of Islam, that U.S. forces had been based since the end of Operation Desert Storm. During the course of the next year, however, Khalil's political and ideological beliefs became clearer. Using the pseudonym Ziyad Sadaqa, he registered as the operator of www.palestine-info.net, a Web site supporting the Palestinian terrorist organization Hamas. Through the global reach of the Internet, the young American student landed on the radar screen of other radical Muslims in other parts of the world. It was then that bin Laden and his lieutenants recognized that Khalil could one day be of use to al-Qaeda.

---

[8]   Ibid.
[9]   Ibid.

-.-. -.-- -... . .-. - . .-. .-. --- .-.

Despite an unprecedented effort to develop a global communications capability to link its regional offices in New York, London, Peshawar, and elsewhere, al-Qaeda's vast command and control network was in need of an upgrade. By 1996, Khalid al-Fawwaz, bin Laden's chief information officer and the head of al-Qaeda's London office (named by bin Laden as the Advice and Reformation Committee), became concerned about the ability to keep communications links open to bin Laden, who was now in the process of moving his headquarters from Sudan to Afghanistan. Al-Fawwaz ran the London office, located in an old Victorian townhouse on Beethoven Street, Queens Park, as a media and information hub designed to publicize the statements of bin Laden as well as to provide a cover for al-Qaeda's military activities, including recruitment, money laundering, and procurement of weapons and high-tech equipment.

Al-Fawwaz collected anonymous fax reports from various al-Qaeda cells at a corner store called The Grapevine, which served as a fax, Internet, and international call bureau. Sometimes he used the Formosa Street sub–post office in Maida Vale. He then translated the messages and used the same commercial establishments to transmit them to al-Qaeda leaders. It would be through this anonymous, commercial fax network that Osama bin Laden would, on February 23, 1998, communicate his *fatwa*, or religious ruling, titled "International Islamic Front for Jihad on the Jews and Crusaders." It would be in that *fatwa* that bin Laden would issue a "call on every Muslim who believes in Allah and wishes to be rewarded to comply with Allah's order to kill the Americans and plunder their money wherever and whenever they find it."[10] But in 1996, the fax system was proving too difficult and inflexible to keep up with bin Laden's constant movements. It was absolutely necessary, therefore, that al-Qaeda make use of the most economical and mobile modern communications devices. That's when al-Fawwaz came up with a plan and identified the perfect agent for procuring the new equipment.

---

[10] Jihad Against Jews and Crusaders, World Islamic Front Statement, 23 February 1998.

"To solve the problem of communication, it is indispensable to buy the satellite phone," he wrote to al-Qaeda leaders in a memo. And the young college student in Missouri, al-Qaeda's brother in America, would prove to be the perfect conduit for obtaining such a device.

On May 8, 1997, Khalil approached Ogara Satellite Networks in Deer Park, New York, and requested help purchasing a $7,500 satellite telephone and 400 minutes of usage. Marilyn Morelli was responsible for keeping records on each phone the company sold. These records included the purchaser name, address, phone numbers, and credit card information. She also maintained a database that generated a random number for the user to add prepaid minutes to the phone. The phone also came with an access telecard that the user inserted to make calls and add minutes. Morelli processed the minute orders for the customers and downloaded all of the call records from the ISPs (Inmarsat service providers) for billing purposes. The call records showed phone numbers and country codes. Little did she know that information pertaining to the world's most wanted terrorist would soon be among the many records she tracked.

Khalil purchased the phone and the minutes using his own money and shipped it to al-Fawwaz in London. Company records would later show billing information for the number 00-873-682505331 linking it to calls to every country in which al-Qaeda is now known to have had cells. On June 3, he received the following letter from al-Fawwaz, assuring him that his reimbursement money was in transit: "Dear Brother Ziyad: As for the transferred money, the bank assured me that the money was withdrawn on [May 27] a week ago, and they told me that the money will be in your account during this period."[11]

In 1998, Khalil was ordered to purchase an ultra-light power supply and a 12-volt mini–battery charger to support bin Laden's constant movements throughout remote, mountainous regions of Afghanistan. This time, however, al-Fawwaz ordered Khalil to ship the battery to Tariq Hamdi in Herndon, Virginia. Hamdi had been working with reporters from ABC News to set up an in-person interview with Osama bin Laden. On May 17, al-Fawwaz received a fax from the Islamabad Marriott Hotel

---

[11]   Court transcript, U.S. v. Osama bin Laden, May 1, 2001.

in Islamabad City, Pakistan. It was from Tariq Hamdi and read as follows: "Brother Khalid: Peace be upon you. We arrived safely and now we are in the Marriott Hotel. . . ." Two weeks later, on May 26, ABC News was granted an interview with Osama bin Laden in Afghanistan, during which Hamdi delivered the battery packs for the satellite telephone. Soon after that, bin Laden's telephone number was cryptically passed to Mohammed Atef, al-Qaeda's military commander. The communications problem had been solved.

Khalil had become al-Qaeda's procurement officer in the U.S., arranging purchases of the satellite telephone, computers, and other sophisticated surveillance technologies. Like a corporate officer, he acted on the strategic direction of al-Fawwaz, the CIO.

Telephone records show a call from Afghanistan to al-Fawwaz dated July 29, 1998. Al-Fawwaz then called Khalil. The next day, a rush order for 400 additional minutes was faxed to the satellite phone company. "Please try to finish this before noon," Khalil's note to the company read. When the additional minutes were made available, $1,000 was wired to a member of al-Qaeda's Kenyan cell. The terror agent needed the money to plan his escape from the African nation. One week later, truck bombs would tear apart the U.S. embassies in Nairobi, Kenya, and Dar es Salaam, Tanzania, killing more than 200 people.

Between 1997 and 1998, Osama bin Laden used his personal satellite telephone so often that it became known throughout U.S. intelligence circles as the "jihad phone." Osama would use the phone, without expensive or sophisticated encryption software to conceal his discussions, to speak with his mother and members of the ruling Taliban regime in Afghanistan. However, the use of the satellite phone is an example of al-Qaeda's early use of modern communications technologies to carry out remote command and control of offensive terrorist operations. But it wouldn't last long. Later that year, word leaked out to the press that the Clinton administration had used location data derived from intercepted phone conversations to launch a cruise missile attack intended to kill bin Laden. The attack failed. But when the terror leader learned of the National Security Agency's ability to monitor his communications, he stopped using the satellite phone and reverted to trusted messengers. But this was only the beginning. Al-Qaeda would regain its dial tone. The Internet was slowly becoming more critical to the organization's tactics, techniques, and procedures for generating terror.

However, something else happened at the so-called press conference held in May 1998 that few observers have picked up on. In addition to bin Laden's principal deputies, also present at the press briefing were the two sons of Umar Abd al-Rahman (aka the "Blind Sheikh"), the spiritual leader of the Egyptian Islamic Group. Bin Laden had grown close to al-Rahman and had eventually appointed him the successor of Sheikh Dr. Abdullah Azzam, the true founder of al-Qaeda, whom bin Laden had killed. Al-Rahman was arrested in 1993 for plotting to blow up the World Trade Center in New York, a short distance from his base of operations in Brooklyn, New York. However, during the 1998 press briefing, the sons of the Blind Sheikh circulated a photograph of their father along with an appeal to fellow Muslims that read as follows:

> *Divide their nation, tear them to shreds, destroy their economy, burn their companies, ruin their welfare, sink their ships and kill them on land, sea and air.*[12]

The timing and the wording of this message are significant. Although bin Laden would make similar requests of his followers after the attacks of September 11, this is one of the earliest signs of al-Qaeda's focus on economic targets, particularly corporate America. In addition, the order to "ruin their welfare" is vague enough to allow succeeding generations of radical Muslim youth to interpret for themselves the best way to go about doing so. "The joystick generation," as U.S. Deputy Secretary of Defense Paul Wolfowitz has called today's Internet and video game–savvy generation of American military recruits, also exists throughout the Muslim world, where bin Laden finds his followers. America cannot ignore the reality that such groups will act upon these directives using tactics and techniques that they are most comfortable with. And in the near future, that may very well mean acting out in cyberspace, where it is possible to do

---

[12] Quoted in Gunaratna, *Inside Al Qaeda*, p. 47. Emphasis mine.

great damage to the enemy's welfare while at the same time remaining relatively hidden and safe from prosecution.

-.-. -.-- -... . .-. - . .-. .-. --- .-.

By the late 1990s, the Internet and various other computer-based communications and planning technologies had become standard issue for many al-Qaeda cells as well as the terror network's leadership. However, al-Qaeda's vast global network offers many studies in contrasts, and those contrasts are often most noticeable in the terror organization's command and control infrastructure. On the one hand, al-Qaeda has shown itself to have an incessant appetite for modern technology. On the other hand, many of its foot soldiers and fringe supporters can be found in destitute, unwired parts of the world. Al-Qaeda's Kenyan cell, responsible for the U.S. embassy bombing in Nairobi, is a case in point.

In August 1996, the United States Justice Department convened a secret grand jury in New York to investigate Osama bin Laden, who was suspected that year of carrying out a truck bombing of the U.S. military compound in Dhahran, Saudi Arabia, that killed 19 U.S. servicemen. Some of the evidence collected would eventually lead FBI investigators to Kenya.

The FBI dispatched evidence response teams to the East African nation in 1997. One team, headed by FBI special agent Daniel Coleman, was to search the Nairobi home of Wadih el-Hage, a known al-Qaeda member who played an instrumental role between 1995 and 1997 in establishing a terrorist cell in Kenya. Another team, led by supervisory special agent Howard Leadbetter II was ordered to proceed from Nairobi to the village of Witu in northeastern Kenya. There he was to conduct a search of a residence believed to be that of Mohamed Odeh, a long-time al-Qaeda member who studied engineering in the Philippines in the 1980s.[13] In addition to training Somali militia to fight the United Nations, Odeh would be in the company of al-Qaeda terrorists in the days leading up to the 1998 U.S. embassy bombing in Kenya.

---

[13]   Peter L. Bergen, *Holy War, Inc.: Inside the Secret World of Osama Bin Laden* (New York: Touchstone, 2002), p. 56.

Coleman's team, operating under the pretext that they were searching for stolen goods, proceeded to 1523 Fedha Estates, the suspected residence of el-Hage. Walking through the main door to the house from the porch, the team encountered an office space with two desks and a telephone. Also discovered in that room was an Apple Macintosh Powerbook 140 laptop computer and a user's manual for the system. In a bedroom directly adjacent to the front office, atop a shelf in a closet, agents discovered power cords for computers, a Canon BubbleJet printer, a Kodak Diconix printer, assorted floppy disks, and a computer mouse. The search lasted an hour.

Although the investigators had not discovered a hotbed of hacking activity, they did uncover the operations of a highly sophisticated information broker who relied on computer technology to keep the wheels of terrorism in motion. Although el-Hage denied having had any communications with bin Laden during the FBI interview, his computer would tell a different story.

The job of conducting the forensic examination of el-Hage's Macintosh computer fell to FBI special agent Robert Crisalli, a computer crime investigator with Squad C37, the FBI's Computer Crime Squad in New York. After making a mirror image of the hard drive to work from (a critical step that ensures data and dates of files are not changed when the computer under investigation is powered on), Crisalli began the tedious process of digging through the documents. He ran the hard drive in his examination computer and began recovering deleted files and hidden or invisible files. On most computers, hidden files are often system files that are critical to the operation of the computer. But on el-Hage's hard drive, nothing was what it seemed.

Crisalli left no file unturned, including the "games" file. But when he clicked the file, it was immediately clear that the file was not a game, but a resource editor file. Known by computer administrators as a ResEdit file, the file was actually a program that holds formatting codes for files, including one for invisibility. Among the secret files discovered on el-Hage's computer was a letter, which the FBI said was authored by Fazul Abdullah Mohammed, aka Haroun Fazul, another suspected bin Laden associate who had been living with el-Hage. The letter outlined the presence of an al-Qaeda terrorist cell in Nairobi and stated clearly el-Hage's knowledge of bin Laden's fatwa to kill Americans.

From Nairobi, Leadbetter and his team traveled by air. The thriving, fertile greenness of the East African landscape below emitted a thick, sticky humidity that could be felt inside the aircraft even before it reached the ground. The team of FBI agents landed on a small airstrip located on Manda Island just across the murky channel from the town of Lamu, close to the border with Somalia. The locals were dressed in traditional Muslim garb; the men wore full-length white robes and the women were covered head to toe in black, some of them peering out into the world through a thin slit cut out around their eyes.

The team traveled by boat across the channel to the mainland, where Kenyan police officials, accompanied by one of Odeh's relatives and military escorts, picked them up in three Land Rovers and drove them along the narrow, winding dirt and mud roads from Lamu to Witu. They drove for an hour and a half along the countryside roadways, crowded with pedestrians, buses, and lorries. Then, finally, the road widened and to the left Leadbetter and his team could see a fairly large village with buildings and homes with thatched roofs. They had arrived in Witu.

The motorcade of four-wheel-drive vehicles proceeded down the main street of the village past a building with a tin roof and a painted sign on the wall that read "Witu General Store." Goats and other animals wandered about outside the store.

When they arrived at Odeh's former residence, they found a home with no electricity, telephone, or running water. The bathroom area was simply an opening with a pit dug out of the ground. An FBI bomb technician collected cotton swabbings that could be used to detect bomb residue that might connect the residence and its occupants to the bombing in Saudi Arabia. Dozens of papers written in Swahili were also collected. Not surprisingly, computers and other high-tech gadgetry were conspicuously absent. Witu was definitely different and as far away from the copper and fiber-optic paved lanes of the information superhighway as one could get.

This was the true, schizophrenic nature of al-Qaeda that often misled people into believing it to be a mindless horde. To the contrary, it is an organization of multiple dichotomies that moves on the sophistication and high-tech skills of a small cadre of leaders and apparatchiks, while its true capabilities remain shrouded by the hand-to-mouth existence of its foot soldiers and devotees.

-.-. -.-- -... . .-. - . .-. .-. --- .-.

In June 1998, only two months prior to the East Africa embassy bombings, CIA director George Tenet told the Senate Committee on Governmental Affairs that terrorist-sponsors such as Iran, Iraq, and Libya were actively pursuing information warfare capabilities and, furthermore, that terrorist groups were actively monitoring U.S. responses to hacker attacks as a way to refine their own tactics. During his testimony in a packed Senate hearing room, Tenet said a group that calls itself the Internet Black Tigers took responsibility for attacks in 1997 on the e-mail systems of Sri Lankan diplomatic posts around the world, including those in the United States. In addition, he outlined how Italian sympathizers of the Mexican Zapatista rebels crashed World Wide Web pages belonging to Mexican financial institutions.

Tenet's remarks would meet with the all-too-predictable criticisms and jeers from those who view cyber-terrorism as strictly an act of political "violence" that cannot be achieved through computers in the first place. Of course, given what we now know about the extent of our nation's vulnerability to cyber-intrusion and disruption of critical infrastructure services, we can safely discard the opinions of those who argue that cyber-terrorism (e.g., the disruption of control systems at a power plant) is impossible. That sort of thinking, which ignores the potential role of cyber-attacks in the larger scheme of future terrorism, will, in fact, get you killed. More importantly, such skepticism ignores the true reality of cyber-terrorism: its ability to disrupt critical services and inject a sense of fear and apprehension in a population that felt removed and safe from such acts. Therefore, it is important to accept Tenet's remarks for what they were: a warning. Signs were clearly emerging by summer 1998 that terrorism was changing and growing in its sophistication and willingness to adapt to the modern world around it.

By 1999, the U.S. national security community began warning the Defense Department about subtle changes that were taking place in international terrorism as a result of the global explosion in information technologies. Reports by respected analysts began surfacing that predicted the rise of a revolutionary form of terrorism that would make great use of advanced communications and computer networks to organize and carry out quicker, more flexible, and more deadly attacks against Americans.[14] Analysts cautioned that the technology-enabled revolution in military affairs—so-called because of the dramatic increases in flexibility, command, and control that the U.S. military had realized by digitizing its operations through computers and networks—would eventually find its way to America's enemies, particularly terrorist groups like al-Qaeda.

In many ways, the U.S. war on terrorism, launched shortly after the September 11, 2001, attacks in America, is helping to advance the rapid adoption of cyber-tactics by terrorist organizations. The decimation of al-Qaeda's centralized command and control structure as it existed in and around Afghanistan has forced the group to rely on a much more loosely knit cell structure and less on hierarchical forms of command and control. The Internet is a perfect vehicle for a variety of operations, including maintaining rapid communications with cells in far-flung corners of the world; helping to lift the "fog of war" that has resulted from the group's defeat in Afghanistan; and potentially providing an avenue of attack for younger generations of sympathizers located outside of the core of the group who feel helpless to act. And it is this last group that may form the beginnings of al-Qaeda's hacker contingent.

However, the problem that has plagued the national security community's proponents of increased cyber-defenses has been convincing lawmakers, government, and corporate leaders and average citizens that cyber-terrorism represents a clear and present danger to the security of the United States. Absent an example of cyber-terrorism to point to, the repeated warnings and recommendations to prepare in advance for obvious threats that are on the horizon have fallen upon deaf ears. One would think

---

[14] See Daniel Verton, "New Cyberterror Threatens AF," *Federal Computer Week*, May 3, 1999.

that after September 11, this would not be a problem. But America has missed the indications and warnings of terrorism's changing tactics before.

For example, America should have been tipped off to al-Qaeda's interest in using commercial airliners as attack weapons at least eight years prior to September 11. It was then, in 1994, that al-Qaeda plans to crash airplanes into prominent buildings and landmarks first emerged, first targeting the Eiffel Tower in Paris and then the CIA headquarters complex in Langley, Virginia. In addition, interviews given by al-Qaeda operatives to foreign journalists, most notably an Italian journalist who quoted an al-Qaeda member in 2000 that he and others were being trained as pilots to carry out "kamikaze-style attacks," went undetected by American and Western intelligence agencies. Still, most experts chose to characterize the September 11 attacks as unprecedented examples of a major change in terrorist tactics and a new threat that nobody saw coming. In the cyber-realm, therefore, the only question that remains to be answered is if it will take a major terrorist attack on the cyber-infrastructure and economy of the United States for the nay-sayers and disbelievers to accept cyber-terrorism as a clear and present danger.

-.-. -.-- -... . .-. - . .-. .-. --- .-.

During the six years that I've spent searching for bin Laden's hackers, one of the most important lessons that I have learned about trying to chart the future terrorist threat is that while not all expert predictions are wrong (many are), most are ignored.

One example was the September 1999 report of the United States Commission on National Security/21st Century, titled "New World Coming: American Security in the 21st Century." In that report, delivered to then Secretary of Defense William Cohen by former Senators Gary Hart and Warren Rudman, a commission of experts warned the administration that "Americans will likely die on American soil [and] possibly in large numbers." Although it would be unfair and wrong to use this as an example of a prediction of things to come on September 11, 2001, other parts of the study are instructive as to the changing nature of modern terrorism. In looking at the threats facing the U.S. in the future as far out as 2025, the report warned of the following:

> As a result, for many years to come Americans will become increasingly less secure, and much less secure than they now believe themselves to be. That is because many of the threats emerging in our future will differ significantly from those of the past, not only in their physical but also in their psychological effects. While conventional conflicts will still be possible, the most serious threat to our security may consist of unannounced attacks on American cities by subnational groups using genetically engineered pathogens. **Another may be a well-planned cyber-attack on the air traffic control system on the East Coast of the United States, as some 200 commercial aircraft are trying to land safely in a morning's rain and fog.** Other threats may inhere in **assaults against an increasingly integrated and complex, but highly vulnerable, international economic infrastructure.**[15]

However, what this report and others failed to consider was another, less obvious threat stemming from electromagnetic pulse (EMP) weapons—the so-called e-bombs. Congress had held two hearings on the dangers posed by EMP attacks between 1997 and the first half of 1999. And during one of those hearings, held on June 1, 1999, at the Applied Physics Laboratory at The Johns Hopkins University, Rep. Roscoe Bartlett, chairman of the Subcommittee on Government Programs and Oversight, referred to EMP devices as "the ultimate asymmetric terrorist weapon."[16] However, it wasn't until October of that year that the threat of EMP attacks against both the military and commercial electronic infrastructure by rogue state and terrorist groups caught the attention of the wider media.

On October 7, I attended a hearing on Capitol Hill presided over by Rep. Curt Weldon (R-PA), a leading Republican technology and defense advocate in the House of Representatives. In his opening statement, Weldon

---

[15] "New World Coming: American Security in the 21st Century," *The Phase I Report on the Emerging Global Security Environment for the First Quarter of the 21st Century,* (United States Commission on National Security/21st Century), p. 8. Emphasis mine.

[16] Question raised by Rep. Roscoe Bartlett, chairman of the House Subcommittee on Government Programs and Oversight, during the hearing on "Electromagnetic Pulse (EMP): Should This Be a Problem of National Concern to Private Enterprise, Businesses Small and Large, As Well As Government?," (House of Representatives, June 1, 1999).

outlined a level of threat to the U.S. digital infrastructure that until that time had gone ignored by the bulk of the Internet security and business communities. The dependence of the American way of life on the delicate integrated circuits that power computers, data networks, and various other personal and public safety technologies places the U.S. at great risk of being paralyzed by a rogue state or terrorist group that is able to conduct an EMP attack against the U.S., either via missile attack in the atmosphere or locally through the use of a suitcase-size device, said Weldon. "The widespread paralysis of electronic computer systems, communications, power grids, and transportation systems would not be merely an inconvenience," Weldon told the packed hearing room in the Rayburn House Office Building. "Nor would an EMP attack have only commercial consequences. Our modern way of life, and life itself, depends upon the functioning of our electronic society," he said. "Some have argued that an EMP event could be like putting the United States in a giant time machine and, in the blink of an eye, transforming our high-tech society into a primitive, preindustrial one, circa the 19th century."[17]

First developed in 1870 by scientist Heinrich Hertz, EMP technology can be harnessed by terrorists who have only basic engineering and technical skills, according to security experts. In addition, EMP devices are highly portable, can be operated from a distance, and provide remote security that hackers do not have when they are connected to the system they are hacking. And unlike the somewhat unpredictable nature of malicious software code attacks, a suitcase-size EMP bomb provides terrorists with a surgical strike capability that can be planned well in advance to target strategic regions of the country or facilities.

What makes the EMP threat unique is not only its usefulness to the terrorist mode of operation but the fact that the world's two largest nuclear powers have direct experience with the effects of EMP. The former Soviet Union, for example, was so convinced of the effectiveness of large-scale EMP emissions from nuclear warheads that it integrated EMP attacks into

---

[17] Opening statement of Rep. Curt Weldon, chairman of the Research & Development Subcommittee, Hearing on EMP Threats to U.S. Military and Civilian Infrastructure (House of Representatives, October 7, 1999).

its military doctrine as one of the first stages of war with the United States. In 1962, the U.S. conducted four tests of nuclear explosions at different altitudes in the vicinity of the Kwajalein Atoll in the Pacific, and the results of the EMP emanations were startling. The EMP effects of the blasts reached out approximately 800 miles away to the Hawaiian Islands, killing the signals of radio stations, shutting down street lights, stopping cars dead in their tracks, and frying the major electronic components of the telephone system.[18]

Today, more than 40 years after those tests were conducted, the clear and present danger to the American homeland remains not nuclear war but terrorism and possibly terrorism in the form of nuclear or biological blackmail. The EMP threat, however, remains and may, in fact, be of a more imminent nature than at any other time in history. From a terrorist perspective, EMP weapons are far easier to obtain, transport, and conceal than nuclear devices, and they would be more than sufficient to achieve the economic warfare goals spelled out by Osama bin Laden.

-.-. -.-- -... . .-. - . .-. .-. --- .-.

The cyber-threat from terrorist organizations such as al-Qaeda does not hinge on the willingness of the core leadership or even the most dedicated and radicalized jihadists within the movement to adopt cyber-tactics as a main attack method. There are already a vast number of cyber-based alliances of hackers and Internet activists (aka "hactivists") that have indicated a willingness to engage in what many have called a cyber-jihad movement, or electronic holy war, against the West, particularly Israel and the United States.

Malaysia, for example, is emerging as a cyber-sanctuary for pro-al-Qaeda hackers and virus writers. Malaysia's defense minister recently expressed concern about the increase in hacking activity there, while there has been a significant increase in intrusion attacks originating

---

18 Statement of Lowell Wood, senior staff member, Lawrence Livermore National Laboratory, during hearing on "Electromagnetic Pulse (EMP): Should This Be a Problem of National Concern to Private Enterprise, Businesses Small and Large, As Well As Government?" (House of Representatives, June 1, 1999).

from that country.[19] In addition, various computer security and Internet threat intelligence experts have characterized Malaysia as one of the top three sources of intrusion attacks worldwide. A group known as "MHA," or Malaysian Hackers Association, has been very active in the region and appears to be pro-Islamic, pro-al-Qaeda, and pro-Iraq. One of the group's Web site defacements on September 12, 2002, left the message, "May Allah bless Saddam Hussein and all Muslims." And while Web page defacing is certainly not terrorism, many experts have made the mistake of characterizing defacers as incapable of conducting anything other than nuisance attacks. One cannot rule out more sophisticated attacks by such groups, including diversion attacks, denial of service attacks, or attacks in the form of devastating viruses or worms.

One such Malaysian virus writer is Vladimor Chamlkovic, aka "Melhacker." In an e-mail interview in November 2002, the virus connoisseur told me in his broken English that he had already tested a mega-worm that combined features from three previously released worms—Klez, Nimda, and Sircam—and that he planned to release the worm into the wild if the U.S. attacked Iraq. Although he acknowledged to me that he was not a "real al-Qaeda hacker," Melhacker stressed that he was linked to various Russian and Pakistani hacker groups and was sympathetic to the cause of Muslims around the world. Melhacker had been the subject of a yearlong undercover investigation by various security experts. And while they acknowledged to me that they were aware of his connections in Russia and Pakistan, they were unsure of how strong those ties were at the time.

"This is a real Internet computer worm," Melhacker wrote in his message to me. "I will attack or launch this worm if America attacks Iraq." The worm has been ready and fully tested in his lab since August, he said. This was not a surprise, since Melhacker is thought to have written or been involved in the development of at least five other worms, including VBS.OsamaLaden@mm, Melhack, Kamil, BleBla.J, and Nedal (*Laden* spelled backward).

---

[19] See current intelligence report (ID# 111672, September 12, 2002) from Fairfax, Virginia–based iDEFENSE, Inc., at www.idefense.com.

At least one of these worms, the Nedal worm, contained encrypted code. When decrypted by iDEFENSE, Inc., a Fairfax, Virginia–based Internet threat intelligence firm, the code was shown to contain numerous Arabic names of unknown significance, as well as references to al-Qaeda. In the case of the VBS.OsamaLaden@mm worm, the code leaves a message that refers to the September 11 terrorist attacks and then attempts to shut down a user's system and delete all files in the Windows System directory.

Melhacker has also gone by the name Kamil, and analysts believe he may have been involved in the September 2002 release of the BugBear mass-mailing network attack worm. According to Brian Kelly, chief executive officer of iDEFENSE and a former military special operations officer, Melhacker has close ties to Nur Mohammad Kamil, a hacker who identifies himself as part of a group known as "AQTE Al-Qaeda Network."

The continuing development of malicious code from pro-Islamic and pro-al-Qaeda hackers, especially in Malaysia, is of great concern and one that needs to be closely watched, according to an intelligence bulletin authored by iDEFENSE analysts.

"While it might be true that al-Qaeda operatives are not well organized, skilled, or equipped to mount a serious cyberoffensive, it is likely that al-Qaeda sympathizers will serve as surrogates in their cyberoffensive," said Kelly.

In summer 2002, security analysts began to notice signs that various pro-Palestinian hacker groups were beginning to band together and coordinate attacks in support of the Intifada in Palestine, against the U.S.-led War on Terrorism, and against what they considered to be Indian aggression against Muslims in Kashmir. The groups in question include the Unix Security Guards (USG), World's Fantabulous Defacers (WFD), and Anti-India Crew (AIC).

The Unix Security Guards, which was last known to have consisted of five hackers—Inkubus, rD, krew, ShellCode, and Egyptian Fighter— began defacing in May 2002, but as of this writing they have either gone further underground to conduct more damaging hacking activity or have disbanded. Many of the group's defacements can best be described as multimedia montages often consisting of mournful Arabic music and pictures of the devastation from the Intifada superimposed on a picture of the

Dome of the Rock on the Temple Mount in Jerusalem. One such defacement in October 2002 proclaimed the following:

> *"There is no such thing as Jerusalem the capital of Israel. There is only
> one Arabic Jerusalem. USA I think that you are all about to be some war
> criminals. UK you are a slave to USA. FREE PALESTINE! STOP
> THE PAIN!"*

As of November 11, 2002, USG was credited with a total of 1,903 Web
page defacements, all of which took a stand against Israel and the U.S. In
an interview in November 2002, however, a spokesman for the group denied having any connection or sympathies for al-Qaeda, calling the organization a group of "murderers." The group also denied supporting any
particular Muslim group or Islamist movement.

Hackers who go by the handles M0r0n and Nightman formed The
World's Fantabulous Defacers (WFD: The Cyber-Resistance Movement)
hacker group in 2000 as a response to the renewed wave of violence that
broke out between Arabs and Israelis in November 2000. They were one of
the first groups to join the cyber-version of the conflict, which became
known in the popular press as the Middle East cyber-war. The group
consists of about a dozen members from all over the world and makes no
apologies for its pro-Muslim, anti-Israeli, and anti-India leanings.

Although the WFD was formed haphazardly, they have been able to
carry out very organized operations, the most important (in the opinion of
m0r0n) being the group's hacks of Israeli Prime Minister Ariel Sharon's official election campaign site.[20] In addition, m0r0n counts the group's pene-
tration of the Bollywood Stock Exchange in India and the Indian
government's Ministry of Information Technology as two of the WFD's
most important anti-India hacking stings.

The WFD's intrusion into Ariel Sharon's election Web site stands out as
one example of a defacing group that was in a position to do far more
damage and possibly cause a national crisis in Israel. "It was a very
well-planned, well-executed attack, and we defaced his site only a few
hours before the Israeli election result, in which he went on to become
the Prime Minister of Israel," said m0r0n. "It wasn't so difficult, but we

---

[20] Author interview, July 23, 2002.

had to execute it in a way that we went into the site, stayed in it for hours, knew we could hack it, and come out secretively without the administrator of the site knowing about it. We were also able to gain access to and download a database in the server related to the Israeli election."[21]

At the peak of the Middle East cyber-war that had broken out in late October 2000, two other hackers, Cyberpunk and B_Real, approached the group and joined forces with them on what m0r0n refers to as a "global awareness" campaign. Then other hackers, referred to by m0r0n as "cyberwarriors," like Sub-0 and n00gie, "shook hands with the truth."

While many security experts classify groups such as WFD as nuisance defacers, they can be highly organized and deliberate in their targeting. "Each person has a different job to perform," said m0r0n. "I can't tell you what jobs are assigned to what member, but the jobs range from preparing [scripts and Web pages] to creating flash movies and finding high-profile targets," he said. "And then finally going into the Web site and defacing it. We're very organized, and this is what makes us the best hacktivist group known to the world today."

The individual members of WFD are also more skilled than most security experts give them credit for. M0r0n, for example, was ranked first in his class throughout his schooling career and then claims to have attended one of the best high schools in his hometown, which he refuses to identify. Nightman has also been ranked in the top ten at his school. CyberPunk has a steady job as a security administrator for a company that provides security services for various other firms. "We're not a bunch of screwed-up loners or teenagers," said m0r0n. "We know what we're doing and that's exactly why we've been intermittent with our defacements. We don't go around defacing like a bunch of monkeys."

The WFD also identifies closely with known terrorist organizations such as Hezbollah, the Islamic Resistance group in Lebanon. "What Hezbollah accomplished should serve as a role model for all occupied and subjugated populations in the world," said m0r0n. "Through their fervent faith, courage, and guerilla warfare, Hezbollah defeated the occupying Israeli military power in South Lebanon. The mujahideen (freedom fighters)

---

[21] Ibid.

of Chechnya earn our utmost respect and support for fighting against, and defeating again and again every day, the human-rights-abusing Russian army."

The ultimate goal of the WFD "is to open the eyes of the world to the suffering of innocent people in Kashmir and Palestine," said m0r0n. "All oppressed societies in history have risen up and fought for their rights. It's nothing new that Kashmiris and Palestinians are fighting for their rights, as both societies have been dispossessed and are living under brutal military occupations. The Armed Resistance in Kashmir and in Palestine will continue, till both peoples gain AZADI (freedom)."

An FBI official confirmed to me in an interview in November 2000 that the "electronic holy war" attacks conducted at that time by a multitude of pro-Palestinian hacker groups had "moved beyond what we've seen in the past in terms of sophistication."[22] In fact, some hackers had been sharing information on specific port vulnerabilities on individual systems, the FBI spokesman said. In addition, private sector security and intelligence experts later warned that pro-Palestinian groups had entered a new phase in the conflict that aimed to attack "Zionist" e-commerce sites in the U.S. and Israel, as well as other high-profile sites that could help publicize their cause.

Meanwhile, an intelligence report issued by Internet security firm iDEFENSE, Inc., uncovered evidence on hacker message boards that popular U.S. Web sites such as those of Yahoo, Inc., CNN, and AT&T Corporation might be on the target list. There were also clear signs that plans were in the works for a major denial of service attack against U.S. companies. A pro-Palestinian group known as Unity has said publicly that if its Web sites are hacked by opponents, it will begin "attacking Zionist e-commerce sites with millions of dollars of losses in transactions."

In another case, a member of the Xegypt hacker group who goes by the name ReALiST posted a message on an Arab hacker bulletin board asking for help to do just that. "I'm thinking of installing [Tribal Flood Network 3000] servers and doing the CNN.com and Yahoo.com thing again any one

---

[22] Author interview. See "U.S. May Face Net-Based Holy War," *Computerworld*, November 13, 2000.

in, mail me quick [sic]," the message stated. It was an obvious reference to the February 2000 denial of service attacks launched against those companies and many others by the 14-year-old Canadian hacker nicknamed Mafiaboy.

However, the so-called cyber-jihad against those companies passed without incident. But the timing of the threats was important, as they coincided with the beginning of the $19 billion online holiday-sales season in the U.S.

In December 2001, the Anti-India Crew (AIC) launched an attack against the servers belonging to the U.S. General Accounting Office (GAO), the investigative arm of Congress. AIC, which prefers to be referred to as a group of cyber-crusaders rather than cyber-terrorists, identifies itself as part of a hacking coalition known as the Al-Qaeda Muslim Alliance. Other members include the GForce Pakistan hacking group and the Pakistan Hackerz Club. The AIC has also counted among its members individuals who earned professional certifications in various technical areas, such as routers.

In addition to defacing the GAO Web site, the intrusion effectively shut down the GAO's automated system for disseminating its reports on the Internet. The message left by the hacker group stated: "We will hit the [U.S., India, and Israeli] government servers until there is peace around us!"

Government information security sources also expressed serious concern about the security of the Congressional Research Service (CRS), which produces many sensitive reports on behalf of Congress.[23] The sources described constant scanning activity by suspected vandal groups of networks that could be used to gain access to the CRS.

-.-. -.-- -... . .-. - . .-. .-. --- .-.

Today, as the world careens toward an era of cyber-coordinated and Internet-enabled violence, the central question that remains is, what are

---

[23] Author interview with two government IT security administrators who work closely with the CRS, November 2002.

the actual cyber-attack capabilities of al-Qaeda and other terrorist organizations?

We know from watching and tracking the activities of terrorist organizations that they have clearly made the leap from treating information technology as simply a "force multiplier" to using modern technologies as a weapon system in their own right. This is not an alien concept to military planners in the U.S. For the last several years, American military commanders have approached the use of digital networks as a weapon system that enables critical targeting data to get from the "sensor" to the "shooter" in real time. In this way, information technology and communications networks have moved out of the realm of support functions and into the realm of real-time direct action—putting steel on target.

In the Middle East, for example, terrorist groups such as al-Qaeda, Hamas, and Hezbollah have actively used computer encryption technologies and Internet cafés to maintain a high tempo of operations. These groups have also indicated a movement away from the traditional forms of state-sponsored terrorism to using modern technology, including the Internet, to support fund-raising and steady recruitment of new sympathizers to their ideology.

Likewise, counterterrorist operations targeting the Algerian Armed Islamic Group (GIA) bases in the 1990s uncovered computers and floppy disks containing detailed instructions for the construction of bombs. The GIA is now believed to make heavy use of computers to store and process orders and other information for its members, who are dispersed throughout Algeria, France, and other parts of Europe.

The militant Islamic group Hamas also uses the Internet to share and communicate operational information in a way that makes the communications medium a weapon system. Hamas activists in the United States use chat rooms to plan operations and activities. Operatives also use e-mail to coordinate actions across Gaza, the West Bank, and Lebanon. Hamas has realized that information can be passed relatively securely over the Internet because counterterrorism organizations cannot accurately and effectively monitor the flow and content of all Internet traffic.

Despite all of the mounting evidence that suggests al-Qaeda is evolving toward the use of cyber-weapons, the terrorist group that started us down this path and that has posed the greatest threat of all terrorist groups to U.S. national security remains somewhat of a mystery. But the War on Terrorism has helped uncover some of the hidden trends. Al-Qaeda cells now operate with the assistance of large databases containing details of potential targets in the U.S. They use the Internet to collect intelligence on those targets, especially critical economic nodes, and modern software enables them to study structural weaknesses in facilities as well as predict the cascading failure effect of attacking certain systems. But the future may hold something quite different.

Shortly after the September 11 terrorist attacks, the Canadian Office of Critical Infrastructure Protection and Emergency Services issued an obscure report that raised the specter of a possible future cyber-attack by agents or sympathizers of Osama bin Laden's al-Qaeda terrorist organization. The Canadian threat analysis of al-Qaeda's cyber-capabilities concluded that although there have been no examples to date of cyber-terrorist attacks conducted by al-Qaeda, "Bin Laden's vast financial resources, however, would enable him or his organization to purchase the equipment and expertise required for a cyber- attack and mount such an attack in very short order."

In the wake of the September 11 attacks, bin Laden reportedly gave a statement to an editor of an Arab newspaper indicating that "hundreds of Muslim scientists were with him who would use their knowledge. . .ranging from computers to electronics against the infidels," according to the Canadian study. If true, the statement suggests that bin Laden may have been planning cyber-attacks against the West at some point in the future, the Canadian study concluded.

Despite bin Laden's use of telecommunications-deprived Afghanistan as his base of operations, the Canadian study did not rule out the possibility of al-Qaeda agents or sympathizers in other countries carrying out sophisticated and coordinated cyber-attacks against critical infrastructure facilities, such as the U.S. telecommunications grid, electric power facilities, and oil and natural gas pipelines. In fact, bin Laden's foot soldiers, such as Ahmed Ressam, who was convicted of attempting to place a bomb at Los Angeles International Airport on January 1, 2000, have stated that they were trained specifically to attack critical infrastructures, including electric power plants, natural gas plants, airports, railroads, large corporations, and military installations.

The three driving factors behind al-Qaeda's operations—intent, resources, and opportunity—all point to the future use of cyber-tactics. First, the intent of Osama bin Laden is clear. He wants to cripple the economy of the U.S. as a means to force the withdrawal of U.S. military personnel from Saudi Arabia and curtail economic and military support for Israel. The targeting of corporate America and the digital economy is clear in this regard. Second, the growing number of technologically sophisticated sympathizers, especially among Muslim youth, is providing al-Qaeda with a steady stream of new talent in the use of offensive cyber-weapons. In addition to the younger generations of hackers and virus writers, al-Qaeda and other radical Islamist movements can count on the intelligence services of various rogue nations who now and in the future will find themselves in the crosshairs of the U.S. military. Finally, America continues to present al-Qaeda and other radical Islamist groups with ample economic targets in cyberspace, thus driving these groups toward the increased use of cyber-tactics. Unless current trends are reversed and America's digital economy is no longer a target of opportunity, terrorist groups around the world will continue to dedicate time and resources to studying ways to integrate cyber-weapons into their operations.

In April 2002, the CIA reiterated its concern to lawmakers on Capitol Hill regarding the increasing threat of cyber-terrorism. In a letter sent to Senator Bob Graham, chairman of the Senate Select Committee on Intelligence, the agency stated that al-Qaeda and various Sunni extremist groups that support al-Qaeda's goals against the United States are the most likely terrorist organizations to attempt some form of cyber-attack in the future. "These groups have both the intentions and the desire to develop some of the cyberskills necessary to forge an effective cyber attack modus operandi," the CIA letter stated. "We are alert to the possibility of cyber warfare attack by terrorists on critical infrastructure systems that rely on electronic and computer networks. Cyberwarfare attacks against our critical infrastructure systems will become an increasingly viable option for terrorists as they become more familiar with these targets, and the technologies required to attack them. Various terrorist groups—including al-Qa'ida and Hizballah—are becoming more adept at using the Internet and computer technologies, and the FBI is monitoring an increasing number of cyber threats."[24]

-.-. -.-- -... . .-. - . .-. .-. --- .-.

One of the critical areas where al-Qaeda has a long history of experience is the use of front companies to veil its sources of financing. Historically, al-Qaeda has focused on low-tech industry front companies, such as fruit and poultry processing plants and fishing enterprises. However, on December 6, 2002, evidence was uncovered through a six-month, top secret investigation by the U.S. Customs Service, the FBI, and the National Security Council that suggests al-Qaeda may have created various high-tech front companies in the U.S. for the purpose of infiltrating sensitive military, nuclear, and proprietary corporate technologies as well as laundering money to support terrorist operations.

Late in the evening on December 5, as a cold snow blanketed much of the town of Quincy, Massachusetts, federal agents searched the premises of a software firm that had been under investigation for several months for alleged ties to the al-Qaeda terrorist network. It was the end of one phase of Operation Greenquest.

The agents searched the offices of Ptech, Inc., downloading files from the firm's computers searching for evidence that the company—which enjoyed contracts with various government agencies, including the Defense Department, the Federal Aviation Administration, the U.S. House of Representatives, and the Department of Energy's nuclear programs—was involved in helping to finance Osama bin Laden's terrorist activities.

Ptech was believed to have been linked to Saudi millionaire and top bin Laden associate Yassin al-Qadi. Ptech's chairman and CEO, Oussama Ziade, holds a bachelor's degree in physics from Harvard University and a master's degree in software engineering from Boston University. He also participated in the doctoral High Energy Physics program at Harvard. Ziade

---

[24] CIA letter dated 8 April 2002, signed by Stanley K. Moskowitz, Director of Congressional Affairs, CIA.

formed Ptech in 1994 and has raised $20 million in private investment money for the company. But there was no evidence to suggest that Ziade was the subject of the investigation.

However, senior U.S. counterintelligence officials familiar with the case said the U.S. Customs Service initiated the investigation of Ptech after a disgruntled employee tipped the agency off to the company's alleged hidden ownership. As a result, Customs and the FBI began investigating Yacub Mirza, an alleged former member of Ptech's board of directors who also managed a number of other businesses in the U.S.

"Mirza was acting on behalf of Yassin Qadi, the Saudi financier who was on the U.S. [terrorism] watch list and whose accounts here are frozen," said Vince Cannistrano, the former chief of counterterrorism at the CIA.[25] "Qadi is the guy behind Ptech. Although it's not clear if Ptech made any money for bin Laden, Operation Greenquest is trying to determine if it was a laundering entity for al-Qaeda," said Cannistrano.

A senior administration official familiar with the investigation (who spoke on condition of anonymity) said "a body of evidence" about the company's possible links to al-Qaeda was brought to the attention of the National Security Council months before the raid and triggered a government-wide investigation into where Ptech software may have been installed and, more importantly, whether malicious code was involved.

"The good news is we couldn't find anything," the official said, referring to the prospect of malicious software that could have been used for espionage purposes. "The bad news is that something might still be there. We couldn't prove a negative."

The official also said that the investigation into Ptech was not an isolated incident and that there is growing concern about terrorist undercover operations and financing coming out of U.S.-based companies, including high-tech companies. In the case of Ptech, the firm's client list reads like a who's who of the high-tech industry, including the likes of IBM, Booz-Allen and Hamilton, Motorola, Sprint, and The Mitre Corporation, among others.

---

[25] Author interview via e-mail, December 6, 2002.

But one of Ptech's most sensitive contracts involved supporting cleanup work at the DOE's former Rocky Flats facility, which was involved in the development of nuclear weapons and now requires disposal of excess plutonium. In an interview with Notra Trulock, the DOE's former chief of counterintelligence who was responsible for investigating DOE scientist Wen Ho Lee and allegations of Chinese nuclear espionage, Trulock said the possibility that al-Qaeda had managed to form a high-tech front company to infiltrate sensitive DOE nuclear programs was not a surprise. According to Trulock, DOE rarely conducts adequate investigations into the companies it does business with.[26]

As of this writing, the FBI has been unsuccessful in finding any evidence linking Ptech to terrorism financing. In several hours of interviews and dozens of e-mails for this book, Ptech's CEO Oussama Ziade and former employees of the company strongly deny having any ties to terrorism. "I consider myself an American," Ziade told me. "This is my country."[27] In Chapter 10, I tell Ptech's story in detail, including how the media's mischaracterization of the investigation as a "raid" may have robbed Oussama Ziade of his American dream.

Roger Cressey, a former counterterrorism specialist at the National Security Council, said that prior to the September 11 terrorist attacks, the government had not dedicated enough energy toward investigating the use of high-tech companies as front organizations for al-Qaeda. Most of the effort had gone into investigating the use of nongovernmental organizations and charities, he said.[28] "What this investigation shows is that the government is now paying as much attention to the role of high-tech companies in terrorism financing as they are with nongovernmental organizations," said Cressey.[29]

The implications of Operation Greenquest are significant in what its focus teaches us about the true sophistication of al-Qaeda and its vast network of fringe supporters. As we saw with the events leading up to the

---

[26] Author interview via e-mail, December 6, 2002.

[27] Author interview via telephone, January 8, 2003.

[28] Author interview via telephone, December 6, 2002.

[29] Ibid.

attacks of September 11, 2001, the indications and warnings are present that al-Qaeda is learning from its past and adjusting its strategy accordingly. Time is running out. And the weak underbelly that is America's digital economy faces a clear and present danger, a major part of which is our own state of denial.

1*(83)^20=13+01>099*[^(*)()^*20103(*&7]1*(83)^20=13+01>099*[
ood()^*201connect03(*&7]1(83)^20=13+01>099*[^(*)()^*20103(*&
3)(83)^20=13+01>099*[^(*)()^*20103(*&7]1*(83)HEY_LOCAL*(83)^2

6

Web of Terror: What al-Qaeda Knows about the U.S.

Al-Qaeda "was using the Internet to do at least reconnaissance of American utilities and American facilities. If you put all the unclassified information together, sometimes it adds up to something that ought to be classified."

—Richard Clarke, Former Chairman,
President's Critical
Infrastructure Protection Board
February 13, 2002[1]

The dust and debris hadn't even settled yet in and around what once was the World Trade Center in New York when the nationwide purge of sensitive online content began. For a moment, people were nervous and scared; for the first time, we had come to the horrifying realization that there were people in the world, even living and working among us, who wanted to kill us. And for that fleeting moment, nobody in government and corporate America was in the mood to help make the killing any easier for the sleeping murderers who had yet to awaken and strike.

---

[1] Testimony before the U.S. Senate Judiciary Subcommittee on Administrative Oversight and the Courts.

conne
03(*&
1(83)
01*(8
^20=1
01>09
[^(*)
^*201
(*&7]
(83)^
=13+0
099*[
*)flo
()^*2
conne
03(*&
1(83)
0=13+
1*(83
20=13
1>099
^(*)(
*2010
*&7]1
83)^2
13+01
99*[^
)floo
)^*20
onnec
3(*&7
(83)^
=13+0
*(83)
0=13+
>099*
(*)()
20103
&7]1*
3)^20

In the wake of the September 11 attacks, many federal agencies in the U.S. began to proactively scrub their Web sites for sensitive information that could be used by terrorists to plan future attacks. For example, the Environmental Protection Agency removed data from its Web site pertaining to the location of chemical facilities in the U.S. as well as information pertaining to risk management at those facilities. The agency also began restricting access to various online databases that contained information on chemicals and environmental threat issues. The removal of the data sparked a somewhat muted debate between the Bush administration's national security proponents and those who argued that the public had a right to know about the existence, location, and threat posed to their communities from such facilities. But like many of the concerns and newfound realities of the post–September 11 world, that debate faded quickly.

However, the EPA wasn't the only federal agency to scrub its Web sites for information that was of marginal public value but could be used to great advantage by terrorists. The Department of Transportation's Office of Pipeline Safety, for example, quickly announced its intent to remove detailed information on the location of oil and gas pipelines from its Web site. Likewise, the Nuclear Regulatory Commission shut its public Web site down between October 11 and October 17 to protect potentially sensitive information from inadvertent disclosure. Information that was targeted for removal included schematics of power plants and documents that outlined scenarios and responses to severe accidents.

The Web content security review conducted by the EPA, the DOT, and other agencies was not as unique as many had made the process out to be. The Defense Department, for example, had for years been wrangling with the issue of balancing operations security with the public's need and right to know certain things. In fact, long before September 11, in December 1998, the Defense Department issued its long-awaited "Web Site Administration Policies and Procedures" document, which delegated to DOD component and unit commanders the authority to decide whether a command or unit would maintain a Web site, and which listed a broad range of information—such as maps and evaluations of commercial products—as inappropriate for posting. The document directed military commanders to "ensure all information placed on publicly accessible Web sites is appropriate for worldwide dissemination and does not place national security, DOD personnel and assets, mission effectiveness or the privacy of individuals at an unacceptable level of risk."[2] The policy was the brainchild of then Deputy Secretary of Defense John Hamre, who commissioned a joint task force to look into the issue. When the commission finished its work, it recommended that information classified as "For Official Use Only" be studied closely and removed due to the ability of adversaries to derive classified information from bits and pieces of less sensitive data. Included in the list of things to remove from public Web sites were:

Unit organization charts

Detailed mission statements

Specific unit phone numbers

Images of command and control nodes

Command, control, communications, computers, and intelligence architectures

Tactics, techniques, and procedures

Tests and evaluations of commercial products or military hardware

Software documentation

Premature release of information on patentable military systems or developmental processes

Unclassified technical data with military or space applications

Reports of technology innovations from the Centers for Industrial Technology

Maps, charts, and geodetic data

But policies are of no use unless they are followed and enforced, as the Defense Department was soon to find out. In spring 2000, a new reserve unit established by the Pentagon's Joint Task Force for Computer Network Defense was given the task of reviewing Defense Department Web sites for the

---

[2]   See Daniel Verton, "Critics: DOD Web Policies Too Strict," *Federal Computer Week*, December 21, 1998.

continuing presence of classified or sensitive information about military facilities or operations. What they discovered astonished most observers and security experts.

The so-called Web Risk Assessment Team spent one weekend each month digging through the Web sites of the Department looking for information that could compromise military secrets or ongoing operations. The team's survey of 800 major DOD Web sites revealed as many as 1,300 "discrepancies," some of them involving highly classified information, including more than 10 instances where information on Pentagon war plans were posted. Officials also discovered information on computer system vulnerabilities and more than 20 detailed maps of DOD facilities.

Some of the maps and photographs included detailed plans of a facility known as "Site R," which serves as the alternate Joint Communications Center for U.S. nuclear forces. The overhead photo of "Site R" displayed the location of underground tunnel entryways and a detailed floor plan of the facility. This data was also available for some time on the Web site of the Federation of American Scientists in Washington, D.C., which runs a program called the Government Secrecy Project.[3] Also discovered was a Web site for an annual exercise known as "Cobra Gold." The site included an entire list of participating units, communications frequencies, and call signs for aircraft and data on Identification Friend or Foe squawks, which are signals used by pilots to determine if a plane is friendly or enemy.

And in one final instance of irony, the Web Risk Assessment Team discovered a classified excerpt taken from a counterterrorism policy document.

The security implications of making data of this type available may seem obvious to some. However, for those who are still doubtful about al-Qaeda's interest in collecting such data, a look at the al-Qaeda training manual discovered in Afghanistan and on the computers of various operatives arrested since the beginning of the War on Terrorism is instructive.

---

[3]   It is interesting to note, however, that while the Project on Government Secrecy is an effort to lessen the amount of unnecessary classification used by the government, Steven Aftergood, the project director at the FAS, announced shortly after the September 11 terrorist attacks that he removed more than 200 pages of information from the FAS' Web site pending further review for security.

The Twelfth Lesson in the Espionage section of the al-Qaeda training manual includes the following instructions on information gathering:

Information needed through covert means:

Information needed to be gathered through covert means is of only two types:

First: Information about government personnel, officers, important personalities, and all matters related to those (residence, work place, times of leaving and returning, wives and children, places visited).

Second: Information about strategic buildings, important establishments, and military bases. Examples are important ministries such as those of Defense and Internal Security, airports, seaports, land border points, embassies, and radio and TV stations.[4]

When conducting surveillance on foot or inside a vehicle, al-Qaeda operatives were also instructed to monitor and record the following types of information about the specific target area. And while this section of the manual is specifically discussing military installations, the type of data sought provides insight into how an al-Qaeda operative would survey any target area. According to the training manual, the description of the base or camp being targeted should include:

Location

Exterior shape

Transportation to it

Space [area]

Weapons used

Unit using the camp

Fortifications and tunnels

Guard posts

Amount and periods of lighting

---

[4] "Part IV, Twelfth Lesson of Declaration of the Country's Jihad Against the Tyrants, Military Series," located by police in the U.K. and translated into English.

Number of soldiers and officers. Officers' ranks

Ammunition depot locations

Vehicles and automobiles

Leave policy

Commander's name, rank, arrival and departure times

Degree and speed of mobilization

Brigades and names of companies

Sleeping and waking times

Telephone lines and means of communication[5]

The Defense Department continued to lead the way in espousing regular and consistent security reviews of Web content. For years leading up to September 11, few if any other agencies seemed interested or even concerned about the sensitive data that was leaking out through their public Web sites. And while that sense of comfortable oblivion was erased on September 11 and on the days following the attacks, the new sense of urgency surrounding security and Web content control didn't last long and may never have found its way into corporate America. More importantly, many of the so-called Web site security scrubs that had been initiated glossed over volumes of sensitive data that remains available today to anybody with an Internet connection.

-.-. -.-- -... . .-. - . .-. .-. --- .-.

On February 11, 2002, the Manhattan-based security consulting firm Stroz Associates, LLC, a company founded by a former FBI special agent that employs the likes of a CIA psychological profiler and a former Justice Department Computer Crimes specialist, delivered to one of its corporate clients a study that gauged the threat of the company becoming a target of a terrorist attack because of the information made available to the public

---

5   Ibid.

on its Web site. It was the first study of its kind for the private sector, motivated almost exclusively by the September 11 terrorist attacks and the realization that al-Qaeda operatives remained free within the borders of the U.S.

The client was a major financial institution in Manhattan that had specifically raised the concern that its Web presence and the specific information posted there could make it a target of Osama bin Laden's al-Qaeda organization and other terrorists. But Stroz also conducted similar studies of various other companies and uncovered a startling amount of data that was of limited value to the business or its customers but of great value to terrorists who might be putting together targeting packages.

Audits found descriptions of physical locations of backup facilities; the number of people working at specific facilities; detailed information about wired and wireless networks; and specifications on ventilation, air conditioning, and elevator systems that could assist a terrorist operation to introduce a chemical or biological agent into a large office complex. Other sites that were studied gave graphical representations of floor plans, cabling connections, and ventilation ductwork.

But information that could be helpful in planning terrorist attacks isn't the only problem, said Eric Shaw, a former CIA psychologist and profiler and the principal author of the Stroz Associates study.[6] Companies could also be targeted if they post information that terrorist organizations simply don't like, according to Shaw. For example, many corporate Web sites contain messages supporting globalization. Unfortunately, this is a particular message that has been known to stimulate portions of the al-Qaeda organization and could make those companies a potential target. In the case of the Manhattan financial institution, which Stroz could not name for contractual and security reasons, the audit also uncovered files listing frozen bank accounts belonging to known supporters of the al-Qaeda terrorist organization, which also could have provided motivation for members of al-Qaeda in the U.S. to attack the company.

---

[6]   Author Interview. See Dan Verton, "Web Sites Seen as Terrorist Aids,"
       Computerworld, February 11, 2002.

During my investigation into the online prevalence of potential targeting information pertaining to high-profile companies that could be considered American "icons," I came across Philadelphia-based American
Executive Centers, Inc., which leases office space in a 20-story building to
major companies such as Oracle Corporation, Bank of America Corporation, and Ford Motor Company. Since the name of the facility as well as its
list of known corporate residents fit the targeting profile that security experts say could put companies on a terrorist's radar screen, I decided to
take a tour of their Web site. There I found photographs of the facility and
its grounds, floor plans, and virtual tour information.

When I contacted the leasing manager for the facility and told him that
various security experts were warning companies to review what information they post on their Web sites, he said that the company hasn't been
concerned with the level of detail provided on the Web site and that it had
taken steps since September 11 to improve security. "Our floor plan is not a
whole schematic of the building," the manager said, adding that no schematics for underground garages were available on the site.[7]

That lack of concern expressed by some firms contrasted sharply with
the position of the FBI's National Infrastructure Protection Center (NIPC).
The NIPC on January 17 issued a warning to all companies and government agencies to scour their public Web sites for sensitive information pertaining to critical infrastructure systems. It was the second such warning
the NIPC had issued since September 11. Of course, the FBI is often in a
position of being "damned if they do and damned if they don't" when it
comes to issuing warnings. So I decided as part of my reporting for
Computerworld to do some research of my own. I put myself in the position
of an al-Qaeda operative assigned to collect information about critical
infrastructure in the U.S. using only the Internet. What I found was
frightening.

I surveyed a dozen Web sites; in a few short hours, I uncovered interactive maps depicting information such as the location of nuclear waste
storage facilities and detailed diagrams of every major telecommunications network in the U.S.

---

[7]   Ibid.

Large telecommunications firms and local communications companies publish a vast amount of sensitive information on their Web sites about critical nationwide networks. My survey of eight national and local telecommunications service providers uncovered enough information to produce a relatively accurate blueprint of the major network backbones serving businesses across the U.S. In addition to network maps, I found detailed information on the locations of current and planned Internet data centers, router locations, and major nodes of metropolitan area networks. Virtual tours of data centers showing the locations of specific systems, maps depicting East Coast termination points of all long-haul undersea communications cables, and street-level maps of fiber-optic networks were also available.

One of the companies included in my survey, Reston, Virginia–based XO Communications, Inc., offered location information for all of the company's five data centers, as well as a virtual tour inside a "typical" center, including a description of all security systems used to protect the facility. When I contacted the company, a vice president acknowledged the need to increase the focus on physical security. "On a day-to-day basis, most of our concern deals with the logical [network] layer rather than the physical layer," the company vice president said. However, the physical "perspective merits focus," he said. "The entire telecommunications industry has to take it into consideration."[8]

The public availability of maps depicting the nationwide network operated by Sprint Corporation led to a series of "intense discussions" at the company to determine what else can be seen on its Web site, a spokeswoman for the Kansas City, Missouri–based telecommunications firm said.[9]

A spokeswoman for London-based Cable & Wireless, which publishes maps of all of its U.S. and global networks, downplayed the sensitivity of the information contained in the maps. "We give no specificity on our

---

[8]   Dan Verton, "Telecom Infrastructure an Open Book," *Computerworld*,
       February 11, 2002.
[9]   Ibid.

network maps," she said. "It just has the city name and would not give terrorists enough information to locate us. It's really a sales tool."[10]

To my surprise, however, I also found detailed street-level maps of the
fiber-optic cable backbone serving the city of Palo Alto, California, including locations of underground cables and backbone splice points. A typical
fiber-optic cable consists of an inner core of silica glass and optic fibers surrounded by multiple coatings of protection. Jennifer Crossen, a spokeswoman for the City of Palo Alto Utilities, said the department didn't
believe any of the information would be of use to a terrorist. "It's not any
different than what anybody could see walking down the street," she
said.[11]

Not exactly, according to Seth Page, chief executive officer of
Manhattan-based Oyster Optics, Inc., a company that specializes in security for fiber-optic networks. Optical taps placed in public and private optical networks would allow unfettered access to all communications and
information transmitted across the fiber backbone, according to Page.
"Available cheap and legally worldwide from various manufacturers, optical taps currently provide an excellent method of intercepting such data
with virtually no chance of being detected and therefore a very low-risk
chance of the intruder being caught," according to Page.[12] More importantly, most optical network equipment manufacturers and carrier networks do not incorporate protection and detection technologies to
monitor such network breaches in real time, nor safeguard the optical signal,
and therefore cannot hinder the extraction of sensitive data.[13]

Fiber-optic taps could pose a significant economic threat to U.S. companies and would fit well within the current economic warfare scheme of
al-Qaeda. And there are plenty of potential tapping points for terrorists to
choose from out of the more than 180 million miles of fiber cable now in
place around the world. While splicing into the cable to tap the signal
causes minor glitches in the communications signal, network providers

---

[10] Ibid.

[11] Ibid.

[12] Seth Page, "Securing Fiber Optic Communications Against Taps"
(Oyster Optics, Inc., October 16, 2002).

[13] Ibid.

often consider such disturbances simply minor network blips and have no way to determine the location of any potential breaks in the cable, said Page.[14] "In reality, all that is required to extract all of the information traveling through an optical fiber is to introduce a slight bend into the fiber, or clamp onto it at any point along its length, and photons of light will leak into the receiver of the intruder."[15] And tapping devices are available on the commercial market.

In addition, numerous methods of tapping optical fibers exist that do not require the intruder to touch the fiber or "steal" light from the fiber plant. And those methods have been described in detail for millions of Internet surfers to read about, according to Page. For example, a recent U.S. Patent (US 6,265,710 B1), as well as European Patent (EP 0 915 356 A1), issued to Deutsche Telekom, describes in detail "a method or device for extracting signals out of a glass fiber without any detectable interference occurring, in particular without the signals propagating through the glass fiber experiencing any transmission loss."[16]

Experts agree, however, that fiber optic taps remain within the domain of foreign intelligence services and highly sophisticated criminal organizations. The risk is simply too high and the technical capabilities too daunting for a typical hacker to undertake such an operation. In fact, the East German intelligence service, known as the Stasi, conducted physical taps on the communications infrastructure in West Germany for the better part of a decade during the Cold War. When I asked a senior NSA official about the difficulty of conducting such taps today on the fiber networks, the official acknowledged the need for some specialized skills but said it is certainly within the realm of possibility.

"The vulnerability is entirely dependent on how the provider of services handles segmentation of the channels, multiplexing," the NSA official said, describing the process. "If the fiber optic transport is a loop and if there is a common multiplexing scheme and if there is no [virtual private network] or encryption protection for each user, which is usually the case

---

[14] Ibid.

[15] Ibid.

[16] Ibid.

with fiber, then access to a wiring closet is an easy way into a target," the official said. Most corporate building complexes include so-called "wiring closets" where all of the major communications devices are located. "The key is that the wiring closet provide for the termination of the optical fiber into a multiplexer and terminal equipment so that there is no interruption or degradation of the fiber bits. The [attacker] has to know quite a bit about the internal structure of the signals, but that is not that hard in today's world."[17]

Just as easily as one can find information on the Web about the location of fiber-optic cables serving corporations in major cities, you can also purchase detailed digital maps of the locations of long-haul undersea cable termination points. Although the chief executive officer of one such company that sells these maps said he didn't feel that his business offered any assistance to terrorists, he acknowledged in an interview that "if you knew what you were looking for, you could probably find it."[18]

The most unsettling information I discovered, however, pertained to the nation's nuclear power plants and other energy infrastructures. An examination of U.S. Department of Energy (DOE) Web sites revealed maps that provide the approximate locations of all nuclear waste storage facilities, nuclear reactors, and surplus plutonium storage sites in the country. In addition, the Energy Information Administration (EIA), a division within the DOE, offered Web surfers an online database of electric power profiles for every state, plus a database of all operational nuclear reactors and a detailed depiction of a typical uranium mill.

Although the Energy Department declined to comment on the information I discovered, Paula Scalingi, the former director of critical infrastructure protection at the DOE, said the problem needed to be addressed immediately. "The genie is out of the bottle," and steps should be taken to study what value, if any, this sort of information provides the public, she said.[19] Scalingi, who now heads her own private consulting business, tried to conduct such a study last year at the DOE but couldn't get funding.

---

[17] Author interview.

[18] Dan Verton, "Telecom Infrastructure an Open Book," *Computerworld*, February 11, 2002.

[19] Dan Verton, "Energy, Nuclear Infrastructure Exposed," *Computerworld*, February 11, 2002.

Ed Badolato, president of Washington-based Contingency Management Services, Inc., and the former deputy assistant secretary for energy emergencies at the DOE, said the amount of information about critical energy infrastructures available on the Internet provides a blueprint for terrorists. And Badolato understands the challenge of critical infrastructure protection and counterterrorism operations better than most. A retired colonel in the U.S. Marine Corps, Badolato personally headed small unit operations against terrorists in Asia, Africa, the Middle East, and Latin America. In 1967, shortly after the Arab-Israeli Six-Day War, he was stationed on the Golan Heights, where he was one of the first U.S. military officers to actually deal with the emerging Middle Eastern terrorists. He personally organized security operations to protect the Trans-Arabian Pipeline (Tapline) in the Syrian Desert against sabotage attacks. As a deputy assistant secretary of energy from 1984 to 1989, Badolato was the principal architect of the U.S. government's readiness and response plan to terrorist threats to the national energy infrastructure, as well as management of all 58 nuclear weapon facilities—by size, scope, and budget, the largest industrial security operation in the U.S.

According to Badolato, the Federal Energy Regulatory Commission (FERC) realized that there was "a virtual gold mine of information on energy sites that would be useful to terrorists," and soon after the September 11 terrorist attacks, it rapidly removed a huge amount of its Web content from publicly accessible sites. But "our potential adversaries have been at this for a good while and the type of attack planning information that they are interested in probably has been already downloaded," acknowledged Badolato.[20] "Still, it will keep the bad guys from getting all of the updates, and may make them work a little harder to hack their way into critical IT command and control sites."

-.-. -.-- -... . .-. - . .-. .-. --- .-.

On February 13, 2002, Richard Clarke, former top cyber-defense official in both the Clinton and Bush administrations, appeared before the U.S. Senate Judiciary Subcommittee on Administrative Oversight and the

---

[20]   Author interview, February 26, 2002.

Courts. He told lawmakers that al-Qaeda operatives were using the Internet to gather intelligence about critical facilities and infrastructure systems inside the U.S.

Evidence had been found in caves in Afghanistan that al-Qaeda "was using the Internet to do at least reconnaissance of American utilities and American facilities," said Clarke.[21] Clarke said al-Qaeda was gathering information from public Web sites. "If you put all the unclassified information together, sometimes it adds up to something that ought to be classified," he said.[22]

Within two weeks of Clarke's testimony on Capitol Hill and publication of my story in *Computerworld* about the online availability of sensitive targeting information, New York Governor George Pataki ordered a statewide scrub of government agency Web sites to remove sensitive information that might help terrorists plan and carry out attacks on the state's critical infrastructure. Among the data that was earmarked for review and potential removal from the state Web sites was information on state government offices, dams, maps, and power stations.[23]

Experts were quick to point out that while Pataki's efforts to impede future terrorist plans were laudable and logical, most of the detailed information about sensitive infrastructures that is available on the Web doesn't belong to the state. Most of the data that has been out there for years was put there by private companies that own and operate the facilities and by the federal government, experts said. "This action is like locking the barn after the horse has been stolen," said Ed Badolato, in an interview I conducted with him shortly after news of Pataki's order broke.[24] However, many state agencies have regulatory ownership and even managerial responsibility for various critical infrastructures and potential targets, said Badolato. Although most of the information that would be useful to attack

---

[21] See Patrick Thibodeau, "Official: Terrorists Used Internet to Get Info on Potential Targets," *Computerworld*, February 13, 2002.

[22] Ibid.

[23] See Dan Verton, "New York Pulls Sensitive Data from State's Web Sites," *Computerworld*, February 26, 2002.

[24] Ibid.

planning has probably already been downloaded, "I can't fault [Pataki] for carrying out his responsibilities," Badolato said.

According to Eric Shaw, who has studied terrorist behavior as a CIA expert, "over the last 25 years, we have found that as we harden facilities, terrorists pull back and attack the periphery, including personnel."[25] The New York plan is "much more concerned about personnel and facility information that could be used to carry out bombings," he said.

Even Shaw's former employer, the CIA, discovered that it too could be the subject of online surveillance. In March 2002, a London-based Internet security and risk consulting firm published the results of a two-day study that highlighted in surprising detail what the company called the CIA's primary points of presence on the public Internet. Using open, legal sources of information and without conducting any illegal port scanning or intrusive network probes, Matta Security Ltd., produced a detailed map of unclassified CIA networks, including several that aren't readily available to the public. Matta's study also uncovered the names, e-mail addresses, and telephone numbers of more than three dozen CIA network administrators and other officials.[26]

A CIA spokeswoman downplayed the significance of the report, stating that many IT professionals within the agency are "overt" employees and need to have Internet access. However, some security experts, although vague about the specific nature of potential vulnerabilities such information could be used to exploit, noted the possible threat from determined adversaries who might be able to use the information to obtain more sensitive or secret information or for other forms of attack planning. In the intelligence world, this is called derivation—the process of deriving tidbits of classified information from large volumes of unclassified, open-source data.

"The points of presence all seem to be overt CIA links, and the names are of overt employees who seem to be either system managers or points of reference for billing purposes," said Vince Cannistrano, former chief of

---

[25] Ibid.

[26] See Dan Verton, "Study: Web Exposes Data on CIA Networks," *Computerworld*, March 11, 2002.

counterintelligence at the CIA, who reviewed the report. "It doesn't tell you anything about the clandestine side of CIA networks over which classified information flows and which has no public points of presence. But perhaps these are good starting points for less-scrupulous elements to begin cyberattacks."[27]

Cannistrano was correct in his analysis. Simply knowing the names and e-mail addresses that Matta turned up would be enough for some social engineers to get the rest of the information necessary to mount a cyber-attack. The network map produced by the company was also of sufficient quality and contained enough details to provide a good starting point for sophisticated hackers.

And that was the whole point of the study, said Chris McNab, the report's primary author. "We wanted to draw attention to the risks of publicly available data that could be mined by determined attackers when targeting large organizations," said McNab.[28] "Through issuing simple search engine requests, combined with [Network Information Center] and [Domain Name System] querying, we were able to build good pictures of the CIA's primary Internet presence, without ever port-scanning or probing their networks directly."

—.—. —.—— —... . .—. — . .—. .—. ——— .—.

The security challenges posed by the hard-wired Internet pale in comparison to the challenge that wireless networks pose to the FBI in its antiterrorism efforts. Of particular concern to law-enforcement officials is a phenomenon known as "warchalking," a process by which wireless Internet enthusiasts place physical chalk markings on sidewalks and on the sides of buildings where open, unsecured wireless networks and Internet connections are present.

But while many wireless Internet enthusiasts chuckle at the notion of warchalking providing any sort of assistance to terrorist operations, the FBI thinks differently of the practice. So differently, in fact, that in July 2002

---

[27] Ibid.

[28] Ibid.

special agent Bill Shore from the FBI's Pittsburgh field office sent an e-mail message to private-sector members of the local FBI InfraGard chapter warning companies throughout the Pittsburgh area of what he described as a systematic effort to mark and map unsecured wireless access points throughout many of the nation's major metropolitan areas.

Shore likened warchalking to hobos marking public facilities that are willing to provide a hot meal, or the way spies mark dead-drop locations to exchange packages clandestinely. Although the markings can be used for legitimate purposes, such as denoting a free public Internet access point, officials fear that the markings being made on corporate buildings are actually enabling hackers, and possibly even terrorists, to more easily locate vulnerable wireless LANs that can be used for surreptitious communications.

"In Pittsburgh, the individuals are essentially attempting to map the entire city to identify the wireless access points," Shore said in an interview.[29] In addition, Web sites have popped up that provide interactive digital maps denoting the precise locations of dozens of wireless access points in cities such as Pittsburgh, Philadelphia, Boston, and Berkeley, California, as well as regions of northeast Texas and various college campuses.

For example, a Web site called Zhrodague Wireless Maps (ZWM) allows war drivers—hackers who drive around in automobiles with laptop computers equipped with antennas looking for wireless networks to tap into—to submit output from their war-driving adventures and then creates digital street-level maps that show the locations and signal strengths of wireless access points. And in some cases, satellite photos are used to denote precise locations.[30] The site includes more than 28,000 entries from war-driving results in Boston alone. It also provides maps for Germany and Okinawa, Japan.

Another Web site, Warchalking.org, includes a message board where computing enthusiasts often post messages about their warchalking plans. One

---

[29] See Dan Verton, "Mapping of Wireless Networks Could Pose Enterprise Risk," *Computerworld,* August 14, 2002.

[30] Ibid.

user bragged about his warchalking excursion in Santa Monica, California, where he marked the "corrugated metal wall of an art gallery."

Shore acknowledged the threat such markings and Web sites pose to ongoing criminal and counterintelligence investigations, especially antiterrorism investigations. The ability of criminals and terrorists to spot these markings while simply walking down the street and then use vulnerable corporate wireless networks for anonymous Internet access "poses a real problem" for law enforcement, he said.[31]

-.-. -.-- -... . .-. - . .-. .-. --- .-.

One of the more obvious corporate uses of the Web is to advertise to the world a company's latest and greatest line of high-tech gadgetry or details of a series of high-profile, and sometimes not so high-profile, government and private sector contracts to work on major information technology programs. But while such use of the Web has been a boon to the technology industry, it has also on various occasions been a national security nightmare. This is a fact that has not been lost on the Defense Department.

On the morning of September 11, 2001, I began the difficult process of reporting on the physical destruction of communications facilities from my office, a short 20-minute drive from the Pentagon. Naturally, I began making telephone calls to my contacts within the "building," as those who work at the Pentagon know the place. One call was made to a U.S. Army press contact. Although I never reached him, my contact's voice mail continued to operate. However, in his message he offered details about the extent of the damage to communications capabilities, including which wings of the building were without telephone service or electric power.

Within days of the attacks, however, the Web sites of technology companies came alive with news that the Pentagon had submitted emergency orders for various types of equipment, including communications gear, and that officials had sped up delivery time lines for previous contracts that had already been negotiated. For the companies involved, it was a public relations coup to be able to say that the Defense Department had turned to

---

[31] Author interview. See Ibid.

Richard Clarke (left), chairman of the President's Critical Infrastructure Protection Board, shares a laugh with National Security Advisor Condoleeza Rice during a meeting of the President's National Security Telecommunications Advisory Committee (NSTAC) held at the U.S. State Department in 2001.

Dan Verton

Tom Ridge announcing the release of the National Strategy to Protect Cyberspace and the National Strategy for the Physical Protection of Critical Infrastructures and Key Assets, February 14, 2003. Both documents owe their success to Dick Clarke.

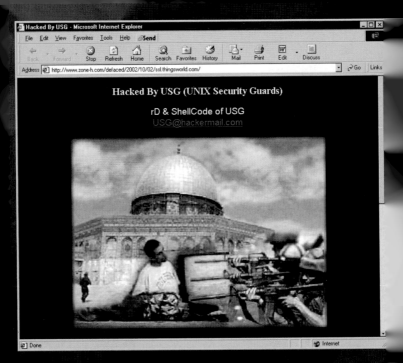

Hacked By USG (UNIX Security Guards)

rD & ShellCode of USG
USG@hackermail.com

cement conducted by the Unix Security Guards, a group dedicated
their hacking skills to spread anti-Israeli propaganda.

THE FACE OF THE WORLD'S BIGGEST MURDERER:

Ariel Sharon - A determined and decisive murderer

- Ariel Sharon Election Campaign 2001 has been hacked.
- Sharon killed 30,000 people.
- A vote for Sharon is a vote for murder and genocide.
- A vote for Barak is a vote for racism and oppression
- Sharon is a war criminal.
- Long live Hizballah!
- Comments? Suggestions? Contact Us

IMPORTANT

A Message from Ariel Sharon himself to all the viewers of this site:

(By the great grace of God, this site, Ariel Sharon Election Campaign 2001, has been hacked by the MEMBERS of the World's Fantabulous Defacers. Why? To reveal the truth about Ariel Sharon, a pathetic, sub-human man who was and is responsible for the tortures, rapes, beatings, and cold-blooded killings of over 30,000 people. [He] is now about to become prime minister of Israel, a racist, fascist state that denies a whole people of the independance free people take for granted. Here is the truth...)

defacement of the official Web site of Israeli Prime Minister Ariel S
e hacker group known as the World Fantabulous Defacers (WFD).

An example of the WFD's anti-Israeli propaganda hacking campaign.

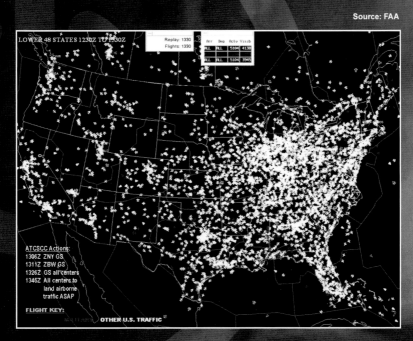

An FAA computer screen depicting radar indicators for more than 4,500 commercial airliners in the skies above the U.S. between 7:30 A.M. EST and 8:30 A.M. EST on the morning of September 11, 2001.

A young Afghan boy sells beads in downtown Kabul, Afghanistan, on July 16, 2002, to help earn money for his family. Experts fear al-Qaeda can succeed in radicalizing young Muslims who will use computers to conduct and support future terrorist attacks.

structure of the building and collapse the area where the plane hit and all the floors above it only. This is all that we had hoped for.

Frame grab from the Osama bin Laden videotape released by the Department of Defense on Dec. 13, 2001.

FBI photo of Mohammed Sher Mohammad Khan released February 7, 2003. He is believed to have entered the United States illegally after September 1, 2001 and is wanted for questioning for possible terrorist links.

DoD photo by Staff Sgt. Stephen Lewald, U.S. Army (Released)

Al-Qaeda's new home since the start of the War on Terror. A detention unit at Camp Delta, Guantanamo Bay, Cuba, on December 3, 2002, showing bed, comfort items, toilet, and sink with potable water.

izon technicians work on restoring critical communications capabilities
ving Wall Street and other areas of lower Manhattan.

e extent of the damage to the Verizon offices at 140 West Street.

The attack on the Pentagon (shown here) destroyed various critical communications systems, including classified network connectivity.

President George W. Bush and Secretary of Defense Donald Rumsfeld survey the

Accompanied by Tom Ridge and White House Chief of Staff Andrew Card, President Bush visits the Homeland Security Complex in Washington, D.C., September 19, 2002.

Secretary of State Colin Powell tells members of the National Security Telecommunications Advisory Committee (NSTAC) on March 13, 2002 that he "never felt more useless in my life than on the morning of the 11th of September" due to the massive loss of communications that resulted from the attacks.

them for help in a time of national crisis. For the military, however, the deluge of press releases being posted on the Internet and faxed to news organizations around the country became a national case of loose lips potentially sinking ships.

Within a week of the attacks, Carlsbad, California–based Holocom Networks issued a statement on its Web site stating that the Pentagon placed an emergency order for 1,000 secure desktop communications enclosures. Likewise, Cryptek Inc., formerly Cryptek Secure Communications, LLC, in Sterling, Virginia, issued a statement that the Army had stepped up its delivery date for 1,400 of the company's secure battlefield fax machines. And Redwood City, California–based BroadVision, Inc., issued a press release that outlined the Air Force's plans to consolidate hundreds of databases into a single portal holding everything from "personnel data to frontline combat intelligence."

As a result of these and other statements, Pentagon officials felt pressured to issue a series of memos urging private industry contractors to think twice about the information they release to the public and post on their Web sites.

"I would also like to stress, during this national emergency, the importance of the use of discretion in all the public statements, press releases, and communications made by your respective companies and by your major suppliers," wrote E.C. "Pete" Aldridge, Jr., undersecretary of defense for acquisition, technology, and logistics, in a letter to businesses on October 2. "Statistical, production, contracting and delivery information can convey a tremendous amount of information that hostile intelligence organizations might find relevant."[32]

Air Force and Navy acquisition chiefs quickly followed suit. And in an e-mail sent on October 4 to ten senior officials in the Air Force, Darleen Druyan, deputy assistant secretary of the Air Force for acquisition and management, went one step further by prohibiting Air Force acquisition officials from speaking to the media.

---

[32] Letter obtained by author dated October 2, 2001, E.C. "Pete" Aldridge, Jr., under secretary of defense for acquisition, technology, and logistics (AT&L).

"Effective immediately, I do not want anyone within the Air Force acquisition community discussing any of our programs with the media [on or off the record]," wrote Druyan. "This includes presenting program briefings in any forums at which the media may be present."[33]

The issue of public disclosure boils down to whether or not the public benefits in any way from having access to the information being disclosed. In many cases, such as data pertaining to the location of hazardous materials or chemical processing facilities, a valid argument can be made for the public's right to know. However, in many other cases, such as ongoing military deployments and equipment support to military forces taking part in the War on Terrorism, an argument can be made that the corporate gold rush now underway to tap into the multibillion dollar market in homeland security technologies can put lives at risk by enabling terrorists and other enemies to derive classified information about capabilities and plans by weeding through mountains of seemingly harmless marketing data.[34]

But while the Web may seem like a gold mine for terrorists, it is important that we as a free nation do not allow the government to use terrorism as a pretext to withhold information that the public has a right and a need to know. This is one balancing act that truly does have life and death consequences.

---

[33] E-mail message obtained by author, dated October 4, 2001.

[34] Likewise, the 24-hour cycle of online news coverage is such that our enemies often know about military plans and deployments in near–real time. This is in stark contrast to my father's generation. My father was one of 13 survivors of the Destroyer U.S.S. Sims (DD-409), sunk in action on May 7, 1942, during the Battle of the Coral Sea, but my grandparents did not receive word of the battle or the sinking of the Sims until the end of June. This was a deliberate effort by the Navy to deprive the enemy of information on the U.S. status of forces.

9/11: The *Cyber*-terrorist Attack

> *If it's a major cyber-event, it's going to have a physical tail. If it's a major physical event, it's going to have a cyber-tail. And as a result you can't separate physical from cyber.[1]*
>
> —Brenton Greene
> Deputy manager, National Communications System

> *The great uncertainty of all data in War is a peculiar difficulty, because all action must, to a certain extent, be planned in a mere twilight, which like the effect of a fog or moonshine, gives to things exaggerated dimensions and an unnatural appearance.*
>
> —General Carl von Clausewitz
> On War, 1832

It was 8 o'clock in the morning on what was shaping up to be a sun-drenched, breezy, and cheerful day in September when Brenton Greene sat down in a secure facility outside of Washington, D.C., for a classified briefing from the CIA. A 25-year veteran of the Navy's submarine force, the so-called "silent service," his career had taken him from the helm of the USS Skipjack and USS Hyman G. Rickover, both

---

[1] Author interview, October 29, 2002.

nuclear attack submarines, to service as a civilian member of the President's Commission on Critical Infrastructure Protection. The former sub commander was used to classified briefings and operating in the shadows, far behind the newspaper headlines and away from the television cameras. But this briefing promised to be different from any other he had taken part in. And Greene's relaxed, contemplative demeanor belied his true interest in what the CIA had to say.

He had been in his latest job for only six months. But as the deputy manager of the National Communications System (NCS), a relatively small agency established by President John F. Kennedy to ensure the uninterrupted availability of critical communications networks during times of national crisis, Greene's role in the meeting was crucial. But he wasn't alone. With him were representatives from seven other federal agencies and more than 40 technology and communications companies that own and operate many of the nation's most critical communications networks.

Once the briefing started, the CIA representatives began to outline what everybody in the room already knew in a general sense: that the international terrorist threat to the U.S. telecommunications infrastructure was real and growing more serious every day. But the CIA officers quickly captured the attention of their audience as they began to delve deeper into one of the first intelligence threat assessments to deal with the issues of cybersecurity and cyber-terrorism. Despite the obvious vulnerabilities to the nation's most critical systems and infrastructures from information warfare and cyber-terrorism, the CIA had only recently completed its estimate—five years after principle members of the National Security Telecommunications Advisory Council (NSTAC) forwarded a memorandum to President Bill Clinton that stated: "[the] integrity of the Nation's information systems, both government and public, are increasingly at risk to intrusion and attack. . .other national infrastructures. . .[such as] finance, air traffic control, power, etc., also depend on reliable and secure information systems, and could be at risk."[2] More importantly, the current sense of urgency, if there was one, was due in large part to Pennsylvania Republican

---

[2]   "Information Sharing for Critical Infrastructure Protection," *Task Force Report of the President's National Security Telecommunications Advisory Council* (June 2001).

Curt Weldon, chairman of the Research and Development Subcommittee of the powerful House Armed Services Committee. During a hearing on March 8, 2000, Weldon harshly criticized the CIA for not yet having produced a National Intelligence Estimate (NIE) covering cyber-war and cyber-terrorism threats to the U.S. Much of Weldon's wrath also fell upon the shoulders of Clinton for failing to adequately address the issue of cybersecurity and critical infrastructure protection in his State of the Union address that year. "If this isn't the state of the union, I don't know what is," Weldon had said.[3]

The CIA and other participants at the NCS briefing agreed that although a strategic cyber-attack on U.S. critical infrastructures had not yet occurred, there was a growing body of evidence relating to the increased sophistication in information warfare (IW) capabilities of foreign nations. Many countries thought by the CIA to be developing IW programs considered cyber-attacks against public and private computer systems in the United States to be the kind of asymmetric warfare option they would need to level the playing field during a conventional military conflict with the U.S. In addition, the agency had previously warned that an attack would likely cut across the public and private sectors and civilian and military domains.

As the briefing continued, the conversation between the meeting participants began to take form. Such an attack would likely involve a major disruption of key telecommunications infrastructures serving other sectors of the economy, including banking and finance, electric power, and air traffic control.

"Everything runs on telecom," recalled Brenton Greene.[4] "If it's a major cyber-event, it's going to have a physical tail. If it's a major physical event, it's going to have a cyber-tail. And as a result you can't separate physical from cyber."

---

[3] Author present at Hearing of the House Armed Services Committee, Research and Development Subcommittee, Rayburn House Office Building, March 8, 2000. Weldon's remarks were in part driven by recent events, including the February 2000 denial of service attacks against some of the biggest e-commerce companies on the Internet that would later be attributed to a 14-year-old Canadian hacker nicknamed "Mafiaboy."

[4] Author interview.

As such, major disruptions could have a strategic economic impact on the U.S., including possible loss of public confidence in the delivery of services from those infrastructures. And the list of potential adversaries that could employ physical or electronic attacks against critical infrastructures was growing longer every day. Foreign governments, for example, continued to pose a serious and structured threat because of their access to sophisticated technology as well as intelligence support, funding, and organized cadres of professional technologists.

But terrorist organizations were also becoming more aware of the targeting potential offered by the telecommunications infrastructure, according to the CIA. And this was a lesson that had not been lost on the members of the NCS. Drawing on previous CIA testimony, the NCS had come into this meeting with the following analysis already having been conducted:

> *The global dependence on interconnected computers and the vulnerabilities thereof fostered the emergence of cyberterrorism. Furthermore, the manner in which terrorist groups have evolved renders them especially suited to using the Internet to achieve their goals. Many terrorist groups have undergone a transformation from strictly hierarchical organizations with designated leaders to affiliations of loosely interconnected, semi-independent cells that have no single commanding hierarchy, like Hamas and the bin Laden organization. Through the use of the Internet, loosely interconnected groups without clearly designated leaders are able to maintain contact and communication.*
>
> *Many terrorist groups are just becoming aware of the advantages that IT can deliver. As individuals within these groups become better at employing IT, they may become more aware of the potential damage that can be caused using this technology. Additionally, publicity is one of the primary requirements for a successful terrorist attack. Extensive coverage has been given to the vulnerability of the U.S. information infrastructure and to the potential harm that could be caused by a cyberterrorist attack. This may lead terrorists to feel that a cyber attack directed at the U.S. may garner considerable publicity. Terrorist groups may also feel that even an unsuccessful attack against the U.S. information infrastructure could gain tremendous publicity. It is possible*

that the publicity given to the potential of cyberterrorism could become a self-fulfilling prophecy. This will require an unprecedented degree of collaboration and cooperation between industry and government.[5]

Despite years of foot-dragging by the Clinton administration to direct the intelligence community to develop a cybersecurity threat assessment, the composition of the NCS briefing audience was a testament to the commitment of career government employees to build and maintain that "unprecedented" partnership with the private sector. All of the representatives from the private sector were senior executives from their respective companies, and all had government security clearances that granted them access to the most sensitive intelligence data pertaining to threats to the infrastructures that formed not only the lifelines of their businesses but the lifelines of the nation as well.

At approximately 8:46 A.M., Navy Captain J. Katherine Burton quietly entered the briefing room and walked calmly to where Greene was sitting. She leaned over his shoulder and whispered in his ear that an airplane had just crashed into the north tower of the World Trade Center in New York.

"We weren't sure yet if it was a Piper Cub, a 737, or what," recalled Greene.[6] With no other information to go on and no indications that this was anything more than a horrible accident, Greene calmly informed the other briefing participants in the room of the news and ordered the briefing to continue. For now, September 11 was simply another day and the accident in New York simply that—an accident.

In Washington, however, where Richard Clarke, Former National Coordinator for Infrastructure Protection and Counterterrorism at the National Security Council, had been giving a speech on the importance of cybersecurity, the world had already changed. Unable to get through his speech due to the incessant signaling of his pager, Clarke cut his presentation short and called back to his staff at the Old Executive Office Building adjacent to the White House to see what the emergency was. It was then that he was told a plane had crashed into the World Trade Center in New York.

---

[5] "The Electronic Intrusion Threat to National Security and Emergency
    Preparedness (NS/EP) Internet Communications" (Office of the Manager,
    National Communications System, December 2000), pp. 28–31.
[6] Author interview.

Clarke rushed back to the White House. His first stop was to see Condoleezza Rice, the president's National Security Advisor, in her corner office of the West Wing. But Rice was already down the hall conferring with Vice President Dick Cheney. Clarke, knowing already that the plane crash was no accident, proceeded down the hall and interrupted the meeting between the vice president and Rice. "They asked me 'what do you think,' and I said immediately that it was a terrorist attack," recalled Clarke.[7] "Planes don't fly into the World Trade Center, I said."

There were few people in government at that time more qualified to make that call. A career government national security expert, Clarke had advised two former presidents on the threat of terrorism on U.S. soil. Educated at the Boston Latin School, the University of Pennsylvania, and the Massachusetts Institute of Technology, Clarke had spent his entire career focused on national security issues before becoming the nation's first counterterrorism chief under President Bill Clinton. He had even spent the better part of New Year's Eve 2000 locked away in a classified communications center watching for indications and warnings of pending terrorist attacks by Osama bin Laden's al-Qaeda terrorist organization. And while nothing happened that night to derail America's New Year celebration, Clarke had no doubt on the morning of September 11 who was behind the crashing of a jetliner into the World Trade Center.

Before a decision could be made on how to proceed, the Secret Service rushed in and told the vice president that he and Condoleezza Rice needed to be moved immediately to the East Wing bomb shelter, known as the Presidential Emergency Operations Center, or PEOC. Clarke then recommended that he remain behind in the West Wing and convene a secure video teleconference between all of the members of the president's cabinet and begin the process of coordinating the crisis response from the White House. He would maintain a direct secure telephone link with the vice president at all times.

Within minutes, the faces of the president's national security team, including Secretary of Defense Donald H. Rumsfeld, CIA director George J. Tenet, FBI director Robert Mueller, Attorney General John Ashcroft, and various

---

[7]   Author interview.

others, appeared on the video screens of the secure teleconferencing system. The FAA informed Clarke that they thought there were multiple hijackings taking place. When asked how many, the FAA representative said as many as 10 or 11. It was then that the White House ordered the FAA to get every plane they could on the ground as fast as possible.

At the NCS briefing, the CIA managed to get through 17 more minutes of material when word reached the briefing room that a second aircraft had sliced through the south tower of the World Trade Center. It was exactly 9:03 A.M. Officials turned to the televisions, where CNN was showing live footage of the unfolding horror.

"It was clear then that there was some threat," recalled Greene. "When the second plane hit, I said, 'I'm leaving. I need to go look at the implications of this.'"

-.-. -.-- -... . .-. - . .-. .-. --- .-.

One of the first things that all U.S. military officers are taught is to accept the inevitability of the "fog of war," a phrase that refers to the uncertainty and confusion that often arises in the heat of battle as a result of a commander lacking adequate information about the enemy and terrain, or receiving faulty intelligence. More importantly, however, is the emphasis that U.S. military officer training courses place on being able to operate effectively and decisively under such circumstances. And on September 11, 2001, that training would be put to the test in America's own backyard.

On the fifth floor Strategic Information and Operations Center at the FBI's headquarters facility in Washington, D.C., Ron Dick, former director of the FBI's National Infrastructure Protection Center and a 24-year veteran of the FBI, began the process of setting up a 24-hour Cyber-Crisis Action Team (C-CAT) that would be responsible for not only helping Brenton Greene's physical recovery effort in New York but also monitoring the Internet infrastructure for signs of a follow-on cyber-attack that might target additional sectors of the economy. "There were a lot of unknowns," recalled Dick.[8]

---

[8]   Author interview.

For the NIPC, September 11 and the days that followed would be a defining moment, more so than any other previous incident involving strictly Internet security. The NIPC had many enemies on Capitol Hill who believed that a law-enforcement agency such as the FBI was incapable of shifting its focus from prosecution to prevention. Prior to September 11, those critics had pointed repeatedly to studies by the General Accounting Office, the investigative arm of Congress, which routinely criticized the NIPC for failing to do its job—infrastructure threat detection, analysis, and warning—as if the NIPC were the only agency tasked to carry out such a mission.

The truth of the matter was that the NIPC was only one of many agencies and private-sector organizations that had a role to play in cybersecurity. And many of the shortcomings cited in the various GAO reports were shortcomings that could be fixed only by senior administration officials. Others were things the NIPC was never intended to do in the first place.

For example, a lack of timely warnings about viruses and other potentially dangerous security incidents was one of the main deficiencies routinely cited by the GAO. Some of the more than 80 warnings issued by the NIPC between 1998 and 2001 were issued in time to prevent widespread damage, but most, particularly those related to viruses, often came after the fact, said the GAO. In interviews, Dick often fought back in defense of his fledgling agency, stating vehemently, "You don't want the NIPC solely in the virus-warning business. There are plenty of other organizations that do that, including dozens of anti-virus companies."

The GAO also criticized the agency for its inability to conduct strategic analysis of threats to the critical infrastructure, a lack of staffing and expertise, and an inability to share information with the national security community that stemmed from its predisposition to treat everything as a law-enforcement investigation. But Dick would find an ally in Clarke, who repeatedly directed attention away from the NIPC's minor shortcomings and toward the true crux of the matter, which was the existence of multiple "stovepipes" in the federal government and the private sector. Although there is "a series of rich deposits" of data on vulnerabilities and threats, there is "very little capability to do data mining across the public/

private gap," Clarke had said publicly. "The expertise lies far more outside the government than in."

None of those issues, however, stopped the NIPC from responding to the catastrophic events of September 11 in a timely and aggressive manner. The NIPC's Cyber-Crisis Action Team began immediately to put together and activate contingency plans and information-sharing mechanisms with dozens of other federal, state, local, and private-sector organizations that could be put into action in the event of a major follow-on cyber-attack. And although that attack would not materialize during the immediate aftermath of the initial attacks in New York and at the Pentagon, the teams became a critical asset in the analytical effort to understand the infrastructure interdependencies and damages caused by the collapse of the World Trade Center towers. "We began to use the Cyber Crisis Action Team in coordination with the Special Technologies and Applications Unit to store and mine tremendous amounts of data to determine who may or may not have been in the buildings or on the flights that crashed, if there were other terrorists who were poised to strike, and a host of other normal investigative procedures," recalled Dick. Within two weeks of the attacks, the NIPC's C-CAT would be able to provide detailed briefings to the president and the vice president about how the terrorist cells used technology to carry out their murderous activities.

While Greene was rushing back to the NCS operations center to get a better understanding of what had happened in New York, civilian and military officials were boarding a militarized version of a Boeing 747, known as the E-4B National Airborne Operations Center (NAOC), at an airfield outside of the nation's capital. They were preparing to conduct a previously scheduled Defense Department exercise.

There are four E-4Bs, code-named "Night Watch," in the U.S. military arsenal. They exist to provide the president, vice president, and Joint Chiefs of Staff with an airborne command center that can be used to execute war plans and coordinate other emergency government operations in the event of a national emergency or destruction of ground command and control centers. As a result, they are often referred to unofficially as "the doomsday planes." One E-4B remains on alert at all times.

As the crew of the E-4B was preparing to begin the regularly scheduled training exercise, including the use and testing of the aircraft's various advanced technology and communications equipment, the Federal Aviation Administration was ordering all New York City area airports to cease flight operations. Minutes later, the Port Authority of New York and New Jersey ordered all bridges and tunnels in the New York area closed. The fog of war was thick and officials were left wondering if other airplanes were about to come careening out of the haze like jet-powered artillery shells.

President George W. Bush, who had been speaking to second graders at the Emma E. Booker Elementary School in Sarasota, Florida, was notified immediately of the unfolding crisis. At 9:30, Bush informed his audience and the nation that America had become a victim of "an apparent terrorist attack." Ten minutes later, the FAA ordered a historic nationwide grounding of all air traffic. It was clear to many officials, however, that the crisis was far from over. And that fact was driven home at 9:43, when American Airlines Flight 77 plowed through the thick concrete walls of the Pentagon.

There were thousands of airplanes still in the air and heading toward airports all over the country. And one of them, a 747 code-named "Night Watch," had only just taken off and was immediately ordered to cease the military exercise it was conducting and prepare to become the actual national airborne operations center. America was under attack.

-.-. -.-- -... . .-. - . .-. .-. --- .-.

As the president was being whisked off to a secure command and control facility at Offutt Air Force Base in Nebraska, the White House began an evacuation of all nonessential personnel. Specific concerns had been relayed by the intelligence community about the potential targeting of the White House and the Capitol building. It was an apparent effort to decapitate the government and sow mass confusion.

Clarke, acting on direct orders from the president and vice president, then initiated the emergency continuity of the government plan, which called for all federal departments to relocate to alternate sites and for the Speaker of the House of Representatives to be moved to a secure location outside of Washington. Although the secretary of defense remained at the

Pentagon, Paul Wolfowitz, the deputy secretary of defense, was moved to an alternate military command and control center. Shortly thereafter, all ports and border crossings were ordered closed, and all available military fighter aircraft were launched.

For Clarke, most of the morning was spent ensuring that all of the various orders relating to the emergency action plan were being carried out. Members of Clarke's staff would remain in close contact with the FBI's National Infrastructure Protection Center. Meanwhile, as the public watched the horrible human tragedy unfold live on television, Clarke, Dick, and their respective staffs were forced to deal with another possibility: that the morning's attacks could be one phase of a multipronged assault that could include attacks against the digital infrastructure of the U.S. economy. If that was the case, then they were staring at the one scenario that had often kept them awake at night.

Across town at the NIPC, Dick summoned his key advisors into an emergency meeting to analyze all available cyber-intelligence. Among those Dick relied on for expert advice were Bob Gerber, a career CIA officer who had been detailed to the NIPC to serve as the agency's chief of analysis and warning; Navy rear admiral James Plehal, who served as Dick's deputy and was a key link to the Defense Department establishment; and Les Wiser, the FBI agent responsible for tracking down CIA spy Aldrich Ames. A major cyber-attack now would prove absolutely devastating to the rescue and recovery effort and would almost certainly amplify the sense of fear and uncertainty far away from the epicenter of the main attack in New York. Such an assault had to be stopped at all costs.

But with the crash of hijacked American Airlines Flight 93 in Pennsylvania, the fog of war had settled firmly over official Washington. Despite the billions of dollars invested every year in advanced information technology designed to provide key government and military decision-makers with what is known in military parlance as "situation awareness," the fog of September 11 proved too thick to see through. America's national security community was thrown off-balance and had lost (in fact, may never have had) the initiative. What should have been an offensive war of maneuver had quickly turned into a reactive war fought from trenches and hardened bunkers.

-.-. -.-- -... . .-. - . .-. .-. --- .-.

September 11 was far from over when a small cadre of highly respected national security experts began warning of the potential for the physical attacks to be followed by cyber-attacks.

Marv Langston, the former deputy CIO at the Defense Department, characterized the events during an interview with *Computerworld* magazine as an act of war and said the country needed to be on alert for what he described as an "electronic Pearl Harbor."[9] Likewise, retired Air Force Lt. General Al Edmonds, who at one time headed the Defense Information Systems Agency, said he feared a cyber-attack could be next and added that such an event would be "absolutely paralyzing."[10]

Meanwhile, Atlanta-based Internet Security Systems, Inc. (ISS), which operates the IT industry's Information Sharing and Analysis Center (ISAC), placed its operations center on what it called AlertCon 3 (the highest is AlertCon 4), "in order to focus IT security efforts on the potential for (and defense against) an Internet component to these attacks." The IT-ISAC was one of several ISACs established in cooperation with the FBI and the NIPC to share information between the government and the private sector about cyber-threats.

In a threat assessment issued to the private sector members of the ISAC, ISS stated, "This is a time to partner all security assets on what is most important to your enterprise. While physical security concerns are paramount, it is essential to keep some eyes on the networks focused on malicious activity. We can expect a significant increase in disaster-recovery activity—plans being activated, dusted off, etc. No doubt the [disaster-recovery] industry will be sorely stressed at this point, and it would behoove staffs to consider security as a move to alternate sites is contemplated or enacted."[11]

At FBI headquarters, the NIPC began what Dick characterized as "harvesting" physical threat information pertaining to critical infrastructures

---

[9] See Dan Verton and Bob Brewin, "Companies Warned about Possible Cyberattacks," *Computerworld*, September 11, 2001.

[10] Ibid.

[11] Ibid.

and pushing that data out to thousands of private-sector companies that owned and operated those facilities, such as power plants, telecommunications facilities, water companies, and financial institutions. Dick relied on the FBI's InfraGard program and the various private-sector-run Information Sharing and Analysis Centers for much of that outreach effort. On September 11, ISACs had already been established in the Financial Services sector, the Electric Power sector, the Telecommunications sector, the Information Technology industry, and the computer software anti-virus industry. In addition, the NIPC would set in motion a daily threat briefing schedule for the Water sector, the Oil and Gas sector, and the Aviation and Railroad sectors.

Accurate and timely information was the only thing that could cut through the fog of war. And the government was doing everything it could to get that information flowing to the right people at the right time.

-.-. -.-- -... . .-. - . .-. .-. --- .-.

In the blink of an eye, the situation in New York went from horrible to unthinkable. Within 23 minutes of each other, the south and north towers of the World Trade Center collapsed, sending one million tons of concrete and steel crashing down on the city streets below, crushing the stuff of life into thin air. The scene was enough to take a person's breath away, like a punch to the stomach from a heavyweight boxer. But for Brenton Greene at the National Communications System operations center, it was immediately obvious that the series of murderous tragedies had now become a massive regional communications disaster extending from New York to the nation's capital.

When the last of the rubble fell to earth, the silence was deafening. Sound was muffled from the thick layer of dust and ash that blanketed the city like a snow. The face of lower Manhattan had changed. Through the grayness it appeared more like Stalingrad in 1943 or Berlin at the end of World War II. But the eerie silence, the gray of the fog of war, and the unnatural stillness of human life within the "red zone" concealed the massive digital disruption that had already begun to eat away at the nation's economic arteries and would only get worse as the day wore on. Lower Manhattan was not only the site of the worst terrorist attack in human history, it was also home to one of the most critical communications facilities in the nation. And that also made it the site of the worst cyber-terrorist attack in history.

The massive brick building located at 140 West Street, across the street from the World Trade Center and directly adjacent to #7 World Trade office complex, was built in the 1920s by the New York Telephone Company. It was known for its "exterior ornamental motifs, veined marble walls, travertine floors with bronze medallions, and a vaulted ceiling embellished with murals depicting the stages in the evolution of human communication."[12] On September 11, however, the building's more than 1,700 occupants knew it as the main regional switching station of Verizon Communications and the digital heartbeat of the nation's economy on Wall Street. The computers and switching equipment inside the facility were responsible for managing billions of bits of electronic data and tens of millions of telephone calls every day. And that was on a normal day.

With the disintegration of the two World Trade Center towers and the collapse of #7 World Trade later that afternoon, that digital heartbeat began to flat-line. Verizon's call volume reached twice the normal daily rate of 115 million calls in New York City and 35 million calls in the Washington, D.C., area. And although it remained operational, the wireless network experienced massive congestion that prevented most calls from getting through. During the peak of the chaos, Verizon experienced nearly 100 percent more traffic than normal on its nationwide wireless network. There were as many as ten wireless cell sites in New York City that were not operating, including those that were located at the top of the north tower of the World Trade Center. In addition, the infrastructure that connected the sites to the landline network went through the basement of the World Trade Center.

"We knew the damage was absolutely major," recalled Brenton Greene. "In the basement of No. 2 World Trade Center, there were two central office switches. You could characterize the World Trade Center buildings as being like two cities, and there was a major switch that controlled telecom-

---

[12] From New York City Landmarks Preservation Committee. Also known as the Barclay-Vessey Building, 140 West Street, it was designed by architect Ralph Walker and erected between 1923 and 1927.

munications for each of the buildings, and both of them were in the basement of No. 2 World Trade Center. And they just went away," he said. "We knew there would be a major impact, but the degree of the impact was not yet known."

In Washington, D.C., the impact was becoming clearer by the minute. Lack of interoperability between the communications equipment of the various agencies assisting in the search and rescue effort at the Pentagon forced officials to raid a local warehouse and commandeer radios for emergency workers. In addition, telephone and wireless cellular service in and around the nation's capitol remained unavailable to civilian users for most of the day. But there was one very important user who felt the impact of the massive communications loss several thousand miles away.

Secretary of State Colin Powell was in Lima, Peru, attending a meeting of the Organization of American States when he received word of the attacks. He immediately cut his trip short and boarded a government aircraft for the seven-hour flight back to Washington. The former chairman of the Joint Chiefs of Staff understood and appreciated the advantage the U.S. enjoyed over most nations when it came to the advanced electronics and communications capabilities. The former Army General had put his name on various Pentagon war-fighting manuals that outlined the Department's commitment to what the military called "network-centric warfare" and "information superiority." He had even written an article in *Byte Magazine* in 1992 titled "Personal Computer Technology May Determine the Outcome of Future Conflicts." But what really made Powell's experience on September 11 unique was his understanding and continued devotion to the military's decision cycle, known as the *OODA loop*. OODA is an acronym for the cycle of Observation, Orientation, Decision, and Action. For Powell, it was absolutely critical that he be inside of his counterpart's or enemy's loop. But on September 11, Powell got a taste of what communications must have been like for his early nineteenth-century counterparts.

"I never felt more useless in my life than on the morning of the 11th of September," Powell told members of the National Security Telecommunications Advisory Committee (NSTAC) during a meeting held at the State Department on March 13, 2002.[13] For most of the seven-hour return flight, Powell was unable to communicate with other senior government leaders in Washington. "Phones [were] gone because of what happened here and what happened to the [communications] system here in Washington," he said. "They couldn't get a phone line through. I was able to get some radio communications—two radio spots on the way back—but for most of that seven-hour period, I could not tell what was going on here in my capital, and I'm the Secretary of State."[14]

The implications of the communications failure on September 11 went beyond the seven-hour window during which Powell was unable to communicate with Washington. For Powell, this meant that there was the chance he and his Department could be severed from the world again in the future, removing the initiative from America's diplomatic and foreign policy efforts around the world. "Power to me now, as Secretary of State, is to be inside of everybody else's information loop or decision loop," he told the group of telecommunications experts. "I had called the President of Pakistan last Friday [March 8] to talk some business and just as I was concluding I said 'I'm sorry to hear about the deaths that occurred in Karachi today.' And he said, 'what deaths?' I'm inside his information loop."[15]

Powell was not alone in his distress. The National Airborne Operations Center that had converted literally on the fly from exercise status to real-world crisis management also had its share of trouble deciphering what was happening around the nation. Although the details are not known, a classified after-action report was produced that, according to one official who was on board the aircraft on September 11, does not paint a favorable picture of the government's overall crisis management capa-

---

[13] Steve Barrett, "Powell Asks NSTAC to Keep Nation Inside the Information Loop," *Telecom News,* Issue 1, 2002, p. 4.

[14] Ibid., p. 5.

[15] Ibid., p. 4.

bilities.[16] According to one government official, the nation was "deaf, dumb, and blind" for much of that horrible day in September.[17]

Back in Arlington, Virginia, Brenton Greene and the NCS staff began preparing for 24-hour operations—a state they remain in as of this writing. As afternoon turned to evening, officials began to piece together the true nature of the digital devastation in and around New York City and the Pentagon. In short, the destruction amounted to "the most significant challenge that the National Communications System had ever seen," recalled Greene.

In addition to the immediate wireless circuit overload, the collapse of the towers sent a massive steel beam slicing through a bundle of critical fiber-optic communications cables buried eight feet below the streets of Manhattan. The hulk of steel destroyed more than four million high-speed access lines and ruptured water lines that filled underground switching vaults with more than ten million gallons of water. As many as 300,000 voice telephone lines and 139 fiber rings in surrounding buildings and 26 building-specific fiber rings also failed as a result of the physical devastation. The damage also knocked out 1.5 million circuits that served the financial district, threatening the country's economic stability with each passing minute. The loss of connectivity to Wall Street was so severe that President Bush would soon establish three top priorities and communicate them personally to the NCS managers: rescue, recovery, and getting Wall Street back online.

The collapse of the towers had knocked out all primary power for much of lower Manhattan, and backup power, which was running on diesel fuel generators, began to fade quickly. Emergency responders and corporate disaster recovery specialists had failed to anticipate the physical impediments to getting fuel and spare parts onto Manhattan Island, which was now essentially surrounded by a blockade of bridge and tunnel police officers and military personnel at sea and in the air. Complicating matters was the fact that air transportation was no longer an option. Therefore, getting

---

[16] Author interview with sources either aboard the NAOC or familiar with the events of September 11.

[17] Ibid.

fuel delivered to keep the back-up power generators running was delayed due to the significant preplanning that was required to pass through security. In fact, security precautions and lack of planning denied Verizon officials timely access to their own facilities at the disaster site. Other telecommunications companies who had pledged support to the restoration effort had been completely denied entry into the disaster site and would only be able to get through using Verizon identification badges. Those delays had a direct impact on the time it took to restore services to the financial district.[18]

The electronic damage also extended to the transportation industry, cutting the electronic circuits that fed data to the tollbooths on the various bridges in the New York Area. When the first jetliner struck the north tower of the World Trade Center, it destroyed the Port Authority of New York and New Jersey headquarters facility, which housed 2,000 staffers and the central host servers for the E-ZPass electronic toll collection system. It would take a team of 15 engineers to recover the toll system, helping to ensure the flow of traffic, including emergency vehicles, into and out of Manhattan. When the towers collapsed, 75 Port Authority workers were among the more than 2,800 who perished.

Despite these difficulties, Greene was amazed at the sense of community and patriotism that had taken hold throughout the various private companies that only a day earlier considered each other ruthless competitors. Lucent Technologies, Inc., in Murray Hill, New Jersey, one of Verizon's main systems providers, rushed a 100,000-line switch to the scene to replace another massive switch that had been sent crashing through the window of the Verizon building at 140 West Street. The company also put all of its customer requirements on hold and made its entire inventory available to rescue services.

"Companies that were competitors with each other were all bending over backwards to help each other," recalled Greene. "There was a clear recognition of the urgent need to get our economic machine—Wall Street—back online."

---

[18] Steve Barrett, "NSTAC Chair Recaps Committee's Recent Accomplishments at March Meeting," *Telecom News*, Issue 1, 2002, p. 5.

Although the attacks had not caused any major disruptions in the military's command and control capabilities, the attack at the Pentagon also caused widespread damage to a host of highly sensitive computer networks and communications capabilities. Offices and facilities destroyed in the Pentagon attack included the U.S. Navy's Telecommunications Operations Center, sensitive chief of naval operations offices, and help desk operations within the U.S. Army's Information Management Support Center. Personnel, including telecommunications specialists and intelligence analysts assigned to those areas, were also among the casualties.

At the Pentagon, emergency orders were quickly put together for new secure communications equipment and computers. One such order involved more than 1,000 proprietary Secured Desktop Gateway communication enclosures to secure information stored on Pentagon workstations that had been set up temporarily in unclassified office locations away from the destruction. Pentagon officials were forced to establish a makeshift sensitive compartmented information facility (SCIF) to handle top-secret data securely. The delivery of the security equipment took two weeks to complete.

Although the Navy and the Defense Department refused to acknowledge any loss of communications capability as a result of the attack (it is traditional practice and prudent not to inform the enemy of your own losses or lack of capability), a former Navy intelligence officer who spoke on condition of anonymity said the location of the crash caused significant damage to many top-secret network operations within the Department of the Navy. The National Military Command Center was also filled with smoke. But the loss of the Navy offices and networks had little or no impact on the Navy's ability to communicate intelligence or orders to Navy warships at sea.

At the FAA and at airport control towers across the country, the situation was quite different. FAA officials around the country were reliant upon a basic voice teleconferencing link established on the morning of September 11 that the FAA called "an events network" to stay abreast of the situation. The teleconferencing line was and remains as of this writing nothing more than a 24-hour, always-open party line. It would be a year after the attacks before the FAA began providing the Pentagon's North American

Aerospace Defense Command (NORAD) with FAA control systems, specifically radar and voice, to improve military air defense operations in the event of another terrorist hijacking.

Despite the low-tech nature of the FAA's crisis coordination network on the morning of September 11, the agency managed in just three and a half hours to clear the skies over the entire U.S. of more than 4,500 commercial flights. During that time, there were at least 11 "suspect airplanes" that officials feared could have been hijacked; four of those aircraft did, in fact, take part in the attacks. Although the hijackings were not the classic hijackings FAA officials had been trained for and experienced over the years, "the calls to NORAD were timely," remarked an FAA official.[19] "We were all kind of coming to the same conclusion at the same time," the official said.

However, there were at least a few instances where critical information on flight restrictions did not reach its intended audience. While thousands of commercial jetliners were being ordered to land or diverted to airfields in Canada, several civilian general aviation flights took off from civilian airstrips. According to the FAA, either those pilots did not receive the order to cease flight operations or they ignored it.

-.-. -.-- -... . .-. - . .-. .-. --- .-.

As corporate requests for relocation and disaster recovery services began to climb, so did the death toll in the technology industry. The trauma caused by the unspeakable loss of life was compounded further during the restoration effort through the loss of critical expertise. Although no person is defined wholly by his or her profession, the economic attack perpetrated by al-Qaeda on that day extended beyond the digital arteries of corporate America and into the ranks of the personnel that watch over those arteries, which give life to the computers and databases that maintain client information to power the corporate decisions that determine a corporation's placement and direction in the

---

[19] See Dan Verton, "FAA Moving to Enhance Integration with NORAD," *Computerworld,* August 13, 2002.

market. For the first time, the saying "our people are our most important asset" was more than a slogan. Skilled people with corporate knowledge of systems and databases and business requirements were a critical infrastructure, too. And people had come under direct attack along with the structural symbols of America's economic and military strength.

Among those technology executives that lost their lives in the attacks were: a cofounder and chief technology officer of Akamai Technologies, Inc., in Cambridge, Massachusetts; the chief financial officer of Chatsworth, California-based optical networking company MRV Communications, Inc.; the vice president of market development and interim chief executive officer at ELogic Corporation; the director of business development at ELogic; the CFO of Netegrity, Inc., in Waltham, Massachusetts; the CEO and president as well as the director of development and the director of human resources of BCT Software AG, in Willstaat, Germany; the chief operating officer of Metrocall, Inc., in Alexandria, Virginia; an engineer with BEA Systems, Inc., in Liberty Corner, New Jersey; a director of horizontal scaling with Sun Microsystem's Software Systems Group; a senior mechanical engineer with Raytheon's Electronic Systems division; a senior quality control engineer at Raytheon; a vice president of operations for Raytheon's Electronic Systems; and hundreds from Cantor Fitzgerald financial services. There were many, many others.

By late afternoon on September 11, disaster declarations began pouring in to companies that specialize in helping other firms recover from major catastrophes. One of the largest such firms recorded 62 disaster declarations from 31 companies in the financial service industry. However, the panic and fear had quickly spread to other major cities around the country, such as Boston and Chicago, which have high concentrations of large office buildings. As a result, disaster recovery firms were forced to field multiple requests from companies that were dealing with voluntary building evacuations. Likewise, companies all over the country lost productivity as a result of the psychological impact that the human tragedy had on their workers, many of whom were too upset and distracted to continue working. In other cases, people who normally conducted business downtown in Manhattan's financial district were too afraid to venture into that part of the city for months.[20] It is nearly impossible to quantify the financial impact of such productivity losses. In the end, however, the first few hours after the initial attacks on September 11 surpassed all previous disasters that the business continuity industry had ever dealt with. Hurricane Floyd, for example, in 1999, produced 32 disaster declarations, and the World Trade Center bombing in 1993 led to only 8 disaster declarations.[21]

-.-. -.-- -... . .-. - . .-. .-. --- .-.

On September 12, the fog of war began to lift slowly and then the sun shined. That was also the first full day governed by an advisory issued by the FBI's National Infrastructure Protection Center. According to the advisory, all public- and private-sector members of the FBI's InfraGard program were to beef up physical and cybersecurity to protect against the potential for follow-on attacks, especially cyber-attacks. If a computer system was not absolutely mission-critical to the operation of the business, it should be shut down for the time being, advised the FBI.

"The FBI has no information of any additional specific threats directed against additional targets or critical infrastructures in the United States; however, infrastructure owners and operators should be at a heightened state of alert and should implement appropriate security measures—both physical and cyber," the advisory stated. An advisory is the second-highest alert condition that can be issued by the FBI to members of InfraGard, a joint program between the government and industry designed to share threat information about possible cyber-attacks and cyber-crime.

Lawmakers on Capitol Hill also wasted no time in focusing on the obvious vulnerability of the nation's critical cyber-infrastructure to terrorist attack. At a September 12 hearing of the Senate Governmental Affairs

---

[20]   Several months after the attacks, I gave a speech at a technology user group association in upper Manhattan. The meeting organizer asked for a show of hands of how many people were still too afraid to hold their monthly meetings in their usual location downtown in the financial district. Standing in the front of the room, I looked out at the audience and watched dozens of hands being lifted into the air.

[21]   See Carol Sliwa, "IT Disaster Declarations Flooding into Comdisco," *Computerworld*, September 11, 2001.

Committee, Senator Joseph Lieberman (D-Conn.) said, "Our enemies will increasingly strike this mighty nation at places where they believe we are not only dependent but unguarded. That is surely true of cyberspace infrastructure today."[22]

By September 14, officials began to get a glimpse of the financial toll on Wall Street stemming from the digital destruction. Preliminary estimates put the cost of rebuilding or replacing the information technology infrastructure for financial services companies whose offices were destroyed by the attack at anywhere from $3 billion to $5 billion.

The Bank of New York and Cantor Fitzgerald financial services were the stock brokerage companies that suffered the most damage on September 11. Cantor Fitzgerald lost nearly 700 people in the World Trade Center—a catastrophic loss by any estimation. The Bank of New York lost telecommunications connectivity to one of its primary data centers and several other facilities. The Bank of New York's communications failure, however, resulted in a cascading failure effect because that bank not only was responsible for clearing security transactions on behalf of its customers but also facilitated the flow of funds between the Federal Reserve and its member banks. "This telecommunications failure on the part of a single institution was large enough to damage critical components of our marketplace pending recovery," according to analysis by a senior member of NYFIX, Inc.[23]

For Richard Clarke, the digital destruction that severed Wall Street from the world was a nightmare come true. It had been only a month since he had toured the Verizon and stock market facilities and asked questions about the security precautions that were in place to protect such a large concentration of critical communications equipment. "What they told us was that after the 1993 attack against the World Trade Center they had diversified some of their routing capability," recalled Clarke. "We also talked to the stock market [officials] about the need for alternative sites and backup facilities." And while some of the work that was required to protect the heart of the nation's economy from life-threatening palpitations

---

[22] See Patrick Thibodeau, "Senate Committee Looks into IT Vulnerabilities," *Computerworld*, September 12, 2001.

[23] See Warren Pollock, "The Nation's Stock Brokerage System Must Fortify Itself Against Future Attacks," *The Journal of Homeland Security*, February 2002.

had been completed, it wasn't enough to withstand the devastation of September 11.

Within 18 hours of the attacks, however, Verizon had rerouted more than two million of the four million data lines that had been destroyed. Within two days, the wireless telecommunications industry deployed mobile "cellular on wheels" units that were capable of providing 125 percent of the wireless capacity that had been in the New York metropolitan area before the attacks.

Fortunately for the NCS, the Government Emergency Telecommunications Service, known as GETS, had reached full operational capability one week prior to the attacks. By September 11, 45,000 government officials and emergency workers had received GETS calling cards, granting them priority access to the nation's telecommunications networks. At the height of the chaos, more than 10,000 GETS calls were processed with a success rate greater than 95 percent, allowing key decision makers to communicate. As of this writing, the number of GETS cardholders has increased to more than 65,000. And in addition to government and emergency service personnel, senior officials from private-sector companies that own and operate various critical infrastructures are now among those carrying the cards.

However, the lack of wireless priority access was one of the most glaring shortfalls of the recovery and restoration effort. Although the GETS program had assisted officials who were trying to make emergency calls on the wired telecommunications network, those who were in remote locations and were trying to coordinate emergency and government response efforts using a cell phone were greeted with a busy signal. For Brenton Greene, it was a thorn in his side. Since arriving at the NCS in April 2001, he had been espousing the need for priority wireless services to anybody who would listen. Career NCS staffers had developed the idea for the program years earlier. "It was absolutely vital, but it wasn't funded," recalls Greene. "And it became crystal clear within minutes on 9/11 that we needed wireless priority capability for key decision makers and key first responders."

As of this writing, the NCS now has an initial operating capability for priority wireless access. The agency signed a contract in April 2002 with

VoiceStream Wireless Corporation to provide priority wireless access to the cellular telephone system serving the New York and Washington metropolitan areas. The goal, according to Greene, is to have a full, nationwide priority wireless capability in place by the end of 2003.

One of the most important factors in the recovery effort may have been a program formed by the Federal Communications Commission in 1998 known as the Telecommunications Service Priority Program, or TSP. The TSP program serves as a central database of the nation's most critical telecommunications circuits and infrastructure equipment, such as switches. Prior to the attacks of September 11, more than 40,000 switches were registered in the TSP database. And as it turned out, hundreds of those switches were key telecommunications circuits that supported Wall Street. In the days following the attacks, more than 598 TSP provisioning requests poured into the NCS from 46 different organizations. The ready availability of data on the switches and circuits that had been destroyed, coupled with the superhuman efforts of employees from the telecommunications industry and the government, was a critical factor in the reopening of the financial markets on September 17.

-.-. -.-- -... . .-. - . .-. .-. --- .-.

By September 18, the fog of war had thinned into a thin layer of silver haze that hovered above lower Manhattan. If there was a sense of clarity, however, it was in the extent of the devastation and the human loss, not in the predictions of what might happen next. The fear of the unknown took the form of crop dusters spraying deadly chemicals, biological agents being spread through the mail or through the ventilation system of a large building, or a crude nuclear weapon, known as a dirty bomb, making its way to the shores of the U.S. stowed away inside one of the six million cargo containers that arrive aboard foreign ships from faraway ports every year. Nobody thought that the next major crisis would occur on the Internet and come in the form of a devastating worm.

On the morning of September 18, the world woke up to the Nimda Internet worm, malicious code that can destroy data and has the ability to self-replicate and find its way through the Internet to other vulnerable computers. Nimda, which contained five different malicious payloads, infected all 32-bit Windows systems it encountered, including Windows 98, 2000, Millennium Edition, XP, and NT. It scanned systems for as many as 100 different vulnerabilities and automatically exploited them when found. Within 30 minutes of being discovered, Nimda had become a global problem.

At the White House, Clarke was immediately alarmed. Nobody could tell him who was responsible for the worm, which meant anybody could be responsible, including a nation-state sponsor of terrorism or some other surrogate of Osama bin Laden. Almost immediately, experts were warning that Nimda was spreading faster and more aggressively than any other worm they had ever seen and could easily begin to have an impact on overall Internet performance. Although there was no way to know for sure, this could have been part of the series of follow-up attacks that the national security community had been expecting.

"Nimda was a devastating attack," recalled Clarke, who remained on a 24-hour rotation in the White House Situation Room. "We had been expecting another wave of attacks. We were all still worrying about conventional terrorism. We didn't know if it would be more airplane attacks, truck bombs, chemical or biological or cyber attacks. And suddenly the cybersecurity team came to me and said there was a major worm going through the Internet and it was knocking off major companies."

Initially, the consensus among Clarke's staff of experts was that Nimda could have been related in some way to the September 11 attacks. "We still don't know for sure," he recalled during an interview in his office in December 2002. "But had Nimda happened on September 5, it would have been a big news story. A lot of companies, particularly in the financial world, shut down major pieces of their operations. It destroyed and corrupted databases. It was quite devastating, causing several billion dollars in damage."

It took some companies weeks to completely scrub their systems and networks of Nimda. One frustrated administrator told *Computerworld* that the worm infected "50,000 to 100,000" files in his company's data center. "We are smart people," he said. "This one just won't be stopped."[24]

Whether the Nimda worm was part of the September 11 effort to inflict even greater financial damage to the U.S. economy or simply the work of a crackpot, nuisance virus writer is a question that has yet to be answered as of this writing. Although Richard Clarke has his gut feelings about the worm, he acknowledges that it could have come from anywhere. "There are a lot of different people who can conduct cyber-warfare," he said. "There are countries that are creating cyber-warfare units. There are criminal groups engaging in cyber-crime. There are also some terrorist groups that we know are looking at using cyber-attack tools. But I don't spend a lot of time trying to figure out who's going to be the next attacker," said Clarke.[25]

"Let's assume for the sake of argument that the next cyber-attack is being planned by al-Qaeda. Well, we're trying to get al-Qaeda and we'll probably eventually either eliminate the group or reduce it to a small group that we don't have to worry about," he said. "But that won't end the threat to us from cyberspace. Someone else will come along who can use the vulnerabilities in our infrastructure to attack us. Don't worry about who is going to be the next attacker. You'll find out eventually, and you'll do what you can about them. Instead, worry about the vulnerabilities that are out there. Until we fix the vulnerabilities, we are at risk."[26]

-.-. -.-- -... . .-. - . .-. .-. --- .-.

Regardless of the mode of attack employed by terrorists in the future, September 11 showed how people, infrastructure, and technology are the three primary ingredients of a functioning U.S. economy in the twenty-first century. Remove any one ingredient from the equation, and you cause disruptions that have the ability to ripple across many sectors of the

---

[24] See Jaikumar Vijayan, "Nimda Needs Harsh Disinfectant," *Computerworld*, September 24, 2001.

[25] Author interview.

[26] Ibid.

economy, eventually having the potential to impact national security or public safety.

Despite these lessons, revealed as they were through the crucible of war on September 11, many in corporate America remain unconvinced. Two months after the attacks, the wounds still wet and raw, a survey of 459 chief information officers at major private companies found that just 53 percent of firms had business continuity plans, and less than half had information technology security awareness and training programs for employees.[27] The private sector remains drunk with denial.

But if the private sector has been operating under the influence, its bartender has been the federal government and its policy of allowing market forces to determine the level of investment in security. In an interview with former Virginia Governor James S. Gilmore III more than a year after the attacks, the former Republican Party chairman said the Bush policy of relying "on private sector willingness to take certain security measures and bear their costs" has had little impact to date on the state of security readiness in the private sector.

"Cyberterrorism is a threat to critical infrastructure," said Gilmore, who is the chairman of the congressionally appointed Advisory Panel to Assess Domestic Response Capabilities for Terrorism Involving Weapons of Mass Destruction.[28] "So far, pure public-private partnerships and market forces are not acting to protect the cyber-community," he said. "Our major concern is that there will be a major conventional attack and then they could launch simultaneously a cyber-attack in order to sow panic," said Gilmore. "The essence of guerilla warfare is that they choose the time, place, and method of attack. Cyberterrorism is a clear and present danger."

The terrorist attacks of September 11 clearly demonstrated the interdependencies that exist between physical and cyber-infrastructures and how the destruction or degradation of one can have catastrophic consequences for the other. And in the days and weeks that followed, Osama bin Laden praised the attacks not only for the human losses they inflicted, but also for

---

[27] See Dan Verton, "Disaster Recovery Planning Still Lags," *Computerworld*, April 1, 2002.

[28] Author interview.

the economic impact that the destruction had on American companies and the financial markets.

"They used to be interested in killing as many people as possible," said Clarke, referring to the changes taking place in the strategic focus of international terrorism. "They talked about creating a Hiroshima-like event. I think that was September 11," he said. "But then if you look at the messages from bin Laden after September 11, he starts talking about destroying the American economy. He refers to the glorious events of September 11 costing the Americans a trillion dollars. You could employ a lot of truck bombs and not really do much damage to the economic infrastructure of the U.S., because it is so diverse. But if you attack in cyberspace, you have a chance to hit the entire network, the entire financial services network, for example. Through physical attacks, that takes a lot of people and a major support network. And we would stand a pretty good chance of noticing. But with cyber-attacks you never even have to enter the United States."

Howard Schmidt, Clarke's deputy in the White House and the former chief security officer at Microsoft Corporation, agreed but added that in his mind the days are gone when cybersecurity and physical security could be approached separately. "There's a cyber-dimension to the physical, and there's a physical dimension to the cyber," said Schmidt.[29] "I don't think we can function in isolation in either one of these areas. At the same time a physical event occurs, if there's some disruption in the cyber-world, it could be a lot more problematic than just one or the other."

---

[29]   Author interview.

8

Intelligence: Stopping the Next Attack

People should understand that "we don't have some magical box out there that we're not telling them about."[1]

—William F. Dawson
Deputy chief information officer, U.S.
Intelligence Community

UBL [Usama bin Laden] took technology and used it to his advantage faster than we [did].[2]

—Larry Castro
Director of homeland security
National Security Agency

At noon on September 11, CNN went live atop the roof of a church located across the street from the U.S. Capitol. One of the many guests that

---

[1] Author interview conducted at the Information Sharing and Homeland Security conference in Philadelphia, Pennsylvania, sponsored by the Defense Department and Intelligence Community in August 2002.

[2] Remarks made at the Information Sharing and Homeland Security conference in Philadelphia, Pennsylvania, sponsored by the Defense Department and Intelligence Community in August 2002.

day was Congressman Curt Weldon (R-Pa), a senior member of the House Armed Services Committee who oversaw the military's $38 billion annual budget for research and development in cutting-edge warfighting technologies. When asked for his thoughts about how such horrible, murderous attacks could have taken place, Weldon said it was the result of "a failure of our intelligence system. It's a failure that was caused by a lack of resources and by a complacency that set in over the last 10 years, a complacency that convinced all of us that with the demise of the Soviet Union, there were no more threats."

What Weldon was really saying was that the blame for September 11, particularly the inability of the intelligence and national security community to alert the nation that an attack was being planned against the continental United States, fell squarely on the shoulders of the Clinton administration. Throughout his presidency, Bill Clinton had given the CIA the signal that he appreciated the gritty work of intelligence about as much as he appreciated having pins stuck in his eyes. In fact, career intelligence professionals had often complained about the administration's apparent lack of interest in what the CIA had to say as well as Clinton's predilection to handle every national security crisis with a cruise missile. Guerilla warfare, on the other hand, is an up-close and personal business, they argued.

But Weldon truly believed that America had the technology that could have enabled intelligence analysts to detect the September 11 planning and maybe even have prevented the attacks altogether. The problem was that of the 32 federal agencies that operated some sort of classified intelligence or national security computer system, few if any actually shared information with each other. And Weldon had the perfect example that would not only prove to be an embarrassment for the CIA, but also an indictment of the stovepipe cultures that had been allowed to form within America's national security community.

-.-. -.-- -... . .-. - . .-. .-. --- .-.

The bombing started on March 23, 1999. The Clinton administration was confident that it would end relatively quickly and that the Yugoslav-backed Serbs, who had been carrying out a genocidal war against Muslims in Kosovo, would crumble under the weight of U.S. and NATO air power. In the end, the bombing campaign would last for 78 days. But within two weeks of its beginning, Weldon began receiving e-mail messages and telephone calls from his counterparts in the Russian parliament, the Duma.

"You have a real problem," one of the e-mails read.[3] "Your policy of bombing [Yugoslav President Slobodan] Milosevic and innocent Serbs is causing the Russian people to lose confidence in what America's real intent is, and you are driving Russia further away from [the U.S.]," the note said. The true message of the e-mail was that the Balkan Peninsula was dangerously close to what could be considered Russia's traditional sphere of influence and the U.S. would be wise to include Russia as a full partner in helping to bring peace to the war-torn region.

"What do you want me to do," Weldon responded.

"We need you to convince your president that Russia can help play a role in ending the war and getting Milosevic out of office," said Weldon's Russian contact. The e-mail also outlined Russia's desire for Weldon to lead a congressional delegation to Belgrade, where the Russians would arrange a personal meeting with Milosevic.

Weldon's initial reaction was that such a trip was impossible given the fact that the U.S. was in the middle of a war. In addition, Deputy Secretary of State Strobe Talbot recommended against the trip, stating that the U.S. could not guarantee the safety of the delegation and that there was no guarantee that Milosevic would follow Russia's lead.

In addition, the situation had been further complicated by the fact that Milosevic had taken hostage three U.S. Army soldiers who had blindly wandered across the border between Macedonia and Yugoslavia during a routine patrol. The soldiers had been stationed in Macedonia to help prevent the war from spreading. However, the Army had failed to issue the soldiers a special global positioning system–equipped radio called the Soldier 911. The radio had been rushed into production four years earlier not only to prevent soldiers from wandering into places they should not be but

---

[3]   As described by Weldon in an interview with the author in 1999 and in the Congressional Record, May 21, 2002 (House), pp. H2820-H2834.

also to enable them to alert other Army units of their situation and precise location. The radio included a commercial GPS receiver chip that provided an exact geographic location on the ground, an embedded computer, a modem, and a small display screen. Thousands had been rushed into production. But when asked if the soldiers had been issued the radios, the Army was unable to determine if the radios had been deployed in Macedonia at all.[4]

Russia soon followed up with an official request printed on Russian Duma stationery to meet with Weldon and a delegation of U.S. congressmen with the lofty goal of negotiating an end to the war in Kosovo and forcing Milosevic to step down from power. However, given the uncertain security situation in Belgrade, Weldon and his colleagues (five Democrats and five Republicans) settled on a meeting in a neutral location—Vienna, Austria—with the Russians and a representative of Milosevic. Weldon was told that he would be negotiating directly with Milosevic through one of the Yugoslav President's most trusted associates, Dragomir Karic. Weldon and the other members of the delegation had never heard of Karic.

To prepare for the negotiations, Weldon called CIA director George Tenet and asked for a profile of Karic. "I do not know who this guy is. But the Russians are convinced that he can give us information that will allow us to get Milosevic to agree to our terms," said Weldon. "Can you tell me something about him?"

Tenet returned Weldon's call the next day and provided him with a three-sentence profile. Tenet added that the CIA "thought he was tied in with corruption in Russia but did not know much else about him," Weldon recalled later.

Weldon then remembered a trip he had taken in 1997 to a relatively obscure Army unit operating out of Fort Belvoir in the Northern Virginia suburbs. It was then that the Army had demonstrated for Weldon the capabilities of what it called its Information Dominance Center, otherwise known as the Land Information Warfare Activity (LIWA). Relying on

---

4   See Dan Verton and Bob Brewin, "Captive Soldiers Lacked Critical GPS Radios," *Federal Computer Week*, April 5, 1999.

the expertise of a former CIA profiler, the Army had managed to harness the power of commercial data mining technologies to tap into the mountains of open-source (public) information on the Internet, such as foreign newspapers and academic studies, and synthesize that data with classified intelligence reporting from around the world. Weldon decided he had nothing to lose by repeating his request for a profile of Karic. Only this time he asked the Army's LIWA analysts to produce it.

Using commercial data mining software, the Army's LIWA unit delivered to Weldon an eight-page profile of Karic. According to the profile developed by the Army, there were four Karic brothers and they were the owners of the largest banking system in the Former Yugoslavia. They employed more than 60,000 people, and their bank had been tied directly to an attempt to finance the sale of an SA-10 missile from Russia to Milosevic. The Karic bank had also been involved in a $4 billion German bond scam. But the Karic brothers' ties to Milosevic went far beyond business, according to the profile. One of the Karic brothers had also personally financed Milosevic's election campaign. The house that Milosevic and his wife lived in was actually owned by the Karic family. And Karic's and Milosevic's wives were best of friends. It was the profile of a close confidant who clearly brought true negotiating power to the table.

The Weldon delegation's trip to Vienna would meet with mixed results. Although the negotiations did not result in an immediate end to hostilities, the agreements reached between Weldon, the Russians, and Karic would eventually become the foundation for the G-8 agreement to end the war.

Upon Weldon's return to the U.S., the CIA and FBI rushed agents to interview the Congressman for any information he had about Karic. The agencies had been tasked by the State Department to provide a profile of this relatively new player in the negotiations who apparently was able to speak for Milosevic. Weldon told the agents everything he knew about Karic. When the CIA and FBI agents asked him how he knew so much about Karic, Weldon informed them that the Army's Information Dominance Center had produced a profile of Karic at his request. The response, according to Weldon, was a look of confusion on the faces of the agents, followed by a chorus of "what's the Army Information Dominance Center?"

-.-. -.-- -... . .-. - . .-. .-. --- .-.

Although the CIA and the FBI had not heard of the Army's Information Dominance Center or its massive data mining capabilities, the U.S. Special Operations Command (USSOCOM) had, and they were interested in harnessing the capability for their own intelligence operations.

By fall 2000, USSOCOM had developed a mini-version of the LIWA data mining and profiling system to support their operations planning, which often focused on guerilla warfare, antiterrorist operations, and the like. However, the more important development to come out of USSOCOM's scaled-down data mining system was a profile of the entire al-Qaeda global terrorist network, including clearly defined links to other terrorist organizations around the world. The unclassified version of the profile included a chart that offered a visual depiction of the network and its linkages.

USSOCOM took this information and produced a briefing for then Joint Chiefs chairman General Hugh Shelton. Included in the briefing was a recommendation to "take out" five specific al-Qaeda cells, which would in USSOCOM's estimation significantly reduce, if not eliminate, the terrorist organization's ability to carry out operations. But when that briefing was finally given to Shelton in January 2001, it was condensed down from three hours to one hour. More importantly, the recommendation to move against the five cells in order to cripple al-Qaeda's ability to conduct attacks was never acted upon.

"One year before 9/11, the capability that Special Forces built actually identified to us the network of al-Qaeda," said Weldon, speaking on the floor of the House of Representatives eight months after the attacks of September 11. "And they went beyond that and gave us recommendations where we could take out cells to eliminate their capability. All of that activity could have prevented or helped to prevent 9/11 from ever occurring.

"I briefed our Homeland Security Director Tom Ridge. He agreed with us, but he has not yet been able to achieve this new interagency collaborative center, and that is an indictment of our government that the American people deserve to be outraged over."

Americans were certainly outraged by the terrorist attacks of September 11. They were even more infuriated, however, when they learned the true depth of the intelligence and information-sharing failures that may have enabled the attacks to succeed. But Americans know only part of the story behind America's high-tech intelligence failures.

-.-. -.-- -... . .-. - . .-. .-. --- .-.

On October 1, 1999, a group of 19 mid-level managers at the National Security Agency (NSA), the signals intelligence and eavesdropping arm of the national intelligence community, delivered to NSA director Air Force Lt. Gen. Michael Hayden a stinging indictment of what they described as the agency's leadership crisis and inability to keep up with the breakneck pace of commercial technology development.

The group of managers (11 men and 8 women), who called themselves the New Enterprise Team, or NETeam, argued that the NSA was "an organization ripe for divestiture."[5] The various individual capabilities and organizations within the agency were of greater value than the organization as a whole, they argued. "NSA has lost credibility with its stakeholders and customers and has failed to begin the organizational transformation necessary for success in the information age," the report continued. As a result, the NSA's "legacy of exceptional service to the nation is in great peril."

What they were really saying was that the NSA was an agency that had lost touch not only with its customers—government leaders and various elements of the military and intelligence communities—but also with the new realities of the Internet age. America's terrorist enemies had learned to "operate and thrive in the net." But the nation's premier signals intelligence collector had become buried beneath the unprecedented volume of communications that now needed to be intercepted and analyzed. Although NSA operates the world's largest collection of supercomputers, the New Enterprise Team warned Hayden, the agency's leadership crisis had caused it to lose pace with the deployment of advanced encryption technologies and millions of miles of new fiber-optic cables that carried the communications of

---

[5] New Enterprise Team (NETeam) Recommendations: *The Director's Work Plan for Change, FOR OFFICIAL USE ONLY* (National Security Agency, October 1, 1999), p. i.

America's terrorist enemies. The NSA, they said, was mired in a Cold War footing. As a result, "critical data required by decision-makers. . .are often unavailable or difficult to retrieve, [and] decisions on financial resources, human resources and customer engagement are often late or fatally flawed." Nothing short of reinventing the agency could reverse these trends, the report argued.

"The magnitude of the change we are proposing is tantamount to re-building an aircraft while it is in flight and loaded with passengers," the group of 19 managers wrote.

The NETeam report kick-started Hayden's so-called "100 Days of Change," during which he pledged to overhaul the NSA's outdated and inflexible management style, and its overly secretive, insular culture. In addition to taking immediate steps to develop a strategic business plan to guide the NSA's technology investments and changes in management structure, the agency undertook a massive renovation project focusing on its 129,000-square-foot Operations 1 Building at its Fort Meade, Maryland, headquarters. The project included communications upgrades for more than 1,000 NSA personnel, as well as the addition of Internet access for at least 10 percent of the workstations. It also included construction of an Operations Watch Center, which serves as a 24-hour intelligence collection and analysis center.

The NSA also began to ratchet up work on a massive ten-year, $5 billion contract proposal to outsource the bulk of its unclassified information technology management to a private sector company. "We must immedi-ately begin to invest in our IT infrastructure to secure NSA's agility and adaptability in the Information Age," said Hayden in a written public statement announcing plans to move forward on the contract proposal, known as "Project Groundbreaker." It was Hayden's belief that the best way for the agency to regain the operational flexibility it had lost was to turn over a large portion of its day-to-day technology management to a private company. That was also a major conclusion of the NETeam report.

Hayden's focus on reform and his willingness to accept and act upon the recommendations of the 19 members of the NETeam, who he liked to call "loyal anarchists," did not go unnoticed on Capitol Hill. Shortly after Hayden's 100 Days of Change came to a close, the Senate Select Committee on Intelligence listed rebuilding NSA as the committee's top, near-term priority in the fiscal 2001 Intelligence Authorization Bill. "The NSA systematically has sacrificed infrastructure modernization in order to meet day-to-day intelligence requirements," the committee stated in a report on the bill. "Consequently, the organization begins the 21st century lacking the technological infrastructure and human resources needed even to maintain the status quo, much less meet emerging challenges."

But if Hayden was a reformer who understood the NSA's desperate need for new blood, his choice of deputy director was not proof of that. Shortly after tapping an investment banker to serve as the agency's first chief financial officer, Hayden turned to the Dulles, Virginia, technology corridor outside of Washington, D.C., to find his primary aide and the tactical leader of the internal revolution at NSA. The only problem, however, was that William Black Jr., Hayden's choice for the number two position, was in fact a 38-year NSA veteran who had retired from the agency in 1997. Since that time, Black had spent the sum total of three years in the private sector. The selection of Black, therefore, was not the break with the past that many had thought it was. The rehiring of retirees was viewed by some as evidence of a continuing inability to groom new generations of leaders from within the ranks of the agency and the intelligence community at large.

To be fair, Black understood many of the NSA's main challenges even if he wasn't the protégé of private industry that some tried to make him out to be. And one of those challenges was and continues to be the export and widespread availability of sophisticated encryption technologies. The same technologies that had enabled the U.S. military and intelligence community to scramble sensitive communications and make them invisible to enemies was now increasingly being made available to terrorists. In fact, encrypted files discovered on the laptop computers of some of the al-Qaeda conspirators in the first bombing of the World Trade Center in 1993 are believed to have taken the NSA several months to finally unravel.

Career national security experts, including Black's predecessor at the NSA, had argued for years against allowing the software industry in the U.S. to export encryption tools abroad without a key escrow provision to provide law enforcement with the ability to recover and open encrypted messages in cases involving criminal proceedings or national security. However, it soon became apparent that the genie was already out of the bottle. Software encryption tools focusing on communications were already widely available around the world, and they were being produced increasingly by foreign companies or foreign companies that had been purchased and funded by U.S. enterprises for the sole purpose of being able to develop and sell indigenous technologies abroad.

In the end, the national security community lost the encryption battle to the force of the marketplace. The global push to extend e-commerce was too strong for any one government to overcome. As a result, strong encryption technologies flourished around the globe and are now used by law-abiding citizens and terrorists alike. NSA was on its own to figure out a way to tap back into the communications streams of America's enemies. And for the time being, its hearing was impaired.

Seven months prior to the September 11 terrorist attacks, Hayden did something highly unusual for a director of the world's most secretive intelligence agency—an agency that once half-jokingly referred to the acronym NSA as standing for No Such Agency. He appeared on national television and talked about the NSA's inability to operate effectively in the Internet age.

On February 13, 2001, Hayden told a national television audience on CBS's *60 Minutes* that the NSA remained behind the rest of the world in keeping up with the pace of technology development.[6] "We're behind the curve in keeping up with the global telecommunications revolution," said Hayden. "Our adversary communications are now based upon the developmental cycle of a global industry that is literally moving at the speed of light, . . .cell phones, encryption, fiber-optic communications, digital communications," he said. With every advance and new development in the world of commercial communications, the NSA had to find a way to tap into it. More importantly, it had to find a way to quickly isolate the communications of international terrorist organizations and foreign intelligence

---

6   See Dan Verton, "NSA Struggles to Keep Up with Pace of Technology," *Computerworld*, March 5, 2001.

services from an unprecedented volume of traffic that had been fueled by cell phones and mobile Internet devices.

Hayden's admission that the NSA remained behind the technology power curve more than a year after the NETeam report and his 100 Days of Change led some security exerts to suggest it might be time for the agency to do what the CIA had already done: fund a private venture capital research and development firm to help it regain its technological edge. The CIA had done more than embrace the private sector technology industry; it jumped into the market.

-.-. -.-- -... . .-. - . .-. .-. --- .-.

At CIA headquarters in Langley, Virginia, George Tenet spent much of 1999 "preparing for the future." And much of that work involved researching new and innovative ways to share information throughout the broader intelligence community, which consists of 14 different agencies, the bulk of which are in the Defense Department.

One of the first projects that the CIA worked on that year was the Intelligence Community Metropolitan Area Communications system. The IC MAC system was designed to enhance connectivity between national intelligence agencies and the U.S. Defense Department. Intelligence agencies also teamed up to develop Web-based tools that take advantage of the connectivity offered by the Internet. A secure Web-based application called XLINK, for example, was developed to enhance collaboration between analysts and information collectors. In addition, the CIA established a secret technology laboratory code-named Platinum Rail to better understand how commercial collaboration software can support intelligence work.

Tenet also saw to it that a PolicyNet Program Office was established to oversee a network that links the U.S. Senate Appropriations Committee and other lawmakers to CIA data via a secure Internet connection. The agency also began to research ways to exploit the World Wide Web through language-translation and data-visualization software. For example, the agency integrated two systems to enable analysts to use English to search documents written in Korean or Japanese and to receive summaries of the results in English through any standard Web browser. The agency also completed a proof-of-concept demonstration on a Farsi-to-English tool. That was 1999 inside the agency.

Outside the agency, however, 1999 was the year of tapping into the wave of dot-com successes and using the CIA's funding influence to attract cutting-edge technology companies to help solve some of the agency's most vexing information management and analysis challenges. That meant 1999 would also be the year of In-Q-Tel, Inc., the CIA's venture capital research and development firm.

In February 1999, the CIA invested $28 million to form In-Q-Tel, a name that combines the abbreviation for intelligence (Intel) and "Q," the name of the fictional inventor of spy-gadgets in Ian Fleming's legendary James Bond movies. The goal of the new firm was to tap into the private sector's technology expertise and deliver new commercial technologies to the CIA more rapidly. For years, the agency had been mired in bureaucracy and a culture that was resistant to technological change. According to some agency employees, the CIA had suffered terribly from a "not invented here" syndrome that hamstrung its ability to research and deploy new technologies in a timely manner.

But the agency's problems ran deeper than that, according to an internal memo written in January 2001 by L. Britt Snider, the CIA's inspector general. According to Snider, the agency's inability to tap into the technology revolution in private industry was threatening the CIA's very existence. "I worry that the agency could see its usefulness diminish over time," wrote Snider in a farewell letter to agency officials before his retirement. "I believe the continued ability of the agency to add value will be largely a function of its ability to harness the technological advances being made in the private sector to its tasks, which cannot be done without involving knowledgeable outsiders in its work.

"When I was staff director for the Aspin/Brown Commission several years ago, I came to realize that the world of information technology does not relate very well to the world of intelligence. It thrives on transparency; we thrive on secrecy. It does not want to be tied up by government contracts and classification stamps; we know nothing else. A way thus must be found to identify and harness the capabilities of this world to the Agency's purposes without (for them) the downsides. That is why I believe In-Q-Tel simply has to succeed. Agency managers and overseers must find a way to make it work."[7]

Snider was clearly taking a shot at the CIA's reluctance to embrace a certain amount of transparency as a means to inject new capabilities in a more rapid manner. Like the NSA, the CIA had its own culture of secrecy to learn how to deal with and make more flexible. I recall a conversation I had in 1998 with George Tenet that touched on this issue. It took place at an awards banquet sponsored by the Marine Corps Intelligence Association, of which I would later become a chapter president. I half-jokingly told him that as a journalist I was having a hard time cracking through the thick layers of secrecy and that it would be great if he could help me uncover a few decent news stories. He asked me whom I had been dealing with at the agency. When I told him the name of my primary contact, he smiled and said he planned to promote her when he returned to work the next day.

By August 2001, one month before the terrorist attacks, signs began to emerge that In-Q-Tel was delivering on its promise. In a report that had been ordered by Congress as part of the fiscal 2000 Intelligence Authorization Act, a 30-member Independent Panel on the Central Intelligence Agency In-Q-Tel Venture concluded that In-Q-Tel's business model "makes sense" but stopped short of recommending that the firm's charter be expanded to other agencies, such as the NSA. The important thing, however, was that technology that could be of help to the business of intelligence collection and analysis was finally making its way into the CIA.

One such technology was the Presidential Information Dissemination System (PIDS), an electronic briefing tool used by analysts to brief the president-elect during the transition period from one administration to another. In addition, PIDS serves as the basis for the CIA's iWeb program, which aims to develop a Web-based portal for analyst groups.

In addition, In-Q-Tel commissioned SafeWeb, a leading privacy technology development firm based in Oakland, California, to create an Internet privacy and security product to protect the agency's confidential communications. Through In-Q-Tel, the CIA also commissioned

---

[7]   L. Britt Snider, "A Letter from the Inspector General, Central Intelligence Agency," Internal CIA Memorandum, January 19, 2001.

Intelliseek, Inc., a Cincinnati-based software firm, to develop future Web-based intelligent agent and knowledge discovery technologies to help analysts make better use of open-source information available on the Internet. The company continued to add dozens of private sector R&D efforts to its portfolio and continues to do so today.

It is unfortunate, however, that it took the deaths of 3,000 Americans on September 11 to focus the intelligence community—headed by the director of central intelligence—on developing a master network architecture that may finally enable the type of information and intelligence sharing that could stop future terrorist attacks before they kill innocent people. Critical information sharing projects that had been moving lazily forward before the attacks of September finally began to get the attention they deserved.

One of the most important programs now being deployed is the Intelligence Community System for Information Sharing (ICSIS). It's a Web-based system that comprises both the Top Secret Joint Worldwide Intelligence Communications System (JWICS—pronounced Jay-Wicks) and the Secret Internet Protocol Routing Network (SIPRNET—pronounced Sipper-Net), which the defense and intelligence communities have been using for years to share data. The difference now is that officials from the CIA's Community Management Staff and other agencies are working to build a browser-based front end that won't take users directly to these systems but rather to a role-based common virtual collaboration space. ICSIS, therefore, will provide controlled interfaces that will for the first time let the intelligence community automate the process of stripping out from classified documents top-secret sources and methods of intelligence collection. It will also automate the sharing of that intelligence with analysts and officials with "Secret" or lower security clearances.

The vision of the architects of this system is to create managed entry points into segregated communities of interest for all security levels. One of those entry points will lead to the Open Source Information System, a collaborative, virtual private network (VPN)–enabled workspace for sharing sensitive but unclassified data and open-source news reports from around the world. That's a capability critics have said the U.S. intelligence community has both lacked and ignored. The example cited most often is the al-Qaeda interview conducted in 2000 by an Italian newspaper in which an al-Qaeda operative states that he and others were being trained as pilots to conduct Kamikaze attacks.

Finding a way to scrub the most sensitive and classified information is critical to being able to get actionable intelligence into the hands of the thousands of federal, state, and local officials who are on the frontlines of homeland defense but who are not (and should not be) necessarily cleared to receive top-secret, code-word intelligence data. When I served in the military intelligence community throughout the early 1990s, this was always an issue of great contention that often resulted in delays in getting information into the hands of people who needed it.

Phase 1 of ICSIS development, which was under way as of this writing, involves various collaboration enablers, such as public-key infrastructure encryption technology; a directory of intelligence analysts who can be contacted by means of encrypted community e-mail; a collaboration software tool suite; trusted interfaces for access to replicated data repositories at different security levels; and a metadata markup process to support data discovery throughout the community. Data discovery is critical to saving time. If analysis and intelligence products already exist, there needs to be a way for analysts at all levels and at all agencies to find them and request access to them.

However, this hasn't always been an easy or popular proposition in the intelligence community. I was a member of the intelligence community when Intelink, the community's premier data repository, was just beginning to enter service in 1994. Intelink is the intelligence community's classified intranet system that is still used to this day to share intelligence data and products. One intelligence official characterized it best when he said, "Take AOL, Yahoo, MSN and link it to a bunch of classified data and that's Intelink."

When it was first deployed, Intelink was a dream come true for those of us who operated on the "pointy end of the spear," a phrase used to describe the environment in which deployed military forces work. I can recall being able to surf through the classified Web pages of the CIA, the DIA, the U.S. European Command in Stuttgart, Germany, and even the Joint Analysis Center in Molesworth, England. That was during the height of the war in

Bosnia. Intelink proved to hold intelligence products (maps, imagery, analysis, military order of battle, etc.) that were generally unavailable to my analysts at the Second Marine Expeditionary Force, which was preparing Operation Plan 40104, a dangerous mission to extract (one might say rescue) the United Nations Protection Force (UNPROFOR) from Bosnia.

But not everybody saw Intelink in the same light. The multiple insular cultures within the intelligence community didn't always like the transparency that Internet technologies provided. The CIA, for example, did not appreciate seeing their analysis of events in the intelligence summaries of other agencies (such as the military command I worked for) without proper credit being given. Likewise, senior military commands became suspicious and annoyed by the fact that subordinate commands could now just as easily download imagery and other intelligence products from national agencies without the added red tape of having to first pass the request up through the chain of command. The Internet had challenged the need for the very existence of some organizations. With Intelink, what used to take me weeks to obtain in writing took me minutes to download electronically. And instead of receiving intelligence photos that might be five years old, I was able to search for and immediately download the most recent U-2 imagery from Bosnia. But somehow, that was a threat to the entrenched cultures and stodgy management structures that were in place. Transparency made people in the intelligence business nervous.

In the seven years since I left the intelligence community, the amount of content available through Intelink has skyrocketed. And that has produced new problems for the current generation of intelligence officers. On the one-year anniversary of the September 11 terrorist attacks, there were more than 2.4 million Web pages available through the top-secret version of Intelink. There is now so much content available to analysts that one senior member of the intelligence community said, "Searching Intelink is like shooting craps."[8] Officials are now developing a structured database to help analysts make sense of the mountains of data sitting out there on

---

[8] See Dan Verton, "Searching Intelink Is Like Shooting Craps," *Computerworld*, September 9, 2002.

servers throughout the community. A 24-hour operations center has also been established for the sole purpose of helping Intelink "customers" to find information.

But homeland security information sharing poses other unique security challenges that few people outside the intelligence community appreciate, said William Dawson, the intelligence community's deputy chief information officer.[9] For example, intelligence agencies are for the first time being asked to share information collected from highly sensitive sources with agencies that sit outside of the traditional boundaries of the intelligence community, such as the Environmental Protection Agency (EPA) and the Department of Agriculture. "You really shouldn't have EPA officials surfing through military order-of-battle information," said Dawson, referring to the legitimate security issues that could arise from the granting of wholesale access to intelligence databases. "I can run a wire and give you information, but what do you want, what do you need, and what are you going to do with it?"

While the relentless march of technology has started the process of defrosting the intelligence community, particularly the CIA, out of its Cold War footing, questions still remain about how the CIA, as the senior intelligence agency within the community, should move forward. Are the traditional skills of the CIA still relevant in the information age? Is the way the CIA is organized still relevant? These were questions that very senior and well-respected intelligence professionals were arguing about and continue to debate. And nothing demonstrated the nature of that intellectual struggle more than the differing views of some of the CIA's past directors.

At a conference on the future of the CIA sponsored four months before the September 11 terrorist attacks by the Council on Foreign Relations in New York, four former CIA chiefs—Admiral Stansfield Turner, William H. Webster, James Woolsey, and John Deutch—agreed that despite new threats and challenges presented by the technology revolution, stealing secrets remains the agency's primary mission.

---

[9] Author interview. Information Sharing and Homeland Security Conference, Philadelphia, Pennsylvania, August 19–20, 2002.

The CIA has a "unique responsibility to steal secrets," said Woolsey, who led the CIA from 1993 to 1995. "That is absolutely timeless."

Turner, who served as director of the CIA in the Carter administration, disagreed that the modern age had turned the agency on its head. "I think we overstate the idea that the function of intelligence has changed since the end of the Cold War," he said. The most fundamental issue facing the intelligence community is determining the role of the CIA director and giving that person the authority to direct the community, Turner said. And he was right. CIA directors for years have complained about their lack of budget and investment authority over the whole of the community—14 separate government agencies. The government's bureaucracy and the turf battles that came with it made the notion of having a director of central intelligence a misnomer.

However, Deutch, who served as head of the CIA in the Clinton administration and came under fire for using a home computer with an Internet connection to type and store classified documents, said new threats like cyber-warfare have blurred the line between law enforcement and national security issues. Those distinctions "simply don't make sense" anymore, he said. "The circumstances have changed so significantly. . .that we really ought to rethink the entire business from the ground up."

-.-. -.-- -... . .-. - . .-. .-. --- .-.

One agency that has used the failures of September 11 to rethink the intelligence business from the ground up is the State Department. Although not traditionally associated with intelligence collection and analysis functions, the State Department offers the future practitioners of homeland security intelligence a valuable resource in the effort to prevent future terrorist attacks. But nothing short of reinventing the culture of the agency and rebuilding its information technology infrastructure will be required to make that a reality. And that's exactly what some officials have planned.

The State Department operates 257 diplomatic posts in 180 countries around the world. As a result, "no other federal agency can match that sort of presence," said an official from the department's Office of Intelligence

Resources and Planning division. "We're going to be the largest influence in the secret [intelligence] space in the next two to three years," the official said.[10]

But the State Department can't accomplish that goal without the help of the CIA and the Intelink program office. That's because the State Department's plan is to link its outposts around the world to intelligence analysts in Washington by deploying the intelligence community's secret intranet, known as Intelink, to all of its posts by the end of 2003. Intelink workstations and connectivity currently exist in about 125 posts around the world. Such connectivity allows intelligence analysts in the U.S. to tap into the unique insight of Foreign Service officers and information of intelligence value that can be collected only at the local level in various countries. And while Intelink training has now been made a part of the Department's overall computer training program, as of this writing it has not been made part of the mandatory introductory training for new Foreign Service officers—a policy that clearly needs to be changed.

Speaking at a public conference on homeland security in Philadelphia hosted by the Defense Department one year after the September 11 attacks, Gerald Gallucci, a career foreign service officer at the State Department, agreed that the lack of computer skills have hampered the ability of foreign service officers to support the intelligence community. "Up to a year ago, many didn't even know they had the capability to share classified data via the SIPRNET," said Gallucci. "Right now, we're still using the telegram system to send messages to and from overseas."[11]

And while the State Department is researching new ways to provide Foreign Service officers with Web-publishing tools so that they can maintain their own searchable Web sites, the process of transformation won't happen overnight. "All of this requires a tremendous change in culture," acknowledged Gallucci.

According to one senior State Department technology manager, "Foreign

---

[10] See Dan Verton, "State Department Aims for Bigger Role in Homeland Security," *Computerworld*, September 9, 2002.

[11] Ibid.

service officers do not always take to new technology like fish to water."[12]

But sometimes the technology just isn't there. For example, one State Department official recently visited a consular officer at the Department's Bureau of Consular Affairs and asked how the visa applicant information was shared with other branches of the government. The answer was what many people now know: Sneaker net, point-to-point transfers and in some cases hard copy. "Sneaker net" is a term used by technologists to describe the outdated process of using human couriers to deliver documents and information.

However, if the State Department wants to become a central player in the global antiterrorism intelligence game, it will have to do more than change its cultural aversion to technology. The Department also has a long history of security breaches stemming from an inability to properly manage its technology assets and provide for physical security of its systems and facilities.

One of the most glaring security lapses occurred months after the September 11 terrorist attacks and involved the issuance of visas to 105 individuals who were on FBI and CIA terrorism watch lists. The oversight stemmed from a special system developed by the State Department in November 2001 called "Visas Condor." The system had been developed specifically to handle the processing of overseas visa applications, including the automated checking of applicant names against FBI and CIA terrorism watch lists. However, an audit by the General Accounting Office, the investigative arm of Congress, found that by April 2002, the FBI had a backlog of approximately 8,000 unchecked names from the State Department Visas Condor system. Of the 38,000 Condor applications subsequently processed through August 1, 2002, roughly 280 names turned up on the antiterrorism lists. The State Department issued visas to 105 of those suspected terrorists because of misspelled or duplicate names.

In January 2000, Secretary of State Madeleine Albright fired the deputy director of the Bureau of Intelligence and Research (INR) and officially disciplined six other senior officials for the loss of a laptop computer that contained thousands of pages of top-secret "codeword" information—the

---

12 Ibid.

highest classification in the world of U.S. intelligence—pertaining to weapons proliferation around the world. The laptop vanished from a conference room within the State Department Headquarters facility in Washington, D.C.

But that was not the only incident that would mar the State Department's security program. In December 1999, officials discovered a sophisticated electronic listening device in a chair rail in a seventh-floor conference room at State headquarters in Washington, D.C. Stanislav Gusev, a Russian intelligence agent who worked in the Russian embassy, had planted the device and attempted to monitor it covertly from a car parked outside of the State Department. The discovery of the listening device followed a February 1998 incident in which a man entered the secretary of state's office and made off with top-secret documents. That such an incident could occur was not surprising given the fact that technology contractors hired by the agency were often allowed to roam about the headquarters facility, including in areas they were not cleared to enter without a security escort.[13]

-.-. -.-- -... . .-. - . .-. .-. --- .-.

The information technology revolution has also thrown the intelligence and counterintelligence operations of the FBI into a tailspin, resulting in a series of embarrassing and sometimes deadly security breaches.

FBI director Robert Mueller, who took the helm of the nation's top domestic crime fighting and antiterrorism agency only weeks before the September 11 terrorist attacks, has acknowledged publicly on many occasions since then that the FBI will not be able to provide the American people with the level of protection they expect unless the bureau becomes "better at applying technology to support investigations." The FBI's current IT infrastructure, according to Mueller, is incapable of supporting the robust analysis capability needed by agents in the field. Mueller made these com-

---

[13] See Dan Verton, "State Department to Punish Six over Missing Laptop," *Computerworld*, December 11, 2000.

ments repeatedly to members of Congress during a series of hearings in June 2002 that focused on Mueller's sweeping reorganization plan for the bureau.

The most pressing problem facing the FBI revolves around a lack of tools to conduct data mining and analysis of financial records and communications, Mueller said. Specifically, the bureau needs artificial intelligence tools, such as those in use at the CIA and the National Security Agency, that will allow agents to conduct searches and identify patterns and relationships within large volumes of information stored in different media formats. One FBI agent referred to it as a need for big iron—mainframe computers capable of crunching through volumes of data—and said that in his estimation the FBI was at least a decade behind other organizations in adopting this type of technology.[14] Other long-time agents likened the bureau's technology investment philosophy to that of building a Chinese wall for security. Nobody could get in that wasn't authorized, that's for sure. However, nobody could communicate to the outside world either. In addition, the electronic case management system that had been deployed for years was so difficult to use that some agents simply didn't use it.[15]

Mueller also acknowledged the FBI's lack of connectivity with other federal agencies that are now part of the overall homeland security and antiterrorism infrastructure. More than six months after the September 11 terrorist attacks, the bureau was still clamoring for a secure intranet to help improve sharing of classified and sensitive data between FBI agents and officials from other federal, state, and local government agencies.

However, the FBI's lack of connectivity to other agencies, especially state and local police organizations, may also stem from cultural roadblocks as much as it may stem from technical shortcomings. Although he would later accuse me in a *Computerworld* letter to the editor of using his remarks to suit my own political agenda in a news story, an investigator with the Houston Police Department railed against the bureau's lack of

---

[14] See Dan Verton, "FBI Must Fix Outdated IT Infrastructure," *Computerworld*, June 17, 2002.

[15] Ibid.

information sharing during a presentation he gave at the Government Symposium on Information Sharing and Homeland Security in Philadelphia in August 2002.

"The FBI is the central repository of all counterterrorism intelligence, [contained] in the most archaic database," the officer said in front of a crowd of hundreds of government and private sector officials. "However, they're not disseminating anything.

"The bureau's philosophy is that if there's a problem, we'll come into your office and tell you what it is," continued the officer. The FBI "doesn't disseminate analytical and predictive intelligence reports. That level of information sharing is no longer acceptable. The bureau doesn't have the Internet—they have their own intranet, and they're not in touch."[16]

Houston, however, was not the only city where the police department was having difficulty assisting the FBI-led Joint Terrorism Task Force. As the one-year anniversary of the September 11 terrorist attacks approached, I traveled to Manhattan and met with a local New York City law enforcement officer who agreed to talk to me on condition that I not reveal his identity. He told me that thousands of bridge and tunnel officers and police officers in New York were being asked to watch for known or suspected terrorists who may still be living in the Manhattan area, without any technology support to automate the process of checking suspects against terrorism watch lists.

"Well, if you stop somebody in a car, for example, who you think fits the profile of a wanted terrorist, how do you go about verifying the person's identity?" I asked.

"The names and descriptions of the suspects are called into headquarters using a radio, and the desk officer then checks to see if the name

---

[16] See Dan Verton, "Cops Watching for Terrorists Say IT Support Lacking," *Computerworld*, September 5, 2002. In a subsequent letter to the editor, the police officer in question said the story I wrote based on his comments and the comments of other local police officials from New York was "inconsistent with the message of cooperation and mutual support I conveyed in my presentation. Although I don't dispute the point that the FBI arguably doesn't possess state-of-the-art IT for the war on terrorism, the fact is they aren't alone." To view the entire letter, see "Houston Police, FBI Have Good Relationship," *Computerworld*, www.computerworld.com/letters, September 23, 2002.

matches any of the names on the hard-copy 'be-on-the-lookout' sheets that we have tacked up on a bulletin board," the law enforcement source said. "The person we're looking for might have five different aliases. It's a joke," he said.[17]

"What about documentation?" I asked. "Don't these people have to carry some sort of identification?"

"That's where the joke gets worse," the law enforcement source said. "We ask to see their license and registration and they show us an international driver's license. It's a piece of paper. My son can make one on his computer," he said.

According to state law, foreign nationals who enter the country with international licenses have 30 days before they must apply for a New York state driver's license. However, international driver's licenses are paper-based and can easily be forged.

"So if and when a terrorist is pulled over for speeding, he just shows the officer his international driver's license, and the officer has no way to check who he is through the Department of Motor Vehicles," said the officer. "We usually write them a summons for driving without a license and tell them to have a nice day. Then they change their name on their international license using a computer, rent a new car, and start the process all over again. I'm positive that we have stopped somebody who is on a watch list and let him go."[18]

-.-. -.-- -... . .-. - . .-. .-. --- .-.

To be fair, progress is being made at the federal level, particularly in the application of cutting-edge information technologies to the problems facing intelligence analysis and dissemination.

For example, within the first year following the September 11 terrorist attacks, analysts and field operatives from the CIA and the National Security Agency (NSA) stepped up offensive operations against terrorists around the world using newly developed text and audio search and analysis

---

17   Author interview.
18   Ibid.

technologies. The purchase of the new technologies was a direct response to the failure prior to September 11 to detect, analyze, and disseminate in a timely manner information pertaining to terrorist cell communications, including the use of code words that may have indicated an attack was imminent.

CIA analysts now use what they call the Name Reference Library developed by Language Analysis Systems Inc. (LAS) in Herndon, Virginia. The software analyzes name origins, tells the analyst whether or not multiple middle and last names are in the right order (Egyptian- and Saudi-born citizens often use multiple generational names), and provides a list of the top ten spelling variants as well as gender associations. The CIA is also interested in a product that is currently under development that will enable processing of native scripts. Therefore, if an analyst captures the name Mohamed in Arabic, he or she can be assured they have a match because in Arabic it's spelled only one way.

Signals intelligence analysts at the NSA, who are responsible for intercepting and analyzing hundreds of terabytes of archived and real-time voice, data, and video communications, are also getting help from making use of new information technologies. A new software program purchased by the agency can break down speech into its smallest components, called phonemes. The phonemes can then be indexed and searched for keywords. The software can retrieve any word, name, or phrase from voice recordings, regardless of speaker or dialect, with up to 98 percent accuracy and up to 72,000 times faster than in real time. The software enables NSA analysts to search through 20 hours of audio in less than 1 second. NSA intelligence operatives are now able to take this capability with them into the field using laptop computers.

Despite these technological improvements being made at the individual agency level, many have concluded wrongly that the formation of a new Department of Homeland Security will necessarily mean an instantaneous, marked improvement in information sharing across the government. Nothing could be further from the truth.

From a cultural and security perspective, the integration challenge facing the new department—which will consist of 22 formerly independent federal agencies and 177,000 employees—is so steep that most experts agree that the most basic capability envisioned by the president is a minimum of five years away. And when the integration of all of the various state and local law enforcement bodies, emergency workers, and health care organizations is factored in, a nationwide homeland security information sharing system could take a decade to achieve.

In March 2002, the White House assigned the task of making all of these agencies communicate with each other as if they were truly one agency to Steve Cooper, a former chief information officer at Corning, Inc. As of this writing, Cooper has focused his staff on pilot projects that are designed to act as what Cooper likes to call "pathfinders"—building blocks that will show officials the way ahead to a truly integrated Department of Homeland Security. The initial Pathfinder Projects included an effort to consolidate all of the federal government's various terrorism watch lists so that all intelligence and law enforcement agencies are looking at the same tactical picture. Another project included creating a Web-based homeland security portal focusing on critical infrastructure protection—a way for all agencies with responsibilities in that area to get the latest information. A third initial Pathfinder Project is to create a coalition of law enforcement agencies to begin sharing tactical antiterrorism information electronically. As many as ten states, led by the Florida Department of Law Enforcement, have agreed to cooperate on a massive data mining and information sharing architecture.

However, Cooper understands the size and scope of the challenges before him. "I haven't seen a federal agency yet whose charter includes collaboration with other federal agencies," he said, speaking at the August 2002 Government Information Sharing and Homeland Security Conference in Philadelphia.[19] Cooper made those remarks shortly after Congress had denied the Bush administration's funding request to establish a central integration office within the new Department of Homeland Security. "To the best of our information, they don't believe it can be done," said Cooper.

---

[19]   See Dan Verton, "Congressman Says Data Mining Could Have Prevented 9-11," *Computerworld*, August 26, 2002.

-.-. -.-- -... . .-. - . .-. .-. --- .-.

Given the bureaucratic, cultural, and legitimate information security challenges standing in the way of genuine, timely information sharing, the war on terrorism at home will in the near term depend almost exclusively on the preparations made by state and local police and emergency responders. And the good news is that some of America's major metropolitan areas are beginning to take steps to ensure they are prepared to act.

The city of Boston, for example, initiated a pilot project in the summer of 2000 called the Boston Preparedness Pilot that is tapping into the digital mapping and smart database expertise of the National Imagery and Mapping Agency (NIMA), an intelligence asset of the Department of Defense. The Boston pilot stems from a larger nationwide program known as the 120 Cities Project, the goal of which is to disseminate what one NIMA official referred to as "a minimum level of geospatial preparedness" down to state and local emergency responders.[20]

Boston police officials acquired 100 digital mapping files of the entire Boston area from NIMA, including six-inch-resolution imagery that details the locations of every school, grocery store, hospital, police station, government building, industrial facility, prominent landmark, bridge, highway, parking lot, and water system. But the data from NIMA isn't simply a collection of flat files. It's what officials refer to as "smart data," which allows officials to click on any installation depicted on their computerized maps and pull up a wealth of data about the structure. This enables emergency planners to quickly determine how many beds are available in a given hospital or how many employees might be in an office building on any given day. They also have access to critical engineering data on bridges, sports stadiums, and other large public structures, which are primary targets for terrorists who may be planning a mass casualty event.

Boston and other cities are also taking advantage of a software package known as the Consequence Application Toolset, developed by the Defense

---

[20] See Dan Verton, "GIS Plays Key Role in Homeland Security," *Computerworld*, September 9, 2002.

Threat Reduction Agency and Science Applications International Corporation in San Diego. The software enables planners to quickly analyze a chemical, biological, or nuclear explosion and determine in a matter of seconds what geographic area and how many buildings and people are immediately threatened. It accomplishes this by integrating real-time weather data that assists the software in determining how and in which direction the toxic plume will spread. And given the challenges facing the creation of a nationwide information and intelligence sharing architecture that is capable of getting critical warning data into the hands of the authorities and emergency first-responders who need it, being able to integrate this type of capability into a city's disaster and evacuation plan may mean the difference between saving and losing tens of thousands of lives. Nuclear, biological, and chemical weapons do not discriminate.

9

Dark Winter: Technology and Early Warning

There were not rapid or reliable ways for public health agencies to communicate to doctors and nurses what was happening [during the anthrax attacks of 2001] or what public health was recommending. . . . The chief of infectious diseases at one of America's best hospitals said that in the midst of the crisis he had to get his medical information from CNN.[1]

—Thomas V. Inglesby, MD
Deputy director
Center for Civilian Biodefense Strategies
Johns Hopkins University

Sometime in the past, present or future
How it could happen. . .
. . .If it hasn't happened already.

He was known to be an early riser and the first one to arrive at the office each morning. On a normal day, a good man put in at least ten hours, he often said.

---

[1] Testimony before the Senate Committee on Government Affairs hearing on "The State Public Health Preparedness for Terrorism Involving Weapons of Mass Destruction: A Six Month Report Card," April 18, 2002.

That was his 20 years in the Marine Corps talking, of course. But John Kearns meant what he said and he expected no less from those he chose to be part of his team. Dedication to the firm's marketing mission was nonnegotiable, he told every new recruit who had managed to survive his initial two-hour interview process. People needed to know what was expected of them from the start, John thought. And they needed to see the boss doing more than talking the talk; they needed to see him walking the walk as well. John walked the walk.

It was that image of John Kearns, the former Marine Force Recon officer turned corporate marketing executive for American Defense Systems Corporation, a major U.S. defense contractor, that made his absence at one of the most important Monday morning executive management meetings of the year so unusual. He, along with five of his top managers—two from the corporate headquarters in Atlanta, where John also worked, and three from the Norfolk, Virginia, regional office—had just returned the previous Friday from a whirlwind tour of Europe. They had made a valiant effort to sell their company's expertise in military electronic subsystems to America's NATO allies in Belgium, the Netherlands, Germany, and Great Britain. By any executive's standards, it was a grueling trip—four countries and six presentations in seven days. But the face time was critical to American Defense Systems' long-term viability, and the CEO was eager to hear the results of the trip straight from the mouth of the company's front man for sales and marketing.

The CEO of American Defense Systems, a tall, slender, leathery-faced retired Marine lieutenant general, preferred to wait until all of his principal advisors were gathered in the conference room before breaking away from his e-mail and heading down the hall to the meeting. It was a habit he picked up during a stint as the commanding general of the Second Marine Expeditionary Force. Back then, every minute of the day counted. A military commander had no set working hours— work was continual. And today, for a CEO wearing pinstripes instead of camouflage fatigues, the same rule applied.

"Sir, there's a problem with the meeting this morning," the CEO's executive assistant said, standing at the door to his office.

"What problem is that, Helen?"

"It's John Kearns. His wife Debra just called and said she's taking him to the emergency room at Memorial General. Something about a dangerously high fever that he hasn't been able to get rid of all weekend."

"Ouch! That doesn't sound very good. Keep in touch with Debra today and let me know how he's doing. But for now is everybody else ready for the meeting? I'm sure John's deputy can brief us on some of the material this morning."

"Well, not exactly," Helen responded tentatively. *"Everybody is here except the team that accompanied Mr. Kearns to Europe. I think they all caught the same nasty bug. You know how airplanes are. One sick passenger can make everybody sick."*

"Are you kidding me? All five of them are too sick to. . . ."

Helen cut him off. *"They're all complaining about fevers,"* she said. *"It's not a coincidence. And three of the others called from a cell phone and said they also were heading for the doctor's office this morning."*

"Okay. Can you. . . ."

" I'll reschedule for later in the week." She had cut him off again. But the look on his face showed that the CEO of American Defense Systems had become preoccupied. And Helen knew from experience not to talk to him about scheduling when he was preoccupied. The last time she did that, he tried to be in three places at the same time.

"Thank you. Please stay on top of that situation and let me know what's going on with each one of them."

"I will," said Helen. *"God, I hope they didn't all eat bad beef when they were over there. Isn't Mad Cow disease still a problem in Europe?"*

"I don't know. I haven't the foggiest idea," the CEO said. And that was the truth. He had no idea what malicious form of bacteria had started to run its course through his company. And that's what scared him. The unknown unknowns always posed the greatest danger. He was just glad that Helen had not added a skin rash to the list of symptoms.

-.-. -.-- -... . .-. - . .-. .-. --- .-.

At 9:30 *that morning, the National Security Council gathered in the White House Situation Room to bring the president up to date on the scores of pressing issues that faced the nation. There was, of course, the planning for a possible war in Iraq—both covert and overt—as well as the global war on terrorism and the mounting crisis in North Korea, which had recently evicted United Nations weapons inspectors and reactivated a mothballed nuclear reactor that the CIA said was capable of producing several nuclear weapons.*

As was the standard practice, CIA director James Tenly was the first to brief. He reported that the al-Daura vaccine plant, located outside of Baghdad, had sometime within the past month renewed full-scale production after nearly a decade of inactivity. The official Iraqi statement on the move was that the plant was being used for the preparation of vaccines against foot-and-mouth disease, a highly contagious disease that causes lameness, tongue erosion, and permanent impairment of milk formation in cattle, swine, goats, and other ruminants. FMD, as the disease was known, had reached epidemic proportions in parts of Asia and the Middle East. The economic impact had been devastating.

However, Tenly said, satellite photos and information from paid sources within the Iraqi government supported the conclusion that the facility was actually being used to build chemical or biological weapons. In addition, the CIA now had confirmed reports that several former nuclear and biological weapons scientists from the former Soviet Union were working in Iraq.

"Do we know if any chemical or biological agents have been smuggled out of the country?" the president asked. "Can we be sure that it hasn't already been introduced into the U.S.?" he asked, knowing in his heart what the answer was. "This is a government that directly supports terror, supports al-Qaeda, and we need to find a way to lock them in a box until we can effectively deal with them on our own terms militarily."

Tenly said he would ask his analysts for a detailed assessment, but, he added, right now he was not in a position to provide that level of assurance. One of the reasons he was hesitant, he said, was because last night FBI and Russian agents reported that they were unsuccessful in locating Abu Hamsa Hattab, a known senior member of al-Qaeda. Hattab was believed to have arranged for the delivery of an unknown amount of plutonium and an unspecified array of biological pathogens that had been weaponized by former Soviet scientists and sold on the black market.

"My station chief in Moscow said they were convinced they had found him in an apartment and that he was there," said Tenly. "But when they arrived, it was immediately apparent that he had been gone for days, maybe weeks."

"Where is he, Jim?" the president demanded.

"Mr. President, all I can honestly tell you at this point is that he could be anywhere in Europe or the Middle East. But we're working on it."

Before Tenly could continue with his briefing and the current intelligence situation on the ground in Iraq, his deputy director for intelligence (DDI) entered the room and *handed him a folder with an orange cover that was labeled Top Secret—SI. The SI stood for Special Intelligence. He opened the folder and quickly scanned the contents of the one-page flash message.*

"Mr. President, we have reports of ten confirmed cases of smallpox coming out of London this morning," said Tenly. "Nobody has claimed credit for spreading the disease, but we have to assume that this was a deliberate attack."

Smallpox hadn't been seen in the U.S. since 1949, and the last international case occurred in Somalia in 1977. Derived from the Latin word for "spotted," smallpox is a highly contagious disease characterized by a rash and lumps that form all over the face and body, making its victim's skin appear to be made of bubble-wrap. It has a mortality rate of 30 percent.

"I guess we found out where Hattab is, Jim," the president said, unable to hide the worry in his face. "But who else could have done it, Jim?" the president asked. "Assuming this is a terrorist act or a direct response to our military activity in the Gulf."

"Smallpox is stored officially in only two places, Mr. President. The U.S. and Russia," said Tenly. "But we can't rule out China, Iraq, Iran, or North Korea. Any nation with a rudimentary industrial biotechnology base could have accomplished this. In addition, we know that several of the former Soviet scientists who special-ized in bio-weapons are now in Iran, Iraq, Israel, and North Korea," Tenly said. "We also know that Iraq has experimented with camelpox, a close relative of small-pox," he added. "But the bottom line, Mr. President, is that any terrorist organiza-tion with enough money and access to these scientists and illicit black market cultures of smallpox could have carried out an attack as well."

The vice president jumped in. "Mr. President, the more immediate concern for us is finding out what is going on here in the U.S. We need to talk about in-bound air-craft from London, what the status is of our smallpox vaccination stockpile, what our policy is going to be on vaccinating the U.S. population, and how to control the hysteria if cases begin to pop up here," the vice president said, understanding that the current situation almost certainly meant an extended stay for him and his family in an "undisclosed location" far away from Washington, D.C.

Around the table, briefing books closed as the president's principal advisors each realized that their individual agency priorities had been overcome by events. The president then ordered his national security advisor to get the Secretary of Health and Human Services working with the Centers for Disease Control (CDC) on the current situation in the U.S. Then, he said, convene a principals meeting and prepare policy options for response to a U.S.-based crisis along with domestic and foreign intelligence updates. The NSC would reconvene tomorrow morning with the Secretary of HHS present, he said. America was facing a nightmare of potentially global proportions. And the only way out of it would be to ensure early detection and rapid, reliable information sharing across all levels of government and the private sector health care community—something that the U.S. was still working to achieve.

-.-. -.-- -... . .-. - . .-. .-. --- .-.

At Memorial *General in Atlanta, John Kearns had taken his seat in line at the "emergency" room and was just now—90 minutes later—getting to see a doctor. He told the doctor, who looked more like an intern than a seasoned emergency room vet, that his biggest concern was his fever; it had reached 103 degrees at one point, and he had been unable to get it down below 100 degrees. He was also suffering from general tiredness, aches and pains, and an occasional feeling that he had to vomit. It was nothing he hadn't dealt with before and he was only here to make his wife happy, he said.*

"How long have you been like this?" the doctor asked.

"About two and a half days," John said.

"Flu shot this year?"

"No," said John.

"Okay. Well, let's see what your temp is now," the young doctor said, sticking one of those electronic thermometers into John's ear. "You know you really need to get that flu shot every year."

Three quick, high-pitched beeps indicated the thermometer had recorded an accurate temperature: 102 degrees.

"Well, you're still pretty warm," the intern pretending to be doctor said. "I'm going to give you something that will help with the aches and pains. But for the fever, you're going to have to pump the clear liquids, take some aspirin, and get a lot of rest. I think you're paying the price for not getting that flu shot."

"I think you're right, doc," John said. "I'll make sure I get that shot next year. But for now, I'm going home to get some sleep."

"Do you have a ride home? You probably should not be driving until your fever subsides and your head clears."

"Yeah, no problem. My wife is taking me home before she heads off to work."

-.-. -.-- -... . .-. - . .-. .-. --- .-.

The NSC *policy-planning meeting that the president had ordered went off the next morning as planned. But it wasn't until three days later, a Thursday, when the white snows of December had become darkened by a shadow of death. The crisis was becoming an epidemic, and with the news media finally able to break the story in London, questions were now being asked throughout the U.S.*

At the Thursday morning NSC meeting, the president opened the conversation with the news that the CDC had confirmed 25 cases of smallpox in Denver and at least 10 in Atlanta. Beyond those two cities, however, the situation was unclear, he said. Colorado Governor Robert Gray had been taken to a secure command and control facility at the North American Aerospace Defense Command (NORAD), where he would be able to brief the president and the NSC on the current situation in his state.

"Bob, I know you have things to attend to so I want to start with you," the president said, referring to Governor Robert Gray, whose pale, worried face filled the video monitor in the Situation Room.

"Mr. President, CDC confirmed the 25 cases about an hour ago. It appears that my state has been the victim of a deliberate attack involving at least one biological agent," Gray said. "The truth is we don't really know how many more cases of smallpox are out there or if smallpox is all we are dealing with. The news coverage has resulted in massive crowding at every hospital emergency room in the state. My staff has been unable to maintain reliable communications with hospital officials due to the surge in telephone and cell phone use. There is no integrated medical surveillance network in my state that would have enabled us to pick up indications and warnings that something was wrong. People are in a panic. Mr. President, I am preparing to declare a state of emergency in Colorado and request immediate assistance."

"What's the status of federal response efforts?" the president asked his NSC advisors.

"Mr. President, we'll have CDC personnel on site in a few hours and 100,000 doses of vaccine delivered within 12 hours," the Secretary of Health and Human Services answered.

"Somebody tell me how bad this can get," the president snapped.

"That depends on the delivery mechanism and length of exposure," said CIA director Tenly. *"Weaponized smallpox delivered using off-the-shelf aerosol technologies, such as those used in pharmaceuticals, could infect two to three thousand if dispersed in a fairly large mall complex. And because we have no information about the origin of attack or attacks, we are in the dark when it comes to knowing how many nonsymptomatic carriers are out there. However, we should start to see the second generation of infections in ten days."*

"What's the FBI doing?" the president asked.

"We'll have several hundred agents on the ground in Denver in a few hours," responded the Attorney General. *"In addition, we're sharing information with the NSA and CIA on potential leads that might indicate who's responsible. And once our agents get on the ground in Denver, they will be setting up a Joint Operations Center for information fusion and dissemination."*

"Good," the president said. *"And how are we tying in the rest of the national health care community so that we are alerted to suspicious outbreaks in other parts of the country and can take immediate action to contain those patients?"* The president was looking in everybody's general direction when he asked this last question.

Nobody had a good enough answer that they were willing to take a chance with. The truth was that the nation had the technology capability to do localized medical surveillance during what the government called "national security special events," such as the Super Bowl or the World Series, but a nationwide health care alert network that linked the nation's thousands of hospitals, clinics, and fire and police departments to federal and state government decision makers as well as subject matter experts did not exist. States and communities around the country were on their own and were forced to rely on the news media for breaking information on government activity and guidance.

Hundreds die within six days of the first confirmed cases. Fear and chaos reaches unprecedented proportions as 2,000 confirmed or suspected cases in 15 states, as well as Canada, Mexico, and Great Britain, are being monitored. Tens of thousands of people around the country are swarming hospitals looking either for treatment or for information on what to do. Hospitals in the infected areas in Denver and Atlanta are faced with the worst crises in their history. Medical workers fail to show up for work. Supplies dwindle quickly, and some hospitals warn that bankruptcy may force them to stop treatment even before the epidemic is under control. Riots break out in some areas where vaccine is not available, forcing states to deploy the National Guard to quell the disturbances.

The economic impact is immediate. The borders are closed to any and all who are not immunized. International trade is halted until the situation can be brought under control. Colleges and universities, as well as public sporting events, are canceled around the country. Shopping malls have been turned into empty, cavernous wastelands. Delivery companies are reluctant to send their drivers into the cities and towns where smallpox cases have been confirmed, causing critical shortages of foodstuffs.

One day after leaving the doctor's office, John Kearns developed a rash of red spots on his tongue and inside his mouth. The spots developed into sores that broke and spread the virus into his mouth and throat. He coughed, transferring it to his wife, who took it to her office. John Kearns never had the flu. He was counted among the dead.

Two weeks after the first infections were reported, the disease spread to 25 states, killing 2,000. Why? Decision making was delayed due to the nation's dependence on conference calls to coordinate a national response; that lack of coordination of emergency management resources led to the formation of a disjointed, ad hoc communications infrastructure; and that communications infrastructure was incapable of delivering officials the level of situation awareness they needed to effectively manage the flow of personnel, equipment, and vaccines.

Containment failed because detection, early warning, and communications failed.

-.-. -.-- -... . .-. - . .-. .-. --- .-.

The fictional scenario you just read is based on an actual exercise sponsored in June 2001 by the Center for Strategic and International Studies code-named "Dark Winter." For four days that summer, former senior government officials, including former Georgia Senator Sam Nunn, former director of Central Intelligence James Woolsey, and former FBI director William Sessions, among others, played the roles of the president's National Security Council responding to a biological attack on the U.S. involving smallpox. One of the key lessons to come out of the exercise was the need for significantly better communications and early warning capability throughout the government and private-sector health care community.

A nationwide information sharing network linking together state and local first-responders (e.g., firemen, police, and specialized federal hazardous materials teams), the thousands of hospitals and clinics around the nation, and federal experts and decision makers may be the only thing capable of preventing a catastrophic disaster stemming from a chemical, biological, or radiological terrorist attack. Without such a system, the extent of the disaster will not be known until sick and dying people begin showing up at hospital emergency rooms. On a larger scale, entire communities and cities could be rendered as helpless as those affected by the Black Death of the fourteenth century, a bubonic plague that killed one-third of Europe's population.

In 1999, the Institute of Medicine published an extensive study that outlined the technology research and development imperatives to improve biological and chemical agent detection and warning throughout the health care community in the U.S.[2] Among other things, the study recommended that a formal communications network be established between the intelligence community and the medical community that incorporates local emergency management agencies.[3]

The study also recognized the importance of extending that communications and computer modeling capability down to the first-responder level. After all, real-time consequence management will invariably take place throughout local communities and will be handled by local emergency responders who will have to make judgments about the area of contamination, the presence of toxic plumes, weather conditions, and the effect those conditions will have on the direction of movement of those toxic plumes. Those same emergency personnel will also immediately become the front-line troops in the war of containment as well as the most critical node in the communications network that will enable the rest of the

---

[2] *Chemical and Biological Terrorism: Research and Development to Improve Civilian Medical Response,* Institute of Medicine (Washington, D.C.: The National Academies Press, 1999).

[3] Ibid., p. 33.

health care community to prepare for the crisis. Hospitals will have to be notified about the number of casualties so that the location of available hospital beds can be determined. They will also need to know, as will senior government leaders, the types of chemical or biological agents used so that stockpiles of vaccinations or antidotes can be located and made available.

However, linking America's first-responders to the nationwide health care infrastructure and, in turn, linking that infrastructure to the government is no small order. For example, there are more than one million firefighters, 600,000 local law enforcement officers, and 155,000 emergency medical technicians in the U.S. Capabilities to respond to and manage an attack involving weapons of mass destruction vary widely from community to community. Not only do many communities lack the training, most lack the equipment to detect attacks and communicate information about attacks between agencies and cross-border communities in other states.

President Bush, in his fiscal 2003 budget submission to Congress, requested $3.5 billion for improving the nationwide capabilities of emergency first-responders. According to former Pennsylvania Governor Tom Ridge, the Bush administration's Secretary of Homeland Security, that is a one thousand percent increase in funding. And why is that important? The answer to that question is simple: criminal and terrorist attacks or threats of attacks in the U.S. involving weapons of mass destruction (WMD), particularly biological agents, are rising at an alarming rate. According to the FBI, in 1998 the bureau opened 181 cases related to WMD events, of which 112 were biological in nature. Since then, the number of biological cases has increased, with 187 threatened biological agent releases occurring in 1999, and 115 in 2000. In addition, prior to the terrorist attacks of September 11, 2001, and the subsequent release of anthrax along the East Coast, the number of cases initiated by the FBI in 2001 was 100, of which 67 were biological.[4] In short, although some reports are hoaxes, WMD attacks represent a clear and present danger to communities all across the U.S.

---

[4]   Testimony of James T. Caruso, Assistant Director, Counterterrorism Division, Federal Bureau of Investigation, before the Senate Committee on the Judiciary, November 6, 2001.

That is why a vast majority of the money requested in the Bush administration's 2003 budget proposal has been earmarked for detection and communications equipment, according to Ridge. "Probably one of the first things people are interested in buying because of what they learned about 9/11 is interoperable communications equipment," Ridge told a gathering of first-responders on April 12, 2002, at the Concordville Fire Company 59 in Concordville, Pennsylvania. "You need to empower the men and women who respond, whether it's the state police, the local police, the paramedics, the EMTs, the firefighters—they've got to be able to communicate with one another," said Ridge. "And tragically, one of the things we learned in New York City is that the communications system wasn't as good as it could have been. It's nobody's fault. I'm not casting any finger—pointing any finger of responsibility or blame, we're just saying to be prepared, to be better prepared, we have to do things differently."

"Everything is not okay," wrote Joseph M. Rosen, C. Everett Koop, and Eliot B. Grigg in a National Academy of Engineering article published in spring 2002.[5] "To meet [the threat of bio-terrorism], we need a new strategy that brings together our command, communication, and control technologies," wrote Rosen, a professor of radiology at Dartmouth Medical Center; Koop, the former surgeon general of the U.S.; and Grigg, a researcher at the Dartmouth Institute for Security Technology Studies. "We must be able to mobilize all of our health care resources rapidly wherever the threat appears, even if it appears in many places simultaneously. During a crisis, there is no time to invent a response. We must be prepared, and right now we are not."

How unprepared is America's health care community to handle such a crisis? In a report released five weeks after the September 11, 2001, terrorist attacks, the Centers for Disease Control and Prevention compared the information technology and communications infrastructure supporting the U.S. health care community to the "pony express," adding that most hospitals and clinics are not even connected to the Internet and instead

---

[5]   See Joseph M. Rosen, C. Everett Koop, and Eliot B. Grigg, "Cybercare: A System for Confronting Bioterrorism," *The Bridge* (National Academy of Engineering, Spring 2002).

rely on paper-based reports and telephone calls for coordination. In fact, when the first anthrax attacks occurred on October 4, 2001, only half of the country's 59 state and territorial health departments and 6,000 state and local health departments and boards had full-time Internet connectivity, according to the CDC. Another 20 percent lacked basic e-mail capability.[6]

Around the time that the CDC report came out in late 2001, the CDC had also started to deploy a secure information system called the Epidemic Information Exchange (Epi-X). The system uses digital certificates to ensure the privacy of data. But deployment of the full-scale Epi-X system was restricted to the state level, leaving some state health department officials with read-only terminals.[7]

In addition, the systemic lack of secure communications infrastructure throughout the U.S. health care community has forced most medical facilities to rely on the U.S. Postal Service to communicate medical surveillance data to U.S. laboratories. Furthermore, the state and local heath authorities throughout the country use more than 100 different computer networks that are not integrated and cannot easily share information, according to the CDC study. The recommendation of the CDC report called for Congress to support funding that would enable the health care community to install high-speed Internet access and other information technology infrastructure that most modern organizations take for granted by 2010. The only question that remains to be answered is if 2010 will be too late.

"We have been lucky so far," wrote Rosen, Koop, and Grigg. "But luck cannot be the foundation for a public health or national security policy."

-.-. -.-- -... . .-. - . .-. .-. --- .-.

To date, the nation's capability to defend against a covert attack involving a chemical, biological, or radiological weapon has been confined to specific geographical areas of interest defined during what the

---

6   *Public Health's Infrastructure: A Status Report,* prepared for the U.S. Senate
     Appropriations Committee by the Department of Health and Human Services
     and the Centers for Disease Control and Prevention, p. 15.

7   See Bob Brewin, "CDC Calls Public Health IT a 'Pony Express,'" *Computerworld,*
     October 18, 2001.

government refers to as National Security Special Events (NSSEs), such as the Super Bowl, the World Series, or the Olympics. During the past several years, the government has deployed sophisticated medical surveillance and detection technologies to alert officials to the presence of a chemical, biological, or radiological agent as well as to any suspicious illnesses that show up in local hospital emergency rooms during the time of the event. In order for the technologies to be deployed, however, the CDC must make an official determination that they are needed or local medical authorities must specifically request them.

Within 24 hours of the September 11, 2001, terrorist attacks, which had raised concerns about the potential for chemical or biological agents to have been either on board the hijacked aircraft or hidden in the World Trade Center, the government deployed a system known as LEADERS—the Lightweight Epidemiology Advanced Detection and Emergency Response System. A Web-based system developed by the Defense Department and private technology companies, LEADERS linked 250 hospitals and medical authorities to real-time symptom tracking throughout the New York metropolitan area and enabled them to detect the covert presence of chemicals or biological agents in patients. Components of LEADERS had also been deployed to monitor for anthrax symptoms during the 2001 World Series between the New York Yankees and the Arizona Diamondbacks. During the January 2001 Super Bowl, the system detected a case of meningitis and a minor upsurge of influenza throughout hospitals in Tampa, Florida.

The problem with LEADERS, however, is that it was and remains a pay-for-service system, similar to the services provided by today's application service providers. Hospitals must subscribe to the different modules of the system and pay a fee for access—a tough sell in a cash-strapped health care industry. For example, in Hillsborough County, Florida, where LEADERS has been deployed, federal grants help pay the $60,000 annual cost of the system. And although the CDC had provided states with $940 million in 2001 to develop components of a national surveillance system, the CDC did not set any requirements for how states should spend the money or develop their networks.[8] Therefore, money had been doled out to deploy new technologies with little or no requirements established for technical interoperability across state lines or with existing systems, such as LEADERS. By August 2002, only 70 hospitals across the country had deployed components of LEADERS.[9] This year, 2003, marks ten years since development of LEADERS began. And because of September 11, 2001, the attention and some of the money is finally beginning to materialize.

Although LEADERS and other surveillance systems under development are encouraging, "communication bridges between providers and the public health system are weak and underused," according to an editorial published in December 2001 in the medical technology journal *Healthcare Informatics.* "A LEADERS pilot program in central Florida is encouraging hospitals to feed details of patients' symptoms into the common database. But for such data feeds to be effective, they must become an integral part of data management and extend beyond public health, emergency and acute care facilities to include direct care providers." The estimated price tag of preparing all U.S. hospitals to be able to adequately respond to a biological, chemical, or nuclear terrorist attack is $10 billion.[10]

Rugged, hand-held detection devices make up another key component of any future national chemical, nuclear, or biological terrorism detection and response system. Through the use of these devices, the presence of dangerous substances can be detected and immediately communicated across a Web-based network to subject matter experts, health officials, and political decision makers. It is only through the use of these mobile, hand-held systems that emergency personnel can locate and map "hot spots" for immediate containment.

---

[8]   See Marianne Kolbasuk McGee, "A Prescription for Millions," *InformationWeek,* April 22, 2002. Also, the new Department of Homeland Security has as part of its mission to establish new national policies and guidelines for states and localities to follow to prepare for nuclear, chemical, or biological terrorist attacks.

[9]   See Jordan Lewis, "Software Helps Detect Illness Patterns," *American City & County,* August 1, 2002. Also see Dan Verton, "Bioterrorism Fighters Get Ammo," *Computerworld,* December 3, 2001.

[10]   See Charlene Marietti, "For the Public Good," *Healthcare Informatics Online,* December 2001.

The Defense Department has been a leader in this area. In 1998, the Pentagon announced the formation of a consequence management office and ten Rapid Assessment and Initial Detection units, the so-called RAID teams. The initial goal of the plans was for the RAID teams to act as the nation's "911" force for domestic incidents involving weapons of mass destruction. The RAID units were designed to provide initial detection of a weapon of mass destruction, assess the level of threat it poses, and provide technical advice to local incident commanders. The teams were outfitted with devices that can detect chemical, biological, or nuclear agents and disseminate reports to local- and national-level decision-makers. In 1998, the goal was to station one RAID team in each of the ten federal emergency management regions throughout the country.

Today, RAID teams are known as National Guard Weapons of Mass Destruction (WMD) Civil Support Teams. One month after the September 11, 2001, terrorist attacks, the number of WMD Civil Support Teams stood at 27 teams in 26 states (California has 2 teams), consisting of 22 full-time members of the Army or Air National Guard. Each team is equipped with a mobile analytical lab and a mobile communications facility.

As of October 2001, states with WMD Civil Support Teams included: Alaska, Arizona, Arkansas, California (2 teams), Colorado, Florida, Georgia, Hawaii, Idaho, Illinois, Iowa, Kentucky, Louisiana, Maine, Massachusetts, Minnesota, Missouri, New Mexico, New York, Ohio, Oklahoma, Pennsylvania, South Carolina, Texas, Virginia, and Washington.

-.-. -.-- -... . .-. - . .-. .-. --- .-.

One of the most pressing security concerns remains the potential for a terrorist organization to take advantage of the global shipping industry to introduce a chemical, biological, or "dirty" nuclear weapon into the continental U.S. through a major seaport. Seaports are not only significant to the communities that surround them, but also to the entire U.S. infrastructure. Seaports are the beginning of the homeland supply chain, which includes various other forms of transportation, such as air, rail, and trucking. As a result, any system that is developed to detect, warn, and respond to WMD attacks will need to be continental in scope and will require a first layer of defense that begins far beyond the borders and ports of entry into the continental United States. If terrorists succeed in transporting a chemical, biological, or nuclear weapon across U.S. borders or through U.S. ports of entry, it is too late.

The Bush administration has pledged as part of its effort to set up a Department of Homeland Security to focus on developing new technologies that will enable the advance detection and notification of the presence of weapons of mass destruction that may be stowed away aboard foreign cargo vessels, air shipments, or ground transportation assets. The White House refers to this as a "nuclear denial program," which would develop and deploy new technologies and systems for safeguarding nuclear material stockpiles and for detecting the movement of those materials. In addition, new regulations went into effect in February 2003 that require 24-hour advance electronic submission of cargo manifests before a merchant ship is allowed to enter one of the more than 1,000 U.S. port terminals.

Such regulations will eventually be supported by new container tracking and security technologies. The U.S. Coast Guard, for example, has been studying the use of "electronic seals" to secure cargo containers. The seals will immediately transmit an alert to U.S. officials via a constellation of satellites known as the Global Positioning System (GPS) whenever a container is opened or tampered with during shipping. This would also facilitate development of a vessel monitoring and identification system capable of uncovering suspicious cargoes up to 20 miles offshore.

Since September 11, 2001, defense and intelligence officials have warned the Bush administration repeatedly that the maritime transportation system in the U.S. offers terrorists a particularly attractive target. More than 7,500 foreign vessels make more than 51,000 port calls in the U.S. every year. In addition, more than 6 million containers, including 156 million tons of hazardous material and 1 billion tons of petroleum products, enter U.S. ports each year. The cruise ship industry shuttles millions of people through many of these same ports. However, prior to the September 11 attacks and for more than a year after, port authorities had very little advance information about the specific cargo being shipped in many of the containers. In fact, only 2 percent of all containers that were off-loaded at U.S. ports and transported to other parts of the country via air, road, or rail were inspected prior to arrival, according to government estimates.

However, the ramifications of poor security at the nation's seaports came crashing home in May 2002, when the U.S. Coast Guard issued a terrorism warning that 25 suspected terrorists of Middle Eastern descent and dressed as stevedores simply walked off cargo ships and melted into the cities and towns around ports in Florida, Georgia, and California. That same month, three men in Mexico hijacked a tractor-trailer containing ten tons of deadly cyanide. Officials couldn't find the truck for six days and did not recover all of the 96 barrels of cyanide for several weeks.

"This is a turning point in our history," remarked a senior agent with the U.S. Border Patrol, speaking at a government-sponsored conference on information sharing and homeland security in 2002. "Things are happening, but they're not happening quickly enough," the official said, referring to the issue of securing the nation's border crossing points.[11] To stop terrorists from getting across the border either on foot or in vehicles that may be loaded with cyanide will require a better mix of enforcement and technology, the official said. The INS has apprehended four million individuals attempting to cross the border illegally into the U.S. during the last three years. And that's only the tip of the iceberg. A new integrated video surveillance system deployed along the southwest border region is enabling the INS to "see persons crossing that we've never seen before."[12]

On October 24, 2002, the FBI issued another major warning involving potential terrorist attacks against the U.S. transportation infrastructure; only this time it was the railroad system that was in the crosshairs. The warning read as follows:

> *Information from debriefings of al-Qa'ida detainees as of mid-October indicates that the group has considered directly targeting U.S. passenger trains, possibly using operatives who have a Western appearance. This threat communication followed one issued on October 9, by the FBI, the Office of Homeland Security and other federal agencies, warning of heightened operational intensity on the part of al-Qa'ida and loosely affiliated terrorist organizations.*

---

[11] Author present at public presentation in August 2002.

[12] Ibid.

Additional information suggests operatives may try a variety of other attack strategies, such as destroying key rail bridges and sections of track to cause derailments or targeting hazardous material containers. Recently captured al-Qa'ida photographs of U.S. railroad engines, cars, and crossings heighten the intelligence community's concern of this threat.

The attack of the French oil tanker off the coast of Yemen and additional information from al-Qa'ida detainees suggest plans exist to continue attacks against the global petroleum sector. According to this information, al-Qa'ida plans to weaken the petroleum industry by conducting additional sea based attacks against large oil tankers and that such attacks may be a part of more extensive operations against port facilities and other energy-related targets including oil facilities and nuclear power plants.[13]

The warning was the result of a series of interrogations of al-Qaeda prisoners held at the U.S. military base at Guantanamo Bay, Cuba. Of particular concern to security experts at that time was the security profile of commercial passenger trains, such as Amtrak. Shortly after the warning was issued, Amtrak increased security patrols of its facilities.

At the time of this writing, however, Amtrak subjected passengers to a minimum level of security screening, usually involving nothing more than showing a picture ID to obtain a boarding pass. In addition, passengers were allowed to board Amtrak trains with any number of carry-on bags, none of which were ever searched or screened electronically. I raised these issues to security experts in October 2002 at a conference on homeland security technologies sponsored by the Council of Security & Strategic Technology Organizations. One conference attendee called Amtrak "a disaster waiting to happen."[14]

When I raised the issue to Amtrak's security director, his answer was simple: Amtrak had taken all of the necessary and prudent security precautions in the aftermath of September 11, but airport-like security screening was impossible throughout all of the railroad's 530 stations because

---

[13] "FBI Issues Threat Communication on Al-Qaeda Targeting the U.S. Railway Sector," FBI Press Release, October 24, 2002.

[14] See Dan Verton, "FBI Warns of Possible Rail Terror Attacks," *Computerworld*, October 25, 2002.

many of those stations are nothing more than small cement platforms in remote areas of the country.[15]

That explanation, however, could not shield Amtrak from stinging criticism by the Department of Transportation's Inspector General's Office. In written and oral testimony given before the U.S. Senate two months after the September 11, 2001, terrorist attacks, the DOT's IG faulted Amtrak's use of its government funding, saying security hasn't been a priority. "In recent years, Amtrak's investment strategy has been driven substantially by its need to improve its financial condition," said Mark Dayton, deputy assistant inspector general. "As a result, important projects, including ones that improve operational reliability or enhance security of equipment or infrastructure, have lost out in the past in favor of investments that can provide a quick and significant return on investment."[16]

To be fair, all Amtrak ticket reservations are compared against the FBI's terrorist watch list. But America's real protection from an attack against passenger rail cars most likely comes from the nose of a trusty canine—man's best friend. That's right. Random checks are conducted on many checked bags by bomb-sniffing dogs. However, the quickest and easiest way to spread an infectious disease, such as smallpox, throughout major metropolitan areas of the country may very well be to buy a train ticket and ride the rails. And it's more than doubtful that dogs can smell the presence of smallpox.

-.-. -.-- -... . .-. - . .-. .-. --- .-.

Security in America against the insidious threat posed by weapons of mass destruction is improving, but at a painstakingly slow pace and on a small scale.

However, the lack of financial resources at the state and local levels means that without federal assistance, the first line of defense against a chemical, biological, or nuclear terrorist attack will remain unprepared.

---

15 Ibid.
16 Ibid.

10
Patriot Games:
Security, Terror, Liberty

They that can give up essential liberty to obtain a little temporary safety deserve neither liberty nor safety.

—Benjamin Franklin

We must also reject the false choice of liberty versus security. We can and must have both.

—Tom Ridge
Director, Office of Homeland Security
The White House

The phrase "Freedom Is Not Free" is etched into a granite wall at the Korean War Veterans Memorial in Washington, D.C. Spoken by the veterans of the so-called "Forgotten War," they are words that sometimes confuse younger generations of Americans who have enjoyed decades of unparalleled security and freedom. But make no mistake about it. The price of America's freedom, and the freedom of an untold number of other nations around the world, is measured in lives—the lives of average people with the prescience to see the greater future cost of inaction. It is a lesson that America learned long before Osama bin Laden was even a twinkle in his mother's eye.

But in the same fashion that America has come to learn that freedom is not free, America is also waking up to the reality that security is not free. Al-Qaeda's infiltration of American society and its attempt to pervert America's way of life has led to an understandable desire to use whatever technological advantage that America has against the enemy within. The result has been a frenzied attempt to deploy an unprecedented number of intelligence gathering and surveillance technologies within the borders of the U.S. and the granting of additional powers of investigation to federal agencies that already enjoyed ample legal authority to apprehend known or suspected terrorists. And while nobody is arguing against the need to eliminate terrorism's foothold in America and elsewhere, many people are beginning to ask one very legitimate question: at what price to liberty and privacy?

Former Virginia Governor James S. Gilmore III is one such American who has been asking that question a lot lately. Gilmore, the chairman of the Congressionally chartered Advisory Panel to Assess Domestic Response Capabilities for Terrorism Involving Weapons of Mass Destruction, argued unsuccessfully in December 2002 against his own commission's recommendation to the president and the Congress to establish an independent all-source intelligence collection and fusion center focused on threats inside the United States. The new agency would be separate from all of the existing intelligence and law-enforcement agencies, such as the CIA and the FBI, but would be managed by a coordinating committee of senior federal agency heads, including the U.S. Attorney General. Its focus would be domestic intelligence.

"This has been a matter of serious, serious debate within this commission for a long time," said Gilmore during a press conference in which I asked him to explain why Americans should feel comfortable taking counterterrorism intelligence collection responsibilities away from the FBI—the only federal law-enforcement agency that conducts such activity within the U.S. under specific legal and constitutional guidelines. "But the belief of the commission is that the counterterrorism function must be done, and there is the sense that the FBI is primarily a law-enforcement organization and its agents are there to make cases looking backward and building cases for a courtroom, not looking forward toward the idea of intelligence prevention," said Gilmore.[1]

But then Gilmore unleashed the shocker. When asked to confirm if he had been one of the primary members of the commission to express concern that such an agency could be seen as a "secret police," Gilmore acknowledged that he had been. "Domestic intelligence gathering makes me nervous," said Gilmore. "If you take an organization that has an arrest function and then you place with it a stepped-up intelligence gathering organization against the terrorists and you put these things together, there's the risk that the arrest capacity together with the intelligence operation does begin to create more of a feeling of a secret police. We don't want to create anything like that.

"We believe that this new agency must adhere to the [Foreign Intelligence Surveillance Act (FISA)] and all the other restrictions that have been placed upon intelligence organizations so that we can make sure that we are focusing on enemies here in the country and not upon regular Americans," added Gilmore.

Passed in 1978, FISA established a separate, secret legal regime to regulate the government's collection of foreign intelligence in the U.S. FISA was initially limited to electronic eavesdropping and wiretapping. But in 1994, it was amended to permit covert physical entries in connection with security investigations. It was amended again in 1998 to permit pen register or trap-and-trace orders, surveillance devices that capture the phone numbers dialed on outgoing and incoming telephone calls, respectively. The government obtains legal warrants to conduct such activity through a secret court, known as the Foreign Intelligence Surveillance Court. The law simply stipulates that efforts be made to "minimize" the collection of information on U.S. persons.

"I for one would rather build upon the existing structures of the [FBI], but the commission doesn't feel that way," said Gilmore, adding that he feels comfortable with the protections put in place by the Commission, such as the FISA requirements and the separation of arrest powers. "Protecting this democracy and the individual freedoms of the American people is para-

---

[1]   Press conference and author interview at National Press Club, December 16, 2002.

mount to achieving ultimate victory in this conflict. It's the whole ball game."

But as of this writing, the score of that game is anybody's guess.

-.-. -.-- -... . .-. - . .-. .-. --- .-.

Americans guard their civil liberties like an over-protective father guards his young daughter's virginity—over his dead body. But the modern world of high-tech espionage and counterterrorism has made it harder and harder for Americans to feel confident in their ability to live private lives. The truth of the matter is that Americans now live two lives simultaneously—one in the physical world and one in the digital world. And it is in the places where these worlds meet that the government, in a legitimate effort to carry out its responsibilities as protector of Americans, has run into trouble.

In summer 1999, the winds of a Cold War–era global electronic spy network established through a partnership between the intelligence agencies in the U.S., the U.K., Canada, Australia, and New Zealand began to send chills down the spines of members of Congress. The super-secret network, code-named Echelon, was believed by many to consist of a worldwide network of clandestine listening posts capable of intercepting electronic communications such as e-mail, telephone conversations, faxes, satellite transmissions, microwave links, and fiber-optic communications traffic. It had already created quite a stir in Europe, where the European Union had gone out of its way to hire an investigative journalist to document instances in which the U.S. used the network to target European companies that were competing with American firms for global contracts. The European contention was that America's global electronic espionage apparatus was helping U.S. companies outbid European companies for large commercial contracts. The United States argued that it was simply uncovering corruption, cheating, and stealing on behalf of European intelligence agencies and firms that in turn had created an uneven playing field for U.S. companies that were trying to do business overseas.

Of course, there was ample evidence within the U.S. intelligence community to prove that France and other countries had employed their own versions of the same system to help European companies cheat American firms out of business. The electronic espionage game was a two-way street. And when I finally convinced a former senior member of the U.S. National Security Agency to talk about the European claims regarding Echelon, the answer was straightforward: "I'm going to take you to the edge of the cliff, but I'm not going over," the official said. "Those bastards do the same thing."[2]

But while officials had shifted the focus of the Echelon network somewhat away from economic intelligence collection and toward the tracking of international criminal and terrorist groups, civil liberties advocates soon began accusing the NSA of spying on American citizens under the banner of national security.

On December 3, 1999, the Electronic Privacy Information Center (EPIC), a Washington, D.C.–based privacy watchdog group, filed a lawsuit in federal court that aimed to force the NSA to hand over documents that EPIC believed contained evidence of domestic spying by the agency. The lawsuit centered on EPIC's belief that the NSA was intercepting the Internet communications of law-abiding U.S. citizens during the course of its efforts to intercept the communications of terrorist groups—something that any communications intelligence expert will tell you is unavoidable. The volume of communications around the world had grown to such a level that it was now impossible to search for instances of spoken terrorist code words without coming across the legitimate communications of law-abiding citizens in the U.S. and abroad.

Within two months of the EPIC lawsuit controversy, the NSA made an attempt to calm the fears of many in Congress who felt that the agency had not been as forthcoming as it could have been with details about the legal guidelines that were in place to prevent both inadvertent and intentional domestic electronic eavesdropping. Adding fuel to the fire was a February 17 speech given at the Kennedy Political Union of American University by NSA director Air Force Lieutenant General Michael Hayden, during which he acknowledged that "it is inevitable that NSA will inadvertently acquire information about U.S. citizens in the course of its foreign intelligence

---

[2] Author interview with former senior official of the NSA.

collection activities."[3]

On February 24, Kenneth Heath, chief of staff for NSA's Legislative Affairs Office, sent a letter to Congress along with a list of frequently asked questions concerning allegations that the agency was tuning in on private citizens' communications around the world and rifling through peoples' electronic lives and secrets with the help of the world's largest collection of mainframe computers at its Fort Meade, Maryland, headquarters.

In the letter, the NSA assured lawmakers that the agency's "activities are conducted in accordance with the highest constitutional, legal and ethical standards, and in compliance with statutes and regulations designed to protect the privacy rights of U.S. persons." But the NSA stopped short of confirming the existence of any ongoing intelligence gathering operations or system, such as Echelon.

The NSA's word wasn't good enough for many in Congress. Within four days of receiving NSA's assurances, Representative Bob Barr (R-Ga.) sent a letter to Hayden, outlining "problems" with the current laws and regulations cited by the agency. In his letter, Barr, a former CIA officer, argued that Hayden's assurances that the Fourth Amendment of the U.S. Constitution adequately protects citizens' privacy regardless of the technologies used in NSA's electronic surveillance operations "grossly oversimplifies the difficulty of protecting privacy in light of recent technological advances."[4]

Barr was arguing that U.S. laws designed to protect the privacy rights of ordinary Americans may not be capable of keeping pace with developments in the information technology market. New capabilities were being introduced every day, and with those new capabilities came ever more ways to find and retrieve information that people used to assume was private.

"As past NSA abuses have shown, privacy rights are better protected by relying on an evolving, explicit legal structure than by [relying] solely on the good faith of government employees wielding massive power and reciting generalities," Barr wrote.

---

[3] See Dan Verton, "NSA Moves to Defuse Echelon Controversy," *Federal Computer Week,* February 29, 2000.

[4] See Dan Verton, "NSA's Privacy Pledges Not Enough for Some in Congress," *Federal Computer Week,* March 1, 2000.

The past NSA abuses referred to by Barr include eavesdropping on anti-war protesters such as Jane Fonda and Dr. Benjamin Spock, and the recordings of conversations by American civil rights leaders such as Martin Luther King.

-.-. -.-- -... . .-. - . .-. .-. --- .-.

Since the September 11, 2001, terrorist attacks and America's realization that the people who are trying to kill us have lived in our country for years, the government has renewed its focus on creating, as Barr wrote in 1999, "an evolving, explicit legal structure" to enhance the flexibility of law-enforcement and intelligence agencies in their daily battle with terrorism. But that evolving legal structure has taken some interesting and, at times, disturbing turns.

One of the main concerns of many Americans, particularly civil liberties advocates, is the passage of the Uniting and Strengthening America by Providing Appropriate Tools Required to Intercept and Obstruct Terrorism Act of 2001, better known as the USA Patriot Act. Despite the complex title, the bottom line on the law is quite clear: it introduced a wide array of legislative changes that significantly increased the surveillance and investigative powers of law enforcement agencies. According to privacy watchdog groups, however, the one thing the Act did not provide is a system of checks and balances that have traditionally safeguarded civil liberties in the face of such legislation.

The USA Patriot Act provided the FBI and other arms of the Department of Justice the ability to obtain court orders for intercepting communications regarding suspected terrorist activities, whether they are related to planned attacks or to financing or supporting terrorist networks. The bill also dramatically expanded the FBI's wiretapping capabilities by allowing investigators to listen in on multiple telephones and cell phones used by a suspected terrorist. Prior to the passage of the law, the FBI was required to obtain a court order for every individual phone it wanted to tap, which caused significant problems for investigators who were trying to keep tabs on terrorists who rotated their communications routinely between multiple cell phones and an untold number of Internet accounts.

"Robert Kennedy's Justice Department, it is said, would arrest mobsters for 'spitting on the sidewalk' if it would help in the battle against organized crime," said Attorney General John Ashcroft in a speech on October 25, 2001, at the U.S. Mayor's Conference. "It has been and will be the policy of this Department of Justice to use the same aggressive arrest and detention tactics in the war on terror."

And by that, Ashcroft was referring to the USA Patriot Act and all available technologies. He called the passage of the law the beginning of "a new era" in America's War on Terrorism.

"Agents will be directed to take advantage of new, technologically neutral standards for intelligence gathering," said Ashcroft. "So-called 'roving' wire-taps, that allow taps of multiple phones a suspect may use, are being added as an important weapon in our war against terror. Investigators will be directed to pursue aggressively terrorists on the Internet. New authority in the legislation permits the use of devices that capture senders and receivers addresses associated with communications on the Internet.

"Law enforcement will begin immediately to seek search warrants to obtain unopened voice-mail stored on a computer—just as they traditionally have used search warrants to obtain unopened email. They will also begin to use new subpoena power to obtain payment information such as credit card or bank account numbers of suspected terrorists on the Internet."

When the USA Patriot Act was signed into law on October 26, 2001, privacy groups, such as the Washington, D.C.–based Electronic Privacy Information Center (EPIC), immediately criticized the Congress for succumbing to pressure by Ashcroft to pass the bill before the next major terrorist attack occurred. "The Attorney General warned that further terrorist acts were imminent, and that Congress could be to blame for such attacks if they failed to pass the bill immediately," according to EPIC's analysis of the law. The USA Patriot Act "was introduced with great haste and passed with little debate, and without a House, Senate, or conference report," argued EPIC.[5]

---

5   See the Electronic Privacy Information Center Web site on the USA Patriot Act, http://www.epic.org/privacy/terrorism/usapatriot/.

On May 30, 2002, Ashcroft again added to the FBI's electronic surveillance capabilities when he issued new regulations allowing FBI agents to surf the Internet for clues relating to terrorist plots. Prior to the new regulations being introduced, agents were restricted from surfing the Web in an official capacity unless it was directly related to an ongoing investigation. The new regulations did not require Congressional approval. A representative of the American Civil Liberties Union in Washington, D.C., characterized the spate of new laws and regulations granting the government expanded surveillance authority an exercise in "awarding failure"—a clear reference to the government's failure to detect and prevent the September 11, 2001, terrorist attacks.

-.-. -.-- -... . .-. - . .-. .-. --- .-.

In many ways, starting a debate in 2003 about the right to privacy in America may be more like conducting a post-mortem than holding a debate. Our electronic society, powered as it is by the incessant appetite of big business to know and understand our buying habits and our likes and dislikes, has long ago shattered the right of many people to simply be left alone. If you've made an electronic purchase of any sort in the last decade, you now exist digitally in a multitude of places around the globe. Your personal information is a much sought-after commodity in the world of electronic commerce and unabashed product marketing.

But now the government wants to search through that data too in an effort to uncover possible terrorist financing or activity in support of an impending attack. Through a Pentagon program started in January 2002 called Total Information Awareness (TIA), the government wants to develop the ability to conduct antiterrorism data mining operations to uncover suspicious activities and pattern analysis within the mountains of electronic data that is being collected by credit card companies, rental car companies, and other legal commercial entities in the U.S.

But the program has not escaped the scrutiny of Congress or America's outspoken privacy groups. In a letter sent to Attorney General John Ashcroft on January 10, 2003, Senator Patrick Leahy (D-Vt.), chairman of the Senate Judiciary Committee, requested that the Department of Justice explain the extent to which data mining tools are being used to fight the War on Terrorism at home. Specifically, Leahy expressed concern about the mining of commercial transaction data as part of the Pentagon's TIA program.

"These concerns include the specter of excessive government surveillance that may intrude on important privacy interests and chill the exercise of First Amendment–protected speech and associated rights," wrote Leahy in the letter, which was also signed by Senators Russell Feingold (D-Wis.) and Maria Cantwell (D-Wash.). "TIA is intended, according to Department of Defense officials, to generate tools for monitoring the daily personal transactions by Americans and others, including tracking the use of passports, driver's licenses, credit cards, airline tickets, and rental cars," the letter stated.[6]

The implications of the government rifling through the commercial transactions of ordinary Americans are astounding. In fact, Senators Leahy, Feingold, and Cantwell put it best when they wrote in their letter to Ashcroft that the biggest threat to a commercial entity that makes a mistake in sifting through customer data is investing in a misdirected marketing campaign. A mistake by the FBI in mining private citizen data, on the other hand, could result in false imprisonment and ruined reputations.[7]

In an attempt to clarify the overall intent of the TIA program, Edward C. "Pete" Aldridge, the undersecretary of defense for acquisition, logistics, and technology, told reporters on November 20, 2002, "It is absurd to think that DARPA is somehow trying to become another police agency." (Aldridge was referring to the Defense Advanced Research Projects Agency.) "DARPA's purpose is to demonstrate the feasibility of this technology. If it proves useful, TIA will then be turned over to the intelligence, counterintelligence, and law enforcement communities as a tool to help them in their battle against domestic terrorism," he said.

A reporter was quick to ask Aldridge the tough question. "How is this not domestic spying?"

---

[6] Letter Dated January 10, 2003, United States Senate Committee on the Judiciary. Author copy.

[7] Ibid.

"Once that technology is transported over to the law enforcement agency, they will use the same process they do today; they protect the individual's identity," said Aldridge. "We'll have to operate under the same legal conditions as we do today that protects individuals' privacy when this is operated by the law enforcement agency."

The Pentagon press corps also quickly turned its attention to former Navy Admiral John Poindexter, the Department's choice to lead the new TIA development program. Poindexter, who had served as President Ronald Reagan's national security advisor, was convicted on the felony charge of lying to the Congress during the investigation into the Iran-Contra scandal. Although his conviction was later overturned on appeal, his role in the scandal has raised serious questions about whether or not he is the type of person that should be in charge of such a program. According to Aldridge, Poindexter's role is limited to managing the development of the technologies and he was selected to lead it because it was his idea and "he has a passion for" the project.

On January 14, a coalition of nine separate civil liberties groups called upon Congress to put a stop to the Pentagon's TIA program. "TIA would put the details of Americans' daily lives under the scrutiny of government agents, opening the door to a massive domestic surveillance system," wrote the coalition. "TIA will collect and mine vast amounts of information on the American public, including telephone records, bank records, medical records, and educational and travel data. TIA would expand domestic intelligence activities to include the analysis of innocent people's personal information—credit card transactions, hotel reservations, or even prescription receipts."[8]

---

[8]   Letter dated January 14, 2003. Letter sent to House and Senate Committees on Armed Services, Appropriations, Government Reform and Affairs, and the Judiciary. Letter signed by representatives of the American Civil Liberties Union, the American Conservative Union, the Americans for Tax Reform, the Center for Democracy and Technology, the Center for National Security Studies, the Eagle Forum, the Electronic Frontier Foundation, the Electronic Privacy Information Center, and the Free Congress Foundation.

As of this writing, the federal government has invested approximately $128 million in TIA and included a request for an additional $10 million as part of the fiscal 2003 Defense appropriations bill.

-.-.   -.--   -...   .   .-.   -   .   .-.   .-.   ---   .-.

In addition to the bevy of new surveillance technologies, the War on Terrorism has also unleashed a virtual witch-hunt in cyberspace to uncover the sources of terrorism's illicit funding. Known as Operation GreenQuest, a joint effort between the FBI and the U.S. Customs Service, the global crackdown on terrorism financing has on balance been relatively successful. But the operation has at times employed a scorched-earth strategy that has left many innocent casualties in its wake. One of those casualties was Oussama Ziade, who, in addition to sharing the same first name with the world's most wanted terrorist, is the CEO of a legitimate software company that was brought to its knees by Operation GreenQuest.

The story starts more than a year before federal agents showed up at Ptech's door. On October 17, 2001, Oussama Ziade called an emergency meeting of all his top managers, including his legal counsel, to discuss a CNN report that had aired the previous evening. The story alleged that Yassin al-Qadi, a wealthy Saudi Arabian businessman, had been placed on a U.S. terrorism watch list and that all of his financial assets had been frozen as part of the Bush administration's multipronged effort to strike back at terrorism's bank rolls. But while al-Qadi wasn't a close friend or associate of Ziade, he was one of Ptech's initial "angel" investors who had helped Ziade start the company in 1994. Al-Qadi was a partial owner of an Islamic financial agency called B.M.I. Leasing, Inc., of Secaucus, New Jersey, and a backer of Sarmany Ltd., registered in the Isle of Man. B.M.I. leased Ziade equipment for his new firm, and Sarmany helped with $5 million of the initial $20 million raised by the young start-up. Another company al-Qadi owns, Qadi International, Inc., lists the same address as B.M.I. in its incorporation papers.

During several hours of interviews that I conducted with Ziade, the 38-year-old naturalized American of Lebanese descent remained steadfast in his assertion that his concern about his company's former relationship with al-Qadi was due to his desire to "be a responsible corporate citizen" of a country he claims as his own.

Ziade immediately asked his advisors what the company should do. Al-Qadi was not an officer of the company or a shareholder of record; therefore, there were no particular assets that Ptech was required under the law to freeze. Al-Qadi had sold his interest in Ptech in 1999. "We were sure that all company activities were aboveboard, and we came to the conclusion with the legal counsel that there was no action required," recalled Ziade.

But what Ziade and his managers didn't know was that somebody else had taken matters into his own hands. Jeff Goins, Ptech's former director of government sales, who had violated a noncompete agreement he had signed with Ptech when he left the company to start his own business, was not satisfied with the management's handling of the al-Qadi situation, said Ziade.[9] Goins, according to multiple press reports in which he is quoted, then contacted the FBI about his concerns regarding Ptech's hidden ownership. Goins told New York's Newsday newspaper that he informed the FBI via e-mail that he was concerned "that Boston could be a possible hub for illegal activity regarding this [September 11] event."[10] Goins also identified Yaqub Mirza as a director of Ptech. In March 2002, FBI agents had raided several charities and businesses linked to Mirza through his CEO status of the Sterling Management Group, Inc. Goins also told the Newsday reporters that Ziade had confided to him that Mirza was named to the firm's three-man board by al Qadi. Regardless of Goins' accusations, papers filed in Virginia and obtained by The Investigative Project, an antiterrorism think tank, indicate Sterling controlled a company called "Ptech Fund LLC."

---

[9]   Author interviews. Goins' violation of the noncompete agreement is a matter of public record. Ptech took him to court and won. Surprisingly, it was Goins who eventually sold Ptech software to officials at the White House, shortly before he contacted the FBI.

[10] See Knut Royce, Tom Brune, and Lou Dolinar, "Mass. Tech Company Raided for Alleged Terror Links," Newsday, December 6, 2002.

The investigation into Ptech and its association with al-Qadi and Mirza moved forward slowly through summer 2002 and into November. Federal investigators presented their concerns to officials at the National Security Council in the White House. The NSC then directed a governmentwide scrub of computers where the Ptech enterprise architecture planning software had been purchased and deployed. And it had been deployed throughout some of the government's most sensitive agencies. In addition to various Fortune 1,000 companies, Ptech had been successful in selling its software to the FBI, the White House, the Defense Department, NASA, and the Department of Energy's Rocky Flats facility, which is focused on cleanup and disposal of excess plutonium used in the Defense Department's nuclear weapons program.

A senior Bush administration official familiar with the investigation said "a body of evidence" about the company's possible links to al-Qaeda was brought to the attention of the National Security Council and triggered a governmentwide investigation into where Ptech software may have been installed and, more importantly, whether malicious code was involved. "The good news is we couldn't find anything," the official said, referring to the prospect of malicious software that could have been used for espionage purposes. "The bad news is that something might still be there. We couldn't prove a negative."

Soon, former executives began contacting Ziade to tell him that FBI agents had been asking questions about the company and if they knew of any illegal activities going on related to the company's finances. So Ziade and his lawyer, David Dryer, called the FBI and offered their assistance in whatever matters they were looking into.

"I called the FBI last August [and again in December] with Mr. Ziade in my office," said Dryer. "I never got a call back."

Customs and FBI agents did finally get back to Ziade. But it wasn't until close to midnight on December 5, 2002. That's when they asked Ziade for permission to search Ptech's offices and promised not to make a scene that the media could latch on to. Ziade was more than happy to assist.

Ziade and his lawyer met with agents for several hours prior to the search beginning. It was then that he described for the agents his knowledge of and relationship with al-Qadi. "I don't know him well," Ziade said. "I met him a few times and talked to him a few times on the telephone. He never talked to me about violence. Instead, he talked very highly of his relationship with [former President] Jimmy Carter and [Vice President] Dick Cheney."

Ziade said he then told investigators that al-Qadi had been a member of the board of directors of Sarmany Ltd., which had invested in Ptech when it was first starting in 1994. Yaqub Mirza, Ziade told the federal agents, was a former member of Ptech's board of directors who resigned from the company in March 2002 after the FBI raided several Muslim charities and businesses that had once belonged to the Saar Foundation, a tight-knit group of more than 100 Muslim groups based in and around Virginia that was dissolved in December 2000. Although Saar was originally founded by Suleiman Abdul Al-Aziz al-Rajhi, a well-connected Saudi, Mirza was responsible for starting the foundation in northern Virginia. The Saar Foundation was also connected to al-Taqwa, a shell company formerly based in Switzerland. Eventually shifting its operations to the United States, Al-Taqwa was shut down after September 11, 2001, and its assets frozen by U.S. presidential order. When it was dissolved, however, many of these same businesses, organizations, and charities would go on to become members of Safa Trust, also run by Mirza.

Ptech and Ziade may have been innocent, but the potential linkages to people of interest to government counterterrorist experts grew with every word Ziade spoke. And worst of all, they were links to individuals that government terrorism experts from the CIA say are key players in a new form of money laundering that seeks to use unwitting, legitimate businesses and layered investment funds to hide the transfer of funds to terrorist groups abroad.

U.S. counterterrorism officials also believe that al-Qadi is a major source of illicit funding for Osama bin Laden and his al-Qaeda terror network, primarily through an obscure charity he once controlled and operated called the Muwafaq Fund. He is also believed to have provided a loan for real estate in Chicago that was used to funnel hundreds of thousands of dollars to Hamas, the Palestinian terrorist group. Al-Qadi instructed that the loan be repaid to Qadi International, care of B.M.I., the company that introduced Ptech to Sarmany, and "Attn: Gamel Ahmed." Ahmed was Ptech's comptroller for about one and a half years in the mid

1990s. However, a CIA officer familiar with the transaction characterized it as a new form of money laundering, in which no official paperwork was used and al-Qadi never requested that the loan be repaid.[11]

Ptech also employed Muhamed Mubayyid, who served as the treasurer of Care International, a Massachusetts-based charity investigated for possible financial ties to terrorists. What raised investigators' suspicions about Mubayyid was a $360 donation to the Alkifah Refugees Center in Brooklyn, New York, according to a receipt obtained by The Investigative Project. The center was named by federal prosecutors as the birthplace of the conspiracy to bomb the World Trade Center in 1993. And while there is no evidence that the money was ever used for anything other than charity, a note on the donation's receipt reads: "Make checks payable to Dr. Abdullah Azam." Azam was the founder of the al-Qaeda organization and a mentor of Osama bin Laden.

As of this writing, Ptech still employs Mubayyid. However, Ziade said he remains astounded at the assertion that a donation made in 1988—the height of the U.S. campaign to support the Mujahideen and Osama bin Laden in Afghanistan against the invading Soviet Union—would be looked upon with suspicion more than a decade later.

That investigators from Operation GreenQuest turned their attention to Ptech should be of no surprise. The firm's relationship with the likes of al-Qadi and Mirza, regardless of how innocent or remote, should have raised red flags to investigators. For example, the Operation Green Quest list of indicators that money laundering may be taking place includes the following:

Corporate Layering   Transfers between bank accounts of related organizations or charities for no apparent purpose

Multiple Accounts   Used to collect funds that are then transferred to the same foreign beneficiaries

Overlapping Corporate Officers   Includes bank signatories or other identifiable similarities associated with addresses, references, and financial activities

---

[11] Author interviews with former CIA and State Department intelligence officials.

No Logical Economic Purpose Associated with Financial Transactions (i.e., no link between activity of lender and other parties involved in transaction)

Many, if not all, of these indicators and warnings were present when authorities began to look into the investors behind Ptech. However, in America people are innocent until proven guilty. And while Ptech executives may have made a series of fatal mistakes in terms of their selection of financial backers, ignorance has never been a crime in America. Regardless, Oussama Ziade and his company were about to get a taste of what it's like to live in a prison.

-.-. -.-- -... . .-. - . .-. .-. --- .-.

Investigators searched Ptech's offices all night until the wee hours of the morning. Ziade assisted them whenever they requested it. He didn't mind. After all, they assured him that neither Ptech nor its employees were under investigation. They were there, the investigators said, looking into the activities of other individuals. But the assurances of the federal investigators would not be enough. Ptech was about to be branded a traitor.

At 7 o'clock in the morning on December 6, the parking lot filled up with news media vans, video equipment, and reporters who were foaming at the mouth for information that al-Qaeda had infiltrated one of Quincy, Massachusetts' fastest growing technology companies. They videotaped agents loading cars with boxes of so-called "evidence." Some of the less professional media outlets even reported incorrectly that employees had been arrested and hauled away.

In Chicago, one of Ptech's regional sales executives was approached by a gaggle of reporters at his home, which also doubled as his Ptech office. Unaware of what was taking place at Ptech headquarters, the executive was shocked at the line of questioning. Without warning, the executive's home was surrounded by reporters and staked out by media vans filled with video equipment. His neighbors began to look at him, his wife, and young baby differently. And why would they not? The local media had already branded his home as the headquarters for the Chicago branch of al-Qaeda.

The executive called Ziade and told him what was happening. Ziade explained the search. But then word came from the other end of the telephone that the executive was scared for the safety of his family. Pictures of his home had been broadcast on television, and people were talking about links to terrorism. He said he was loading his wife and baby into the car to leave, but there was nowhere to go. Ziade was helpless to do anything.

Ziade's life also soon became a prison. "I could not sleep in my house for three days," he said. "It was ambushed by the media. And I couldn't send my kids to school for a week."

It was a surreal experience for somebody who considered himself a loyal American who loved the opportunity and freedom provided by his adopted country. "My mother's family came here in the 1950s and died here, and I have two uncles that came here and died here. We love the country, the culture, and the liberty. This is my country," he said.

Former employees of the company who I interviewed, many of whom happened to be Jewish, were stunned by what was happening. They painted a picture of a company that was open and accepting of different cultures and traditions. They described Ziade as a man who encouraged his employees to share their cultures with each other. Non-Muslims were invited to share in the breaking of the fast during Ramadan and were also asked by Ziade to share and instruct the other employees on the traditions of their own holidays and religious observances. It was not a hotbed of radical Islamic beliefs.

By the time the White House had issued public statements clearing Ptech's software of suspicions that it might have contained hidden malicious code that could be used by terrorists to disrupt government services, the damage had already been done. The young company that had managed to survive the economic downturn after September 11, 2001, and that had won nearly every competitive contract bid it took part in was now a shell of its former self. The slump in the economy had forced Ziade to reduce his staff from more than 65 to 35. But the terrorist financing scandal had reduced the company to ten employees, including Ziade and his cofounder.

Business came to a halt. The company lost all of its revenue for the months of December 2002 and January 2003. New business that the firm had been banking on, including a $7 million deal, was put on hold. The legal departments at Ptech's customers and many of its strategic business partners, such as IBM, issued gag orders that prohibited employees from talking about the investigation or providing words of support.

According to Ptech's lawyer, the company had been branded as part of the Fifth Column. If you were a Muslim today in America, you were automatically part of a conspiracy to blow up Americans, he said. And at a time when America was preparing to go to war with Iraq, it was important to have a bogeyman in your backyard, the lawyer charged. America had found its bogeyman in Quincy, Massachusetts.

As of this writing, no charges have been filed against Ptech or any of its employees or executives. But the damage has been done. Ziade says Ptech may not survive in its current form, if it survives at all. And most troubling of all, said Ziade, is the fact that many of the same Saudi investors who he went to for venture capital in 1994 have also invested millions of dollars in a multitude of other U.S.-based technology firms.[12]

"How far are we going to go with making links between people?" asked Ziade. "And how are we supposed to know before the fact?" he added, referring to the investigation into his company for ties to people who were not on any government watch list at the time Ptech approached them before September 11.

"I had a dream that I was going to be a big scientist, a big innovator," said Ziade. "At Harvard, I worked on a project that used a high-energy accelerator to cure tumors in the eyes and brain using proton beams. We treated 250 patients. I was very interested in high-energy physics. But Einstein took it all, and there was nothing left for the rest of us," he said, laughing, during the end of my two-hour interview with him. "So I went into computers. But now, what can I do?"

---

[12] See Dan Verton, "Funding Scrutiny May Spread," Computerworld, January 27, 2003, p. 1.

11

The War on Terror: Mobilizing for the Future

The day of the storm is not the time for thatching.

—*Irish Proverb*

We've learned that vast oceans no longer protect us from the dangers of a new era. This government has a responsibility to confront the threat of terror wherever it is found. And that is why we're taking the battle to America's enemies ...

—*President George W. Bush*
Swearing-in ceremony for Tom Ridge as the
nation's first Secretary of Homeland
Security, January 24, 2003

Our story ends as it began, with many unanswered questions, fear and uncertainty, and the hope that the current generation of Americans will have the wisdom to recognize the greater threat of inaction. It also ends with a plan, a national plan for the defense of cyberspace, our nation's most critical infrastructures, and our way of life.

On February 14, 2003, one week after the president had ordered the national terrorism threat level be raised from code yellow (elevated risk) to code orange (high risk), Secretary of Homeland Security Tom Ridge announced the publication of two major planning documents that he said would form the basis of the future direction of the new department. I attended the nationally televised ceremony in Washington, D.C., where Ridge and his top cybersecurity advisors explained the importance of two national strategies contained in the documents.

The "National Strategy to Secure Cyberspace" and the "National Strategy for The Physical Protection of Critical Infrastructures and Key Assets" will "help guide governments and businesses" in their efforts to defend the homeland from terrorism, Ridge said. Even if the strategies lack teeth in terms of their willingness to force the private sector companies that own and operate the bulk of the nation's most critical infrastructures and cyber-systems to comply with a minimum set of security precautions, they bring valuable awareness to the issues, according to Ridge. "Al-Qaeda will attack when they deem themselves ready to move," said Ridge. "We know that enhanced security and broader awareness is a deterrent."

In recognizing the importance of computers and computer networks to the everyday functioning of our national economy and defense infrastructure, these two strategies established three important goals:

Prevent cyber-attacks against America's critical infrastructures

Reduce national vulnerability to cyber-attacks

Minimize damage and recovery time from cyber-attacks that do occur

One of the first priorities of the administration's cyber-defense strategy is to establish a national cyberspace security response system that will enable the government to work with the private sector on analysis, warning, incident management, and recovery efforts stemming from a coordinated cyber-attack against the U.S. Although the private sector currently operates various information sharing and analysis centers (ISAC) specifically for this purpose, the National Strategy to Secure Cyberspace clearly recognizes the need for a single point of contact on cyber-defense issues in the new department:

> *By 2003, our economy and national security became fully dependent upon information technology and the information infrastructure. A network of networks directly supports the operation of all sectors of our economy—energy (electric power, oil and gas), transportation (rail,*

air, merchant marine), finance and banking, information and telecommunications, public health, emergency services, water, chemical, defense industrial base, food, agriculture, and postal and shipping.

But the strategy also made clear what Howard Schmidt, the acting chairman of the President's Critical Infrastructure Protection Board at the time of the strategy's release, called the "inextricable connection between physical and cyber" infrastructures. "The reach of these computer networks exceeds the bounds of cyberspace," the strategy acknowledges. "They also control physical objects, such as electrical transformers, trains, pipeline pumps, chemical vats, and radars."

But that was not where the potential problems ended. To the contrary, that was merely where the problems began. The real issue was in being able to detect and prevent attacks in cyberspace that could have an impact in the physical world of critical infrastructure. "There is no synoptic or holistic view of cyberspace," the strategy states. "Therefore, there is no panoramic vantage point from which we can see attacks coming or spreading."

This is a critical aspect of the challenge facing the nation that many in the mainstream news media have yet to focus on. During the news conference with Secretary Ridge and Schmidt, Pete Williams, a correspondent for NBC's Nightly News with Tom Brokaw, asked for an explanation of exactly what the threat was stemming from the nation's reliance on computer networks. "What is the vulnerability in the cyber area?" Williams asked. "Is it just a matter of people not being able to use their ATMs for a few days, or is there any real vulnerability attached to the cyber security?"

That was a question that had been answered in the strategy document and by the fact that the president had put his name to it. Perhaps the most important accomplishment of the cybersecurity strategy was its ability to put the presidential seal of approval on the issues surrounding national cybersecurity. Cyberspace is the "nervous system" of the nation's critical infrastructures and institutions, the strategy states. It is the "control system of our country...composed of hundreds of thousands of interconnected computers, servers, routers, switches, and fiber optic cables that allow our critical infrastructures to work. Thus the healthy functioning of cyberspace is essential to our economy and our national security," according to the strategy.

Schmidt, however, answered Williams' question by outlining the much larger threat stemming from what the government calls a "swarming attack" involving multiple attacks, both physical and cyber, targeting multiple infrastructures simultaneously. "As the cyber environment, including the Internet component of it, has been built up we have had dependencies that have now changed dramatically from what it used to be," said Schmidt. "I think the bigger issue we've got to worry about is what we call the swarming attack, where we have a physical event that takes place, be it a natural disaster or an intentional criminal act, that occurs at the same time we have a degradation or an impact on our telecommunications services. That's where we have that interdependency we clearly worry about the most."

Schmidt also said issues such as common router infrastructures and telecommunications systems that serve various infrastructures are responsible for some of the nation's vulnerabilities to potentially debilitating cyber-attacks. The national strategy recommends that corporations "consider diversity in IT service providers as a way of mitigating risk."

It was clear from listening to the line of questioning from the mainstream news organizations that the administration's efforts to communicate the message that cyberspace does not exist outside of the realm of traditional national security was not getting across. In an effort to bring the discussion back on track and to try to galvanize that message for everybody present, I specifically asked Schmidt about how the nation's cyber-defense efforts were being integrated with the overall homeland security alert system. Surely, if cybersecurity was as critical to national security and homeland defense as the government was saying it was, then the overall homeland security alert system would have some applicability to the nation's cybersecurity posture as well.

Schmidt said that the department was considering a cybersecurity alert system that would work in conjunction with the overall Homeland Security Alert System. However, because the Defense Department also operates an Information Operations Condition (InfoCon) alert system, Schmidt said cybersecurity officials were trying to determine how a national cyber-alert system could be done "without causing confusion and undue concern" for agencies or entities that may not be affected by the InfoCon alert status.

-.-. -.-- -... . .-. - . .-. .-. --- .-.

At a Town Hall meeting in Washington, D.C., on December 17, 2002, then-Director of Homeland Security Tom Ridge tried to describe the nature of the homeland security challenge for those who still doubted the importance of cyber-systems to the nation's security.

"When people think of critical infrastructure, they have a tendency to think of bricks and mortar," said Ridge, referring to buildings, bridges, and dams. "But given the interdependency of just about every physical piece of critical infrastructure, energy, telecommunications, financial institutions and the like with the Internet and the cyber side of their business, we need to be focused on both, and will be," he said.

"We need to do a national overview of our infrastructure, map vulnerabilities, then set priorities, and then work with the private sector to reduce the vulnerabilities based on our priorities," Ridge continued. But "there is no conceivable way that this country can harden every target, do everything humanly and technologically possible with regard to every person that comes across the border, every piece of cargo that comes across the border, every potential vulnerability in the private sector or the public sector. We can't possibly do that. We're too open. We're too diverse. We're too large. It cannot be done. So the approach that we have to take—all of us—is manage the risk."

Ridge's comments bring us back to the central question we've been exploring: What is the risk that terrorist organizations such as al-Qaeda will turn to cyber-tactics to further their goals? To answer this question, we would be wise to look at the public comments of some of the terrorists who are trying to kill us. It is only through this type of analysis and discussion—a discussion that was not had prior to September 11, 2001—that we can prepare ourselves for the unseen threats of the future.

Ahmed Ressam, an Algerian member of al-Qaeda who was arrested in December 1999 while trying to cross the border from Canada to the U.S. carrying an explosive device, told U.S. authorities in July 2001 that he had been trained in Afghanistan in how to conduct sabotage operations against U.S. critical infrastructures.

"What types of targets were you trained on?" asked Assistant U.S. attorney Joseph Bianco.

"The enemies' installations, special installations and military installations, such as electric plants, gas plants, airports, railroads, [and] large corporations."

Within five months of the September 11, 2001 terrorist attacks, another senior al-Qaeda operative and a suspected senior strategy advisor to Osama bin Laden, Abu Ubeid al-Qurashi, wrote an article in the bi-weekly publication al-Ansar in which he describes "jihad on the Internet" as one of the "nightmares" that will soon come to America.

"Despite the fact that the jihadi movements prefer at this time to resort to conventional military operations, jihad on the Internet from the American perspective is a serious option for the movements in the future," wrote al-Qurashi. "Remote attacks on Internet networks are possible in complete anonymity" and the "needed equipment to conduct attacks on the Internet does not cost much" nor do they "require extraordinary skill," he wrote. "The targets that the mujahid movements would go after have been extracted from the American experience, ranging from the huge electrical networks that pass through nuclear power stations, to financial institutions to even the 911 network for emergency calls. The American economy is being day by day converted to basically an informational economy, and indicating such is the fact that in 2000, the profits that were extracted from information technology formed one-third of the economic growth in America and that is what makes the possibility of future, focused attacks have effects that should not be underestimated."[1]

On January 28, 2002, al-Qurashi wrote of "fourth generation wars," in which he compared the attacks of September 11, 2001 to the Japanese attack on Pearl Harbor in 1941 and the Soviet invasion of Czechoslovakia in 1968 among others. "In the pain [9/11] caused, [al-Qaeda] surpassed these surprise attacks, because it put every individual in American society on [constant] alert for every possibility, whether emotionally or practically," wrote al-Qurashi. "Preparing an entire society for terrorist attacks appears hard to achieve."[2]

---

1   Excerpted text of article cited in Ben Venzke and Aimee Ibrahim, *The al-Qaeda Threat: An Analytical Guide to al-Qaeda's Tactics & Targets* (Alexandria, Va.: Tempest Publishing LLC, 2003), p. 122.

2   Ibid. pp. 89-90.

Al-Qurashi's assessment should serve as a wake-up call to all Americans, especially to those who view the future with blinders on. Our terrorist enemies understand our weaknesses. It is the responsibility of those in positions of authority in both the government and the private sector not to ignore the increasing vulnerability in cyberspace, but to take the target away from our terrorist enemies. The day of the storm is not the time for thatching, according to an old Irish proverb. This is not about hype or sensationalism; it is about being prepared for an uncertain future and about heeding the warning signs that are available now. It is about understanding the essence of guerilla warfare and the fact that our terrorist enemies will attempt to strike out at our economy and our way of life using any and all available means. That is why the national strategy released by the Bush administration is critical to the future security of our nation and why future versions of that strategy must be willing to use the government's power of regulation if the private companies that own and operate our nation's most critical infrastructures fail to secure them properly. For now, we are banking on the commitment of companies that are in business to make money, not to defend America from its many enemies.

As for the high-tech future of al-Qaeda and America's many other terrorist enemies, Osama bin Laden and his top lieutenants have already delivered that message and have made their intentions very clear. "America should prepare itself. It should be ready," said Sulaiman Abu Ghaith, a Quwaiti-born member of al-Qaeda who served as the terrorist organization's official spokesman.[3] "Despite all of their precautions, we are coming to them where they never expected."

That may be wishful thinking, however. America is preparing. In his State of the Union address delivered at 9:01 EST on January 28, 2003, President George W. Bush pledged to deliver the capability that Representative Curt Weldon (R-Pa.) had argued could have prevented the terrorist attacks of September 11, 2001. "Tonight, I am instructing the leaders of the FBI, the CIA, the Homeland Security, and the Department of Defense to develop a Terrorist Threat Integration Center, to merge and analyze all threat information in a single location," said Bush. "Our government must have the

---

3   Ibid. p. 91. Interview conducted on June 23, 2002.

very best information possible, and we will use it to make sure the right people are in the right places to protect all our citizens."

That new center, known now by its government acronym, TTIC, is scheduled as of this writing to become operational on May 1, 2003. And while the TTIC will not, as former Virginia Governor James Gilmore advised against, have an intelligence collection capability that stands outside the bounds and protections of the U.S. Constitution, it will for the first time in American history enable the collection and analysis of all-source terrorism threat data in one location. A U.S. government officer who will report directly to the director of Central Intelligence will lead the TTIC. In addition, it will be staffed initially by 60 government analysts and will operate a 24-hour watch center located at CIA headquarters until a separate facility can be acquired.

"TTIC will be the principal gateway for policymaker requests for analysis of potential terrorist threats to U.S. interests and will maintain a database of known and suspected terrorists," according to a description offered by the White House. Total staffing will grow to nearly 300 analysts and support personnel, who will be co-located with personnel from the FBI Counterterrorism Division and the CIA's Counterterrorist Center.

In addition to the TTIC, the FBI is establishing an intelligence program to streamline the collection and dissemination of intelligence. But more importantly, the program will elevate the job of collecting and analyzing preventative intelligence to the same status the FBI has traditionally given to collecting evidence for criminal prosecutions. Likewise, a new Executive Assistant Director for Intelligence will have direct authority and responsibility for the FBI's national intelligence program, which will work out of intelligence units in all of the bureau's field offices. The FBI is also developing a new data management system to ensure that it shares all the FBI's terrorism-related information internally and with the CIA, the Department of Homeland Security, and other agencies.

The new focus on intelligence integration is critical to countering the ever-increasing threats from an ever more flexible and elusive terrorist enemy. On February 11, 2003, Navy Vice Admiral Lowell E. Jacoby, the director of the Defense Intelligence Agency, told the Senate Select Committee on Intelligence that not only does al-Qaeda remain an "adaptive, flexible...and agile" enemy that poses the greatest risk to the U.S. at home and abroad, but that the potential use of modern technologies by such terrorist organizations is a critical concern.

"While terrorism, Iraq and North Korea have our immediate attention, they are not the only challenges we face," said Jacoby. "The globalization of…technologies is according smaller countries, groups and individuals access to capabilities previously limited to major powers." It is increasingly difficult to predict what the technologically powered future holds, Jacoby said. "Surprises will result."

The terrorist threat to the U.S. homeland, said Jacoby, stems from the desire of terrorist organizations and rogue nation states to avoid a conventional military conflict with the U.S. in favor of a less direct avenue of attack that is designed to erode the U.S. economy and the nation's will to engage the rest of the world. "Al-Qaeda has spoken openly of targeting the U.S. economy as a way of undermining our global power and uses publicly available Internet web sites to reconnoiter American infrastructure, utilities and critical facilities," said Jacoby. "Our infrastructure is vulnerable to physical and computer attack. I expect this threat to grow significantly over the next several years."

Jacoby's warnings are particularly important given the impact that the U.S.-led War on Terrorism is having on global terrorist networks. The physical destruction of terrorist camps and cells by CIA paramilitary teams and the U.S. military will continue to push terrorist organizations such as al-Qaeda into a less hierarchical structure that will be glued together by information age technologies. Likewise, as fortress America continues to make it more difficult for our terrorist adversaries to cross our borders, information age attack tools will become part of the natural progression of terrorist tactics. That process has already started.

For example, when FBI agents arrested Sami Omar al-Hussayen in April 2003 on 11 counts of Visa fraud and false statements, they discovered photographs of the World Trade Center in New York City that were taken before and after the September 11, 2001 terrorist attacks stored on a computer that al-Hussayen used as part of his graduate studies in computer science at the University of Idaho. Al-Hussayen was also suspected of providing computer services to Web sites that support violence against the United States.

Likewise, his uncle, Saleh Abdel Rahman Al-Hussayen, wired him $100,000, much of which the student then transferred to the Michigan-based Islamic Assembly of North America (IANA), which, according to the FBI, advocated suicide bombing and the use of airplanes as terrorist weapons. But what is most interesting about the 34-year-old Saudi-born graduate student is that he focused his studies on computer security and intrusion techniques, according to the government's indictment.

The indications and the warnings that terrorism is evolving toward the greater use of cyber-tactics are there, if we choose to acknowledge them. The only question that remains to be answered is if America will act before it is too late. From now on, every day is September 10 in America.

A

Critical Infrastructures

Executive Order 13010, signed by President Clinton in 1996, defined eight critical infrastructures whose services are so vital that their incapacity or destruction would have a debilitating impact on the defense or economic security of the United States. All of these infrastructures rely on computers and computer networks, including the public Internet, for their continued operation and daily management. In addition, many infrastructures cannot function under conditions of prolonged outages or failures in other infrastructures.

Electrical Power
Consists of power generation stations, transmission and distribution networks that create and supply electricity to end users, including homes, government agencies, and businesses of all sizes. Depends on natural gas and other forms of energy to power generation facilities.

Gas and Oil Production, Storage, and Delivery
Consists of production and holding facilities for natural gas, crude and refined petroleum, petroleum-derived fuels, and the refining and processing facilities for these fuels. Depends on computers and telecommunications infrastructures for management and control.

Telecommunications

Consists of computing and telecommunications networks, software, processes, and people that support everything from the public switched telephone network to the Internet. Depends on energy infrastructure for uninterrupted operation and backup generators.

Banking and Finance

Consists of banks and credit unions, investment institutions, exchange boards, trading houses, and reserve systems, savings and loans, and associated operational organizations, government operations, and support activities. This industry is heavily dependent on the telecommunications sector, including the public Internet, for real-time transaction processing.

Water Supply Systems

Consists of water resources, reservoirs and holding facilities, aqueducts, and other transport systems. Also includes filtration, cleaning, and treatment systems, as well as pipeline and cooling systems, and other delivery mechanisms that provide for domestic and industrial applications, including systems for dealing with water runoff, wastewater, and fire fighting.

Transportation

Consists of the physical distribution system critical to supporting national security and economic stability. Transportation infrastructure refers to the national airspace system, airlines and aircraft, and airports; roads and highways, and trucking and personal vehicles; maritime commerce; ports and waterways; mass transit; and movement/delivery of natural gas, petroleum, and other hazardous materials; freight and long-haul passenger rail; and delivery services.

Emergency Services

Consists of medical, police, fire, and rescue systems and personnel that are called upon when an individual or community is responding to emergencies. These services are typically provided at the local level (county or metropolitan area).

Government Operations

Refers to all government capabilities at the federal, state, and local levels that are required to provide minimum essential services to the public.

B

PDD-63 at a Glance

Presidential Decision Directive 63 (PDD-63) remains one of the key building blocks in the federal government's effort to protect the nation's critical infrastructures from physical and cyber-terrorism attacks.

What follows is a white paper prepared in 1998 by the Clinton administration to explain what is meant by the term "critical infrastructure" and to outline how the government must work with the private sector to protect those infrastructures from mass disruptions.

White Paper
The Clinton Administration's Policy on
Critical Infrastructure Protection:
Presidential Decision Directive 63
May 1998

This White Paper explains key elements of the Clinton Administration's policy on critical infrastructure protection. It is intended for dissemination to all interested parties in both the private and public sectors. It will also be used in U.S. government professional education institutions, such as the National Defense University and the National Foreign Affairs Training Center, for coursework and exercises on interagency practices and procedures. Wide dissemination of this unclassified White Paper is encouraged by all agencies of the U.S. government.

I. A Growing Potential Vulnerability

The United States possesses both the world's strongest military and its largest national economy. Those two aspects of our power are mutually reinforcing and dependent. They are also increasingly reliant upon certain critical infrastructures and upon cyber-based information systems.

Critical infrastructures are those physical and cyber-based systems essential to the minimum operations of the economy and government. They include, but are not limited to, telecommunications, energy, banking and finance, transportation, water systems and emergency services, both governmental and private. Many of the nation's critical infrastructures have historically been physically and logically separate systems that had little interdependence. As a result of advances in information technology and the necessity of improved efficiency, however, these infrastructures have become increasingly automated and interlinked. These same advances have created new vulnerabilities to equipment failures, human error, weather and other natural causes, and physical and cyber attacks. Addressing these vulnerabilities will necessarily require flexible, evolutionary approaches that span both the public and private sectors, and protect both domestic and international security.

Because of our military strength, future enemies, whether nations, groups or individuals, may seek to harm us in non-traditional ways including attacks within the United States. Our economy is increasingly reliant upon interdependent and cyber-supported infrastructures and non-traditional attacks on our infrastructure and information systems may be capable of significantly harming both our military power and our economy.

II. President's Intent

It has long been the policy of the United States to assure the continuity and viability of critical infrastructures. President Clinton intends that the United States will take all necessary measures to swiftly eliminate any significant vulnerability to both physical and cyber attacks on our critical infrastructures, including especially our cyber systems.

III. A National Goal

No later than the year 2000, the United States shall have achieved an initial operating capability and no later than five years from the day the President signed Presidential Decision Directive 63 the United States shall have achieved and shall maintain the ability to protect our nation's critical infrastructures from intentional acts that would significantly diminish the abilities of:

The Federal Government to perform essential national security missions and to ensure the general public health and safety;

State and local governments to maintain order and to deliver minimum essential public services;

The private sector to ensure the orderly functioning of the economy and the delivery of essential telecommunications, energy, financial and transportation services.

Any interruptions or manipulations of these critical functions must be brief, infrequent, manageable, geographically isolated and minimally detrimental to the welfare of the United States.

IV. A Public-Private Partnership to Reduce Vulnerability

Since the targets of attacks on our critical infrastructure would likely include both facilities in the economy and those in the government, the elimination of our potential vulnerability requires a closely coordinated effort of both the public and the private sector[s]. To succeed, this partnership must be genuine, mutual and cooperative. In seeking to meet our national goal to eliminate the vulnerabilities of our critical infrastructure, therefore, the U.S. government should, to the extent feasible, seek to avoid outcomes that increase government regulation or expand unfunded government mandates to the private sector.

C

Remarks on Cyber-Terrorism

President George W. Bush

The United States and her allies will pursue a balance of world power that favors human freedom. This requires a new strategic framework that moves beyond Cold War doctrines and addresses the threats of a new century such as cyber-terrorism, weapons of mass destruction, missiles in the hands of those for whom terror and blackmail are a very way of life. These threats have the potential to destabilize freedom and progress, and we will not permit it.

—Remarks to the World Bank, July 17, 2001

There are new threats, new forms of terror: cyber-terrorism, fundamentalist extremists, extremism that certainly threatens us, threatens Israel, who is our strong ally and friend, threatens Russia. We've got to deal with it.

—Remarks during roundtable discussion with the foreign press, July 18, 2001

It's time to work together to address the new security threats that we all face. And those threats just aren't missiles, or weapons of mass destruction in the hands of untrustworthy countries. Cyber-terrorism is a threat, and we need to work on that together.

—Remarks at a joint press conference with
British Prime Minister Tony Blair, July 19, 2001

Second, the department will gather and focus all our efforts to face the challenge of cyber-terrorism, and the even worse danger of nuclear, chemical, and biological terrorism. This department will be charged with encouraging research on new technologies that can detect these threats in time to prevent an attack.

—On signing of legislation forming Homeland Security Department,
November 25, 2002

Former FBI National Infrastructure Protection Center Director Ronald L. Dick

With regard to cyber-manipulation, there are growing numbers of water supply systems that use Supervisory Control And Data Acquisition (SCADA) systems, the digital controls for pumps and treatment facilities. There are vulnerabilities in this system that could lead to water supply problems. In addition, more water system operators are being given access to the Internet via the SCADA systems['] local area network[s] (LAN[s]). As a result, water systems are more likely to encounter denial of service attacks, viruses, and other malicious programs, which could severely disrupt the operation of these systems.... There is a great deal of interdependency between water and other infrastructures, the most important being the electric power sector. If power is interrupted or withdrawn, it affects the entire water system. To a lesser degree, telecommunications service outages or system degradations could affect remote control access to pivotal systems....

—Statement before the House Committee on Transportation and
Infrastructure Subcommittee on Water Resources and Environment,
October 10, 2001

Former FBI Director Louis Freeh

The FBI believes cyber-terrorism, the use of cyber-tools to shut down, degrade, or deny critical national infrastructures, such as energy, transportation, communications, or government services, for the purpose of coercing or intimidating a government or civilian population, is clearly an emerging threat for which it must develop prevention, deterrence, and response capabilities.

—Statement before the United States Senate Committees on
Appropriations, Armed Services, and Select Committee on Intelligence,
May 10, 2001

Our Nation's critical infrastructure—both cyber and physical—present terrorists, hackers, criminals, and foreign agents with a target for attacks, the consequences of which could be devastating.

—Statement before the Senate Committee on
Appropriations Subcommittee for the Departments of Commerce,
Justice, and State, the Judiciary, and Related Agencies, February 4, 1999

Leslie G. Wiser, Jr., Chief of Training, Outreach, and Strategy Section, National Infrastructure Protection Center, Federal Bureau of Investigation

In one example, convicted terrorist Ramzi Yousef, the mastermind of the World Trade Center bombing, stored detailed plans to destroy United States airliners on encrypted files on his laptop computer. While we have not yet seen these groups employ cyber tools as a weapon to use against critical infrastructures, their reliance on information technology and acquisition of computer expertise are clear warning signs.

—Statement before the House Committee on Government Affairs
Subcommittee on Government Efficiency, Financial Management, and
Intergovernmental Relations, August 29, 2001

D

The Homeland Security Challenge Source: U.S. Department of Homeland Security

As is evident from the following list provided by the U.S. Department of Homeland Security, the challenge of protecting the U.S. infrastructure from an attack, either physical or cyber in nature, is daunting. However, it is because of the sheer size and distributed nature of our infrastructure that makes the use of modern information and communications technologies absolutely critical to any successful defense of the infrastructure and all of its components. Here's a look at what our government is up against as it tries to rally the private sector to the cause of homeland security:

Agriculture and Food: 1,912,000 farms; 87,000 food-processing plants

Aviation: 5,000 public airports

Banking and Finance: 26,600 FDIC insured institutions

Chemical Industry & Hazardous Materials: 66,000 chemical plants

Commercial Assets: 460 skyscrapers

Dams: 80,000 dams

Defense Industrial Base: 250,000 firms in 215 distinct industries

Electricity: 2,800 power plants

Emergency Services: 87,000 U.S. localities

Government Facilities: 3,000 government owned/operated facilities

Maritime: 300 inland/coastal ports

Nuclear Power Plants: 104 commercial nuclear power plants

Oil and Natural Gas: 300,000 production sites

Passenger Rail &Railroads: 120,000 miles of major railroads

Pipelines: 2 million miles of pipelines

Public Health: 5,800 registered hospitals

Telecommunications: 2 billion miles of cable

Water: 1,800 federal reservoirs; 1,600 municipal wastewater facilities

References

Introduction

Berinato, Scott. "The Truth about Cyberterrorism." *CIO Magazine* (March 15, 2002).

Hudson, Rex A. "The Sociology and Psychology of Terrorism: Who Becomes a Terrorist and Why?" A report prepared by the Federal Research Division, Library of Congress (September 1999).

National Infrastructure Protection Center Highlights (June 15, 2001): 2.

Staten, Clark L. "Asymmetric Warfare, the Evolution and Devolution of Terrorism; The Coming Challenge for Emergency and National Security Forces" (Emergency Response & Research Institute, April 27, 1998).

Chapter 1

Gunaratna, Ronan. *Inside Al Qaeda* (New York: Columbia University Press, 2002).

Shenon, Philip. "U.S. Says Suspects Awaited an Order for Terror Strike." *New York Times* (September 15, 2002): 1.

United States of America v. Osama bin Laden, United States District Court, Southern District of New York. Testimony of L'Houssaine Kherchtou, February 7, 2001.

Chapter 2

"America Still Unprepared—America Still in Danger" (Report of an Independent Task Force Sponsored by the Council on Foreign Relations): 26.

Gellman, Barton. "Cyber-Attacks by Al-Qaeda Feared." *The Washington Post* (June 27, 2002): A01.

Pacific Northwest Economic Region, Partnership for Regional Infrastructure Security Interdependencies Tabletop Exercise "Blue Cascades." *Report* (July 18, 2002).

Pollitt, Mark M. "Cyberterrorism: Fact or Fancy?" *Proceedings of the 20th National Information Systems Security Conference* (October 1997): 285–289.

Staten, Clark. Testimony before the Subcommittee on Technology, Terrorism, and Government Information, U.S. Senate Judiciary Committee (February 24, 1998).

Verton, Dan. "Black Ice Scenario Sheds Light on Future Threats to Critical Systems." *Computerworld* (October 18, 2001, http://www.computerworld.com/securitytopics/security/story/0,10801,64877,00.html).

———. "Corporate America Must Confront Terrorism, Security Experts Say." *Computerworld* (September 12, 2001, http://www.computerworld.com/news/2001/story/0,11280,63751,00.html).

Chapter 3

Badolato, Ed. "Physical Security for Electric Power Systems—A Draft" (Contingency Management Systems, Inc., September 27, 2001).

"The Cost of Power Disturbances to Industrial & Digital Economy Companies" (Electric Power Research Institute, June 2001).

Critical Foundations: Protecting America's Infrastructures, the Report of the President's Commission on Critical Infrastructure Protection (October 1997).

National Infrastructure Protection Center Highlights, Issue 4-01 (FBI, April 18, 2001): 3.

"Utility Companies Face Barrage of Cyberattacks." *Computerworld* (January 21, 2002).

Verton, Dan. "Experts Predict Major Cyber Attack Coming." *Computerworld* (July 8, 2002).

"Vulnerability Assessment Triggers Alarms." *Computerworld* (January 21, 2002).

Wiese, Ian, Principal Officer, SCADA Planning. "The Integration of SCADA and Corporate IT" (Water Corporation of Western Australia, 2002).

Chapter 4

"Airline Web Sites Seen As Riddled with Security Holes." *Computerworld* (February 4, 2002).

"Airport WLANs Lack Safeguards." *Computerworld* (September 16, 2002).

"DOD IT Projects Come Under Fire." *Computerworld* (May 20, 2002).

"Electronic Security: Risk Mitigation in Financial Transactions" (The World Bank, June 2002).

"IT Rolls Out Wireless LANs Despite Insecurity." *Computerworld* (March 25, 2002).

"U.S. May Face Net-Based Holy War." *Computerworld* (November 13, 2000).

Verton, Dan. "American Airlines Secures Wireless LANs in Denver." *Computerworld* (January 6, 2003).

"Wireless LANs: Trouble in the Air." *Computerworld* (January 14, 2002).

Chapter 5

Bakri Muhammad, Sheikh Omar. Author interview, November 2002.

Bergen, Peter L. *Holy War, Inc.: Inside the Secret World of Osama Bin Laden* (New York: Touchstone, 2002).

Cannistrano, Vince. Author interview via e-mail, December 6, 2002.

Caruso, J.T., acting assistant director, Counterterrorism Division, Federal Bureau of Investigation. Author interview, November 19, 2002.

———. Statement for the Record on al-Qaeda International. Before the Subcommittee on International Operations and Terrorism, Committee on Foreign Relations, United States Senate, Washington, D.C. (December 18, 2001).

Cilluffo, Frank, special assistant to the President and adviser for external affairs, Office of Homeland Security. Author interview, June 2001.

Cressey, Roger. Author interview, December 6, 2002.

Gunaratna, Ronan. *Inside Al Qaeda* (New York: Columbia University Press, 2002).

House Subcommittee on Government Programs and Oversight, hearing on "Electromagnetic Pulse (EMP): Should This Be a Problem of National Concern to Private Enterprise, Businesses Small and Large, As Well As Government?" (House of Representatives, June 1, 1999).

iDEFENSE, Inc. Current intelligence report (ID# 111672, September 12, 2002, www.idefense.com).

M0r0n (hacker pseudonym). Author interview, July 23, 2002.

Moskowitz, Stanley K., director of congressional affairs, CIA. CIA letter dated 8 April 2002.

"New World Coming: American Security in the 21st Century." *The Phase I Report on the Emerging Global Security Environment for the First Quarter of the 21st Century* (United States Commission on National Security/21st Century): 8.

"Threat Analysis: Al-Qaida's Cyber Capabilities" (Canadian Office of Critical Infrastructure Protection and Emergency Planning, November 2, 2001).

Trulock, Notra. Author interview via e-mail, December 6, 2002.

U.S. v. Osama bin Laden, February 21, 2002.

U.S. v. Osama bin Laden, May 1, 2001.

Verton, Dan. "U.S. May Face Net-Based Holy War." *Computerworld* (November 13, 2000).

Verton, Daniel. "New Cyberterror Threatens AF." *Federal Computer Week* (May 3, 1999).

Weldon, Rep. Curt, chairman, House Research & Development Subcommittee. Opening statement, Hearing on EMP Threats to U.S. Military and Civilian Infrastructure (House of Representatives, October 7, 1999).

Wood, Lowell, senior staff member, Lawrence Livermore National Laboratory. During hearing on "Electromagnetic Pulse (EMP): Should This Be a Problem of National Concern to Private Enterprise, Businesses Small and Large, As Well As Government?" (House of Representatives, June 1, 1999).

World Islamic Front. *Jihad Against Jews and Crusaders* (February 23, 1998).

Ziade, Oussama. Author interview via telephone, January 8, 2003.

Chapter 6

Aldridge, E.C. "Pete," Jr., undersecretary of defense for acquisition, technology, and logistics (AT&L). Letter obtained by author dated October 2, 2001.

Badaloto, Ed. Author interview, February 26, 2002.

Druyun, Darleen. E-mail message obtained by author, dated October 4, 2001: From: Druyun, Darleen, SAF/AQ, Subject: FW: Suggested E-Mail to DACs—Communications Regarding Programs, Importance: High.

Page, Seth. "Securing Fiber Optic Communications Against Taps" (Oyster Optics, Inc., October 16, 2002).

"Part IV, Twelfth Lesson of Declaration of the Country's Jihad Against the Tyrants, Military Series." Al-Qaeda training manual located by police in the U.K. and translated into English.

Shaw, Eric. Author interview.

Shore, Bill. Author interview.

Thibodeau, Patrick. "'Official' Terrorists Used Internet to Get Info on Potential Targets." *Computerworld* (February 13, 2002).

Verton, Dan. "Energy, Nuclear Infrastructure Exposed." *Computerworld* (February 11, 2002).

———. "Mapping of Wireless Networks Could Pose Enterprise Risk." *Computerworld* (August 14, 2002).

———. "New York Pulls Sensitive Data from State's Web Sites." *Computerworld* (February 26, 2002).

———. "Study: Web Exposes Data on CIA Networks." *Computerworld* (March 11, 2002).

———. "Telecom Infrastructure an Open Book." *Computerworld* (February 11, 2002).

———. "Web Sites Seen as Terrorist Aids." *Computerworld* (February 11, 2002).

Verton, Daniel. "Critics: DOD Web Policies Too Strict." *Federal Computer Week* (December 21, 1998).

Chapter 7

Barrett, Steve. "NSTAC Chair Recaps Committee's Recent Accomplishments at March Meeting." *Telecom News,* Issue 1 (2002): 5.

———. "Powell Asks NSTAC to Keep Nation Inside the Information Loop." *Telecom News,* Issue 1 (2002): 4.

Clarke, Richard. Author interview.

Dick, Ron. Author interview.

"The Electronic Intrusion Threat to National Security and Emergency Preparedness (NS/EP) Internet Communications" (Office of the Manager, National Communications System, December 2000): 28–31.

Gilmore, James S., III, former governor of Virginia. Author interview.

Greene, Brenton. Author interview, October 29, 2002.

"Information Sharing for Critical Infrastructure Protection." *Task Force Report of the President's National Security Telecommunications Advisory Council* (June 2001).

Pollock, Warren. "The Nation's Stock Brokerage System Must Fortify Itself Against Future Attacks." *The Journal of Homeland Security* (February 2002).

Schmidt, Howard. Author interview.

Sliwa, Carol. "IT Disaster Declarations Flooding into Comdisco." *Computerworld* (September 11, 2001).

Thibodeau, Patrick. "Senate Committee Looks into IT Vulnerabilities." *Computerworld* (September 12, 2001).

Verton, Dan. "Disaster Recovery Planning Still Lags." *Computerworld* (April 1, 2002).

———. "FAA Moving to Enhance Integration with NORAD." *Computerworld,* August 13, 2002.

——— and Bob Brewin. "Companies Warned about Possible Cyberattacks." *Computerworld* (September 11, 2001).

Vijayan, Jaikumar. "Nimda Needs Harsh Disinfectant." *Computerworld* (September 24, 2001).

Chapter 8

Dawson, William F., deputy chief information officer, U.S. Intelligence Community. Author interview, August 2002.

New Enterprise Team (NETeam) Recommendations: *The Director's Work Plan for Change, FOR OFFICIAL USE ONLY* (National Security Agency, October 1, 1999): i.

Snider, L. Britt. "A Letter from the Inspector General, Central Intelligence Agency." Internal CIA Memorandum (January 19, 2001).

Verton, Dan. "Congressman Says Data Mining Could Have Prevented 9-11." *Computerworld* (August 26, 2002).

———. "Cops Watching for Terrorists Say IT Support Lacking." *Computerworld* (September 5, 2002).

———. "FBI Must Fix Outdated IT Infrastructure." *Computerworld* (June 17, 2002).

———. "GIS Plays Key Role in Homeland Security." *Computerworld* (September 9, 2002).

———. "NSA Struggles to Keep Up with Pace of Technology." *Computerworld* (March 5, 2001).

———. "Searching Intelink Is Like Shooting Craps." *Computerworld* (September 9, 2002).

———. "State Department Aims for Bigger Role in Homeland Security." *Computerworld* (September 9, 2002).

———. "State Department to Punish Six over Missing Laptop." *Computerworld* (December 11, 2000).

——— and Bob Brewin. "Captive Soldiers Lacked Critical GPS Radios." *Federal Computer Week* (April 5, 1999).

Weldon, Rep. Curt. Remarks made at the Information Sharing and Homeland Security conference in Philadelphia, Pennsylvania, sponsored by the Defense Department and Intelligence Community in August 2002.

———. Author interview, 1999, and the *Congressional Record* (House, May 21, 2002): H2820-H2834.

Chapter 9

Brewin, Bob. "CDC Calls Public Health IT a 'Pony Express.'" *Computerworld* (October 18, 2001).

Caruso, James T., assistant director, Counterterrorism Division, Federal Bureau of Investigation. Testimony before the Senate Committee on the Judiciary, November 6, 2001.

Chemical and Biological Terrorism: Research and Development to Improve Civilian Medical Response. Institute of Medicine (Washington, D.C.: The National Academies Press, 1999).

"FBI Issues Threat Communication on Al-Qaeda Targeting the U.S. Railway Sector." FBI Press Release (October 24, 2002).

Inglesby, Thomas V., MD, deputy director, Center for Civilian Biodefense Strategies, The Johns Hopkins University. Testimony before the Senate Committee on Government Affairs hearing on "The State of Public Health Preparedness for Terrorism Involving Weapons of Mass Destruction: A Six Month Report Card," April 18, 2002.

Kolbasuk McGee, Marianne. "A Prescription for Millions." *InformationWeek* (April 22, 2002).

Lewis, Jordan. "Software Helps Detect Illness Patterns." *American City & County* (August 1, 2002).

Marietti, Charlene. "For the Public Good." *Healthcare Informatics Online* (December 2001).

Public Health's Infrastructure: A Status Report, prepared for the U.S. Senate Appropriations Committee by the Department of Health and Human Services and the Centers for Disease Control and Prevention: 15.

Rosen, Joseph M., C. Everett Koop, and Eliot B. Grigg. "Cybercare: A System for Confronting Bioterrorism." *The Bridge* (National Academy of Engineering, Spring 2002).

Verton, Dan. "Bioterrorism Fighters Get Ammo." *Computerworld* (December 3, 2001).

———. "FBI Warns of Possible Rail Terror Attacks." *Computerworld* (October 25, 2002).

Chapter 10

American Civil Liberties Union, et al. Letter dated January 14, 2003, sent to House and Senate Committees on Armed Services, Appropriations, Government Reform and Affairs, and the Judiciary.

Electronic Privacy Information Center. Web site on the USA-PATRIOT Act, http://www.epic.org/privacy/terrorism/usapatriot/.

Gilmore, James S., III, former governor of Virginia. Press conference and author interview, December 16, 2002.

Leahy, Senator Patrick. Letter dated January 10, 2003, United States Senate Committee on the Judiciary. Author copy.

Royce, Knut, Tom Brune, and Lou Dolinar. "Mass. Tech Company Raided for Alleged Terror Links." *Newsday* (December 6, 2002).

Verton, Dan. "Funding Scrutiny May Spread." *Computerworld* (January 27, 2003): 1.

———. "NSA Moves to Defuse Echelon Controversy." *Federal Computer Week* (February 29, 2000).

———. "NSA's Privacy Pledges Not Enough for Some in Congress." *Federal Computer Week* (March 1, 2000).

Chapter 11

Ben Venzke, and Aimee Ibrahim, "The al-Qaeda Threat: An Analytical Guide to al-Qaeda's Tactics & Targets (Alexandria, Va.: Tempest Publishing LLC).

Appendix A

The White House. *Executive Order 13010* (July 17, 1996, www.ntia.doc.gov/osmhome/cip/eo13010.pdf).

Appendix B

Department of Justice. *WHITE PAPER: The Clinton Administration's Policy on Critical Infrastructure Protection: Presidential Decision Directive 63* (May 22, 1998, http://www.usdoj.gov/criminal/cybercrime/white_pr.htm).

The White House. *Presidential Decision Directive / NSC-63* (May 22, 1998, http://www.nici.org/publications/publications/39%20%20PDD-63.PDF).

Appendix C

Bush, President George W. On signing of legislation forming Homeland Security Department, November 25, 2002.

———. Remarks at a joint press conference with British prime minister Tony Blair, July 19, 2001.

———. Remarks during roundtable discussion with the foreign press, July 18, 2001.

———. Remarks to the World Bank, July 17, 2001.

———. Remarks at a joint press conference with British prime minister Tony Blair, July 19, 2001.

Dick, Ronald L., Former FBI National Infrastructure Protection Center director. Statement before the House Committee on Transportation and Infrastructure Subcommittee on Water Resources and Environment, October 10, 2001.

Freeh, Louis, Former FBI director. Statement before the Senate Committee on Appropriations Subcommittee for the Departments of Commerce, Justice, and State, the Judiciary, and Related Agencies, February 4, 1999.

————. Statement before the United States Senate Committees on Appropriations, Armed Services, and Select Committee on Intelligence, May 10, 2001.

Wiser, Leslie G., Jr., Chief of Training, Outreach, and Strategy Section, National Infrastructure Protection Center, Federal Bureau of Investigation. Statement Before the House Committee on Government Affairs Subcommittee on Government Efficiency, Financial Management, and Intergovernmental Relations, August 29, 2001.

INDEX

INTERNATIONAL CONTACT INFORMATION

AUSTRALIA
McGraw-Hill Book Company Australia Pty. Ltd.
TEL +61-2-9900-1800
FAX +61-2-9878-8881
http://www.mcgraw-hill.com.au
books-it_sydney@mcgraw-hill.com

CANADA
McGraw-Hill Ryerson Ltd.
TEL +905-430-5000
FAX +905-430-5020
http://www.mcgraw-hill.ca

GREECE, MIDDLE EAST, & AFRICA
(Excluding South Africa)
McGraw-Hill Hellas
TEL +30-210-6560-990
TEL +30-210-6560-993
TEL +30-210-6560-994
FAX +30-210-6545-525

MEXICO (Also serving Latin America)
McGraw-Hill Interamericana Editores S.A. de C.V.
TEL +525-117-1583
FAX +525-117-1589
http://www.mcgraw-hill.com.mx
fernando_castellanos@mcgraw-hill.com

SINGAPORE (Serving Asia)
McGraw-Hill Book Company
TEL +65-6863-1580
FAX +65-6862-3354
http://www.mcgraw-hill.com.sg
mghasia@mcgraw-hill.com

SOUTH AFRICA
McGraw-Hill South Africa
TEL +27-11-622-7512
FAX +27-11-622-9045
robyn_swanepoel@mcgraw-hill.com

SPAIN
McGraw-Hill/Interamericana de España, S.A.U.
TEL +34-91-180-3000
FAX +34-91-372-8513
http://www.mcgraw-hill.es
professional@mcgraw-hill.es

UNITED KINGDOM, NORTHERN, EASTERN, & CENTRAL EUROPE
McGraw-Hill Education Europe
TEL +44-1-628-502500
FAX +44-1-628-770224
http://www.mcgraw-hill.co.uk
computing_europe@mcgraw-hill.com

ALL OTHER INQUIRIES Contact:
McGraw-Hill/Osborne
TEL +1-510-420-7700
FAX +1-510-420-7703
http://www.osborne.com
omg_international@mcgraw-hill.com